AN AUTOBIOGRAPHY

A WARRIOR'S JOURNEY

CHIMA OLUGH

This is a work of nonfiction. No names have been changed, no characters invented, no events fabricated. It is also a book of memory, and memory has its own story to tell. But I have done my best to make it tell a truthful story. Any perceived slight of any individual or organisation is unintentional.

Copyright © 2020 by Chima Olugh
First paperback edition 2020

Book cover and interior design by Asya Blue.

ISBN 978-1-9163617-0-6 (paperback)
ISBN 978-1-9163617-1-3 (ebook)

For more information contact chimaolugh@gmail.com.

Website: www.chimaolugh.com

*For my grandma, Nne Agbai,
who inspired me to be the best.*

*For my mum and dad, who pointed
me in the direction of honesty, respect,
morals and integrity.*

*For my two children, Nkechi and Obinna,
who gave me the strength to fight for justice.*

Author's Note

This is an autobiography containing some detailed facts about my life. It contains details of experiences, incidents and special events that shaped my life and made me who I am now.

I started collecting details about my life in 1979. I am unsure why I started writing down my experiences, but once I had started, I did not stop. I wrote my experiences in diaries, on pieces of paper, and on the walls of anywhere I lived.

Finally, in 1989, I made a conscious decision to start writing my memoirs using all the information I had collected over the years. I was unaware that my long journey through life still had many surprises in store; many battles that I would need to fight and win in order to develop the right qualities to be a good dad, role model, leader and husband.

While writing my memoirs, I've had the opportunity to reflect on many things that have happened to me. Now I know that I am meant to be an example of what is possible.

The experiences and events contained herein are all true. They have been documented as I have remembered them, to the best of my ability, and I have also independently verified all the facts that I have included. This is one of the reasons it has taken me thirty years to complete this piece of work.

Most of the conversations I have included come from my diligent recollection of them. However, they are not recounted word-for-word; rather, I have tried to retell my experience in a way that evokes the real feeling and meaning of what happened, in keeping with the true essence of the mood and spirit of each event and the impact it had on me.

Contents

My Early Years
(1966–1976)

My name is Chima Olugh. I was born on 11 December 1966 in London, UK, where I lived until my parents sent me to live in Nigeria. I am the first child of four; two boys, two girls.

As a young child, I always wanted to visit Nigeria – my parents always told me exciting and wonderful things about the country that we called home, even though I hadn't been there. With a name like Chima, which means "God Knows", most Nigerians knew I was Nigerian, and from the Igbo tribe, whilst everyone else just knew I wasn't English. It felt as if I had established my own identity from birth; I felt unique.

My parents had arrived in Britain in the mid-sixties. My dad, Oko Olugh, came in 1964, and my mum, Agbogho Elekwa, came in 1965. Like most Africans and Nigerians in those days, they had come to study – to gain a good education and an understanding of what a good-quality life was like, with the aim of going back to Nigeria and making a better life with better job prospects. Not all black people were welcome in Britain in those days; my parents were no exception, and they struggled with racism and prejudice. Employment was incredibly difficult to come by, but my parents persevered. My dad, using his business perspicacity, his ability to socialise easily and his good command of the English language, was able to find a job fairly quickly – he actually started working less than a week after arriving in London. My mum also managed to find a job not too long after she arrived. They lived with my dad's cousin, Chima Ibiam, for a while. However, Mr Ibiam had a very different set of plans for my parents' future than they did. He wanted them both to work and give him their weekly earnings so that he could fund his medical degree. My dad wasn't having any of that crap. My dad's refusal to give Mr Ibiam any money led to a huge disagreement, a test of resolve, a few physical fights, and ultimately a parting of ways.

When my parents left Mr Ibiam's place in 1966, they had to find somewhere of their own. My mum was pregnant with me during this time, and they had a very hard time finding a place to rent. They ended up spending small amounts of time in different houses throughout that year and were turned away from many places in and around South London. My dad said that it was very difficult for them; the racism, discrimination, the pride – and to top it all, the harsh, cold, uninviting weather.

I eventually arrived into this world on Sunday 11th December 1966 in the grand surroundings of Guy's and St Thomas' Hospital in Westminster, across the River Thames from the Houses of Parliament. My arrival made it difficult for my parents to maintain their rented accommodation. Living in South London was probably even worse than living in other parts of London or the UK, as there was a sudden influx of Africans and Caribbean's taking over the suburbs. A lot of the white folk were getting increasingly pissed off with the incessant increase in black folk invading their country, their local areas, and their territory.

After being turned down for accommodation too many times for his liking, my dad, being a business-minded man, decided to try a different tack; he went to a bank and inquired about taking out a mortgage to buy a house. The fact that my parents were both in good employment helped his case, and after a couple of months of sorting out the small details, he succeeded in securing a mortgage. He went on to buy his own home off Coldharbour Lane, Brixton, in South London for little more than £4,000. Life looked like it was on the up. Coldharbour Lane is a road in South London that leads south-westwards from Camberwell to Brixton. The road is over a mile long with a mixture of residential, business and retail buildings. The stretch of Coldharbour Lane near Brixton market had shops, bars and restaurants, whilst the junction of Coldharbour Lane and Denmark Hill in Camberwell not only led to the prestigious King's College Hospital, but also marked part of the boundary between the London boroughs of Lambeth and Southwark. It was a prestigious location in which to own property in those days.

For me, life really began to get going when I was around the age of three; 1970. I was described as cute, bubbly, intelligent and cheeky. I can remember little from being that age, but the memories I have are happy ones. One question I always asked my parents was why I didn't have any godparents. They always said: "You've got us – what do you need more parents for?"

My parents worked full-time, which meant they had to find someone to look after me. After trying many child-minders, most of whom initially said yes and then let us down at very short notice, my parents decided to look for someone I could live with – a nanny. After I had spent some time with a couple of different nannies, my parents eventually found a middle-aged lady, Mrs Weeks, who lived in Erith, Bexley, South London, with her husband. I went to live with them in early 1970. This meant my parents could focus on their jobs; they still had my younger sister Onyemachi to look after, but I guess it is easier to look after one child than two. Onyemachi was born in August 1969, and at about six months old was lucky enough to have a child-minder near our house, so my parents were able to go to work and pick her up in the evenings. She was named Onyemachi (which means "Nobody Knows Tomorrow") by my mum following the tragedy that befell her parents during the Nigerian Civil War, which took place whilst she was in the UK.

Living with Mrs Weeks was a different experience to living at home with my parents, but it was still an enjoyable one. From what I remember, she treated me well. Her children were grown up and lived elsewhere, but I had someone to play with all the time as Christine, a little black girl, also lived with Mrs Weeks. She was the same age as me, so we got on very well; in fact, we were more like brother and sister. We had a tan-coloured Alsatian dog called Kimmy, who I was very fond of, and she was fond of me too. She was quite big and very obedient; I used to be able to ride on her back sometimes, and I always imagined I was riding a horse. At the weekends, we would often go shopping in Erith town centre. People always stared at us – I guess they were baffled as to how or why a white couple had two black kids. I loved those walks; I pretended I was Mrs Weeks's child and daydreamed of life as a white kid while people looked at me with confused, baffled, or indignant expressions. Afterwards, we would take a taxi back home with all our shopping. It was fun.

I lived with Mrs Weeks until I was about four and a half and ready to start primary school. I still remember the day my dad drove down to collect me from Mrs Weeks for the final time. I was quite sad to be leaving Erith, as I had been treated very well and was going to miss Christine, our walks to the market, and the bedtime stories that we would read to each other. I was, however, happy to going back to my real home, my real parents, and my real sister.

In September 1971, back at home in Brixton, South London, I started school. Loughborough Junior School, on Loughborough Road just on the outskirts of main Brixton town, was literally five minutes' walk away from our house. It was a fairly small school with a mixed popula-

My nanny, Mrs Weeks

tion of black, Asian and white kids. At four years and eight months old, I was the youngest in my class, although I didn't know it at the time. I thoroughly enjoyed school; I was very energetic and intelligent, and my favourite activities were reading, writing, cutting out, acting and playing the piano. I also liked running and playing football in the playground. Like most kids, we played Cowboys and Indians in the playground during lunchtime, and we also played around with marbles, football cards and conkers. After school, I had to join Onyemachi at her child-minder's house, which was one street away from our house on Eastlake Road. We would both then be collected later in the evening by either my mum or my dad after they finished work. Onyemachi's child-minder was a black, middle-aged lady who was very strict. I don't think she liked my sister very much, as she was always shouting at her for no reason.

In March 1972, my mum gave birth to my second sister, Ugo. I don't remember being told we were going to have a new addition to the family. I do, however, remember my mum and dad coming home from the hospital with Ugo. On the day my dad left the house to go and collect my mum from hospital, he left me at home with Onyemachi. We both saw this as an opportunity to have some free time, so we went outside and played around. At some stage, we decided to have a race from halfway down our street to the front of our house. I gave her a head start. As we were racing, Onyemachi kept looking back to see if I was catching up with her. On one occasion she looked back, but as she was about to turn her head to the front again she bumped her face into a lamp-post. She dropped the biscuit that was in her hand and let out a very pained scream. I ran to the finish line before coming back to help her up from the floor. Almost instantly, the side of her face that had hit the lamp-post began swelling. By the time I had helped her inside, the eye on that side of her face was totally closed. When my dad got back from the hospital with my mum and Ugo, I had to explain what had happened. I received a beating for taking my younger sister outside without permission and for letting her bump into a lamp-post – as if I were her eyes.

I used to get beaten regularly, as I was very explorative,

stubborn, energetic and mischievous. My dad tried very hard to get me to be an honest, independent and straight-forward kid, but I did not understand all that at my young age. After a while, the beatings rarely hurt anymore; I just went through the screaming, shouting and running motions to prevent my parents devising alternative methods of punishing me. With the addition of baby Ugo, the house was a lot noisier, and I was expected to take on a lot more responsibilities such as looking after Onyemachi a lot more. I didn't mind; she was very independent and wanted to do as much as possible by herself. Ugo, on the other hand, did cry a lot, and my parents spent a lot of time with her in the evenings after work.

My parents, being one of only a few couples who owned their own homes at that time, used to have guests quite frequently – either for someone's party, for Nigeria's Independence Day, for Christmas, or to celebrate one landmark event or another. These were often fun times for me because the guests usually came with their children and we would play together for hours on end. There was always lots of food and drinks. I used to enjoy playing pranks on the adults. I would sneak into the kitchen where all the drinks were and shake all the fizzy drinks and beers. Then I would quietly stand by the door of the sitting room to watch the guests as they opened their drinks and to see it squirt all over them. What a sight. They never did figure out it was me; they were either too merry to care or thought they must have shaken the drinks themselves by accident.

The weekends were the best times for me. I had time to read my novels and other books, and sometimes to go out onto the streets and play. I was only allowed outside to play if I had been a good boy all week. That was rare, but I did sometimes try to be on my best behaviour so I could play with my friends. The times I wasn't allowed outside, I would stand by the window and watch everyone else playing, I would imagine myself out there with them, riding a bike or scooter, or driving a pedal car.

At the age of six, I was still wetting my bed. It was not something I did intentionally; it just seemed to happen, and although it wasn't every day, it was embarrassing, and it got me down sometimes. My parents vowed not to buy me a bike or scooter until I stopped wetting the bed. I did try explaining that I wasn't doing it deliberately, but they never did believe or understand me. Everything I tried failed, and bed-wetting would haunt me for a very long time, through parts of my life. I never did get a bike or scooter to call my own. This meant that when I played outside with friends, I had to beg them to use their bikes, scooters and other toys. I was lucky because they normally obliged. Nobody taught me how to ride a bike, but I soon became a master, doing wheelies, bunny hops and slides, although I was nearly always cautious not to damage anyone's property.

At the age of seven, I was given my own house key so I

could go straight home after school – seen as an important part of my independence. I didn't always go straight home after school, though; sometimes I would go and play with friends at the adventure playground on Gordon Grove, round the corner from the school. At other times, I'd walk the local streets just for fun, memorising the names of all the streets I went past. I went as far away as possible from the areas and streets I knew and then tried to make it back home without getting lost. This somewhat aimless wandering became the basis for my incredible knowledge of the streets. I did get lost on many occasions, but this just heightened my adrenaline rush, and it gave me a buzz working out how to get back home or to a familiar area.

After a while, walking around on the streets got boring and I started indulging in more interesting and illegal activities, such as stealing sweets, chocolates and drinks from the shops. I targeted small shops, which normally had only one shop attendant, waiting for some sort of distraction before I struck. I always tried to take as much as I could so as to have enough of a stash for the day, the evening, and (if I was lucky) the next day. Again, it was the adrenaline rush that I got when I was successful that I liked the most. I did get caught on many occasions, and was soon banned from most of the shops along Coldharbour Lane. The awful thing about the local shops in those days was that the owners all knew my parents and would report me whenever they met them on the streets or in the shops. Naturally, that information prompted heavy beatings from either my mum or my dad – or sometimes both, with one beating me first, then the other doing a follow-up act some minutes later, as if to complete the work of the first tired parent. Sometimes, whoever got the news first would get back and commence the beatings; they would then wait for the other to get back so they could share the information, and another beating would normally follow. None of this deterred me from continuing my stealing trend. At times, I did it simply to piss them off.

I didn't often get into trouble with other pupils from school, so I was liked by most of them. Nevertheless, there was one Jamaican boy, Paul Williams, who made it his business to bully me whenever he got the chance. Paul Williams was in the same class as me, but he was over five foot at the time and had very long legs, so people – including me – were very scared of him. For some unknown reason, he seemed to pick on me more than anyone else; he used to get me to steal sweets from shops. He picked on me so much that one day my dad took me to go and have a word with his mum. That was a big mistake. His mum cursed us from the fourth floor balcony of her Loughborough Estate flat until we left.

The bullying did not stop; in fact, Paul upped his harassment. On one occasion, he tried to get me to steal a toy gun from a shop on Flaxman Road, round the corner from our house. He wanted me to use a brick to smash the window of the toy shop and grab the gun. I knew that if I smashed the shop window I would be in serious trouble with the authorities and my parents – I had never done anything as dumb as that, and I wasn't going to start. He stood back as I walked slowly towards the shop front. I purposely walked slowly as I plotted my next move. When I got to the shop, I thought of running in and asking for help, but I was not confident I'd get the help I needed. They would possibly mistake me for a kid playing around, especially if Paul came in looking for me. As I continued thinking, I pretended to look for something to smash the window with. I walked slowly around the area, steadily increasing the distance between myself and Paul. Then, all of a sudden, my plan was perfected – I bolted and headed towards our school. It must have taken him a couple of seconds to register that I was actually running away from him, but he followed in hot pursuit on his gangly legs. I headed towards Gordon Grove and then made my way towards the Loughborough Estate. I knew he lived in one of the flats on the estate, and my thinking was that he would slow down or stop pursuing me on his patch because people, including adults, knew him there, and they would surely ask him why he was running after me.

The plan worked, to some degree. He slowed down as he approached the estate, but he didn't stop. I gained a bit of ground and tried to outfox him by running down different corridors, up one flight of stairs, across another corridor, then down to street level again. I began to get tired, and he slowly gained ground. Eventually I came to a stop at the bottom of the estate, facing the busy Loughborough Road. He caught up with me and gave me a slap that blinded me for a couple of seconds. In those seconds, I decided on my next move. As I crouched over, pretending to be in pain, I was looking and waiting for a car to approach. As a speeding car approached, I feigned a dash across the road, putting one foot into the road as the car approached. Paul was taken unawares and ran straight into the middle of the road without looking. The car was unable to stop in time; it hit him head-on, and he landed smack bang on his back in the middle of the road. I took one sly look at him, slowly turned around, and casually walked home. The next day it was all over the school that Paul Williams had been knocked over on Loughborough Road whilst playing. Not many people expressed any sympathy for the bully. He spent weeks in hospital, and more months at home, and the school sent him flowers and a card. When he finally came back to school, he was a totally changed individual, and I secretly took the credit for his transformed character. He was too ashamed to tell anyone what had really happened. It was to remain our secret.

By the time I was eight years old, I had taken a very keen interest in stealing and was doing so on a somewhat professional level. When I was at school, I would sometimes sneak out of the classroom, go to the students' cloakroom, and go through coat pockets looking for money. I was always successful. Fortunately, closed-circuit television was not in existence in those days.

At home, we had one of those fifty-pence gas meters in the basement flat, and my parents always made sure it was fully topped up. I used to use it as my personal cash cow, and I was quite smart with it too. I would only take one or two fifty-pence pieces; this way, when my parents went to empty it, they weren't suspicious. This must have continued for months. One day, though, as I was leaving the house to go to somewhere with my friend Nnamdi, I decided to take a lot more than a couple of fifty-pence pieces – I must have taken up to five pounds' worth and put them in my shoe. As I was coming out of the basement flat, I looked up and saw my mum standing there. She was scowling at me.

"Come here!" she shouted. As I ascended the stairs, I received a stunning slap across my face. It brought instant tears to my eyes. She searched all my pockets, and when she found nothing she looked at me suspiciously. "What were you doing down there?" she asked.

"Nothing," I replied. I knew she didn't believe me; I could see the way her eyes scrutinised me.

"Take off your shoes!" she shouted. I froze. What was I going to do? I contemplated running, but that would only prolong any punishment I was about to get. I took off the shoe that contained all the fifty-pence coins, and out they fell. Another unsuspecting slap connected with my face, knocking me off balance for a few seconds. "You thief!" she screamed, following up with another slap.

She then grabbed my earlobe between her long nails and pinched as hard as she could. This time, the tears that flowed from my eyes were tears of pain. I couldn't move; when I did move, she just pinched harder, and it hurt.

"Who told you to take the money?" she asked. I kept quiet. "Who told you to take the money?" she asked again.

"Nobody," I replied glumly. She looked at her watch and realised the time. With a final pinch of my lips with her nails she told me to go back downstairs and put the money back where it belonged. I walked down the stairs to the basement; when I was out of sight I took off my other shoe, put all the money in it, slipped my shoe back on, and slowly climbed up the stairs. When I got to where my mum was standing, now with Nnamdi, beside my other shoe, I froze – I fully expected my mum to tell me to take off the other shoe. Thankfully she didn't; she hurried Nnamdi and me off. I struggled to walk normally with all that money, but I got away with it. Once we had turned the corner onto Flaxman Road, I stopped, stooped down, and took off my shoe containing the fifty pence pieces. Nnamdi was gobsmacked. He couldn't believe that I was brazen enough to do something as daring as that. I couldn't quite believe it either; I had pulled off a major coup, and there were many more to come in the future. I spent the money on sweets, chocolate and cards.

The few things that interested me when I was in the house were reading and watching the television; at the age of eight I was reading crime novels like Agatha Christie's Elephants Can Remember and Ruth Rendell's Some Lie and Some Die and No More Dying Then. I would easily get absorbed in the storyline and spend hours on end reading; sometimes I would read one book immediately after the other. I also watched a lot of late-night television, mainly when my mum was there. She didn't know this, though, as she always switched on the television and then dozed off on the sofa shortly afterwards. I would sneak in from my room and change the channel to watch whatever I wanted – was normally crime, thrillers or horror movies. Reading all those books and watching the crime thrillers gave me lots of ideas, and I wondered whether they would work in real life and whether I would get away with them. After watching one particular film, I decided to try out the ideas it gave me. My plan was to steal a student's keys from their school jacket, go to their house, take what I wanted, and return. I spent two days planning the heist. I chose someone whose address I knew. I watched them to find out which coat they wore to school and where they usually hung it. I then spent some time running to their house and back to find out how long it would take to complete my operation.

When I had perfected my plan, I struck. I stole the keys during lunchtime, as all the students would be indoors and would not need their coats. I took only cash, as I didn't want to take anything that would get my parents suspicious. The operation took me about fifteen minutes. It gave me a buzz to pull off something of that magnitude. The next day, news of the burglary of my friend's house circulated through the school. My friend said that the police were perplexed as to how the burglar got in, as there were no signs of a break-in. I was thrilled to know the police were involved and to know they would never catch me; I was too young, not a suspect, and I had worn gloves.

Having succeeded in my first major heist, I was keen to carry out more. I completed two more burglaries, and again the rumours circulated through the school. The fact that I did them a month or so apart meant that nobody suspected it could be a student carrying out these raids. In order not to attract any suspicion, I stopped as abruptly as I had started. I would normally wait till the weekends before spending my stash of cash, which I hid under the carpet in the basement flat. Nobody was living there at the time. I would take the money and go on very long bus rides to places I'd never been to on my own before, like Elephant and Castle, Croydon and Peckham, where I would spend the money on sweets, cards and books.

Whilst I was busy being devious and stealing at school, I was also overachieving in most aspects of my academic life. I was lucky to have a great teacher, Mrs Seaman, who spotted my potential and constantly gave me extra work to challenge me and stretch my imagination. She would sometimes take me to her flat on the Loughborough Estate opposite the school and give me private reading and writing lessons.

I think it was probably my academic ability that prevented the head teacher from expelling me. On one occasion, I had to go to the head teacher's office with Mrs Seaman to beg the school not to expel me. One of our teachers had upset me by saying I asked too many questions in class; she wasn't going to allow me to ask any more questions that day. I didn't think I asked a lot of questions. Upset with her decision, I decided to teach her a lesson she'd never forget. When we had a short break and everyone had left the room, I went to her desk and took a handful of drawing pins, which I carefully arranged on the seat of her chair. When everyone returned, we all sat down ready for the next lesson. Nobody else was aware of what I had done. The teacher came back in and sat down on her chair, and as if she had been electrocuted, she let out a pained scream and sprang back up. The entire class was taken unawares, and the sight was so comical that they all burst out laughing, including me. We watched as she gently retrieved the drawing pins from her bum; in tears she rushed to the head teacher's office and reported the entire class.

The head teacher came to our class immediately, slowly looked around the class for a couple of seconds, then disappeared. When he came back he walked up to me, grabbed me by the cuff of my shirt and marched me upstairs to his office. He told me to face the wall and left me there till the end of the day. When I was going home, he gave me a letter to give to my parents. It was a letter of expulsion. My parents were numbed by the news. The next day, I went to the school very early and waited near the gate for Mrs Seaman. As I saw her coming down the road, I ran to her. I explained what had happened the previous day and asked her to please help me beg the head teacher to rescind the expulsion letter. She asked me to wait for her inside the school gates while she got her class ready. Whilst she was talking to me, everyone was staring at us; the news of my expulsion had already circulated. After what seemed like hours, Mrs Seaman emerged and led me to the head teacher's office. She literally begged him to rescind the expulsion; she said she wanted to be personally responsible for me going forward. It worked. The head teacher gave me an unadulterated warning: he said that if I ever had to come to his office again, he'd physically kick me out of his school. That was the beginning of my developmental journey with Mrs Seaman. She made me work hard at school and gave me extra homework every day. She gave me newspapers to read and she got me to write book reviews; she took me under her wing and mentored me until I left the school.

During the weekends when my parents wouldn't let me out of the house, I would wait for them to go shopping – normally on a Saturday morning. Then I would climb out of the window of my basement room into the garden, scale up the lead pipe that rose all the way to the roof of the house, and climb into the house through the window that led to our second floor landing; it was always open, for some odd reason. Then I would let myself out through the front door, leaving it on the latch so that I could always get back in when I finished playing outside. This sneaky system worked for me most of the time, but sometimes I would make the mistake of staying out for too long. I used to play a little, then go and check that the door was still on the latch; the times that I played for too long, I'd get home and the door would have been taken off the latch and locked from inside. That meant my parents were back. On the first occasion, I was able to avoid a beating by telling them that they had not locked the door to my room properly, but this didn't wash with them when I was caught outside the second time, and all the other times subsequently. The fun I used to have when playing outside was just too much for me; I was happy to take the beatings, or any other consequences, just to fulfil my appetite for the fun and happiness.

As my daring expeditions escalated, my mum realised that beatings alone weren't having the desired effect on me, so she amplified my punishment. The two most excruciating new methods she introduced whenever I was caught stealing were to hold my hand over our burning gas cooker or to put hot ground pepper in my eyes.

The first time I got the "pepper in my eyes" treatment

was when I stole some money from Mr Brown, one of our new tenants, who shared the basement flat with me. He had the front room, the kitchen and bathroom, whilst I had the room facing the garden at the back of the house. I didn't have any need to walk through the rest of the flat because there was a staircase leading upstairs to the main house from the basement corridor. One day, he had forgotten to lock his room and went off to work. I went inside his room and took twenty pounds that I saw lying on the bedside table. I was out spending it when he returned. He noticed the money was missing and must have guessed it was me, so reported the incident to my mum. Immediately after I got back from spending the money, my mum cornered me in my room. First, she gave me a very serious beating. Then she dragged me upstairs to the kitchen, lit the cooker and held my hand over the fire. How she did it without actually burning my hand, I'll never know. After what seemed like hours of torture, she finally let me go and sent me to my room. I thought my ordeal had finished and was sobbing quietly when she reappeared with a small bowl in her hand. She locked the door, got me in a headlock, and smeared what was in the bowl all over my face. It was pepper mixed with hot water. I closed my eyes, and almost instantly a sizzling sensation passed through my head. It felt as if it had connected with my brain; it felt like the inside of my head was on fire. I started crying and running around frantically whilst trying to rub the pepper off my face with my hands, but this only made it worse. As my mum left the room, she told me she was going to repay Mr Brown his money, and if I was ever tempted to steal again, she would cut my hand off and tell the authorities it was an accident.

After about twenty or so minutes of screaming, crying and running around the room, I must have dozed off – when I woke up, it was a lot later in the day. All the pepper had dried up and I was able to open my eyes; there was the odd sting here or there, but the worst seemed to be over. For the rest of that day, I spent my time thinking what I needed to do to in order to be a good boy and avoid that sort of punishment ever again. I probably remained a good boy at least for the rest of the day.

The second time my mum gave me the pepper treatment – and this time, it was my entire body – was on a Friday afternoon after school, when I had been playing outside with the rest of the kids. I borrowed a friend's bike to ride round the block, as some of us were taking turns to do. As I was cycling, a thought occurred to me – I cycled round the block once, and when I got back I begged to have one more go, but as I was cycling round for the second time, I took a detour and rode off in the direction of Loughborough Junction, then Brixton, then Stockwell. I rode the bike throughout the afternoon, visiting places I knew and was comfortable in. When I was tired of riding around South London, I decided it was time to go home.

As I was cycling back towards our street, I saw a large crowd gathered outside our house. They must have been either worried about what had happened to me, or wondering why I had deliberately taken another boy's bike, ridden off on it, and not returned. On seeing the crowd, I panicked, turned around quietly (as they hadn't yet seen me) and rode off to Kennington Park, where I spent the rest of the evening. When the park wardens started telling people to get out, I hid behind a large hedge and waited until the park was empty before coming out. I left the bike behind the hedge and wandered off to a nearby fish and chip shop, where I bought my dinner. I took it back to my hiding place and devoured it as quickly as I could. After that, I laid my head down and went to sleep. I was awakened occasionally by sirens; I speculated as to whether they were looking for me, but when they faded into the distance I soon got caught up in the embrace of sleep. In the morning, I went for another long ride around Brixton before finally going home in the middle of the afternoon. My street was eerily empty. I knocked on our front door. My dad opened it. He asked me whether I was okay, to which I responded yes; he then took me to my friend's house, knocked on the door, and waited. My friend's dad opened the door, and my dad told me to apologise for stealing their bike. I didn't want to at first; in my view, I hadn't stolen the bike – I had borrowed it. But there was a look on my dad's face that I didn't like, so I apologised.

When we got back, my dad got ready and went out shopping. When my mum woke up, she told me to go downstairs to my room and wait for her. When she eventually came in she locked the door and told me to strip off my clothes. I did. With one swift swipe of her hand, she had pasted the hot pepper across my face and in my eyes; as I thrashed around in agony, she proceeded to paste the rest of the pepper on my private parts, up my nose, in my mouth and in my ears. It burned like hell. I squirmed and lashed out, trying to stop her putting more on me. She must have become fed up after a while, so she left me in my room and went upstairs, locking the door after her. After a couple of minutes of screaming and thrashing, a thought came to me. I decided to endure the burning sensation and keep quiet, so I sat down on my worn old sofa and mentally counted down the time. After about fifteen minutes, the seething pain began to subside; after another ten minutes or so, the pain had gone. I opened my eyes and laughed out loud; I had found yet another way to beat punishment. I went to the door. My mum had made one vital mistake when locking it; she had left the key in the keyhole.

My years of reading and watching crime stories had taught me how to get past that hurdle. I slid a piece of newspaper under the door, found something to poke the key with until it fell onto the newspaper, and pulled the newspaper with the key on it back under the door. I couldn't believe it at first, but it had worked. I opened the door and snuck upstairs and into the pantry where my mum kept fruit. As I was stealing some fruit to take with me back downstairs, my mum walked in on me. Her face was aghast. She must've thought she was seeing a ghost. She knew she had locked the door, so she asked me how I'd got out. In order to preserve my secret of how I'd escaped, I lied and said the door wasn't locked. I told her that I shook it a few times and it opened. She must have believed me. I was able to use this technique to my advantage on many other occasions before my parents eventually found out.

I think the final straw for my parents came in May 1976, when I was nine. Harold, a school friend who lived on the next street, had invited me to his ninth birthday party. The party was supposed to be from four o'clock till nine o'clock. I had assumed my parents would let me go, as it was literally a minute's walk away. I was wrong; when I asked them, they said no. I begged until I was tired, but to no avail. I hatched a quick plan; I asked if I could go to the library instead. They agreed, so I packed my library bag with my books and headed out. They watched me through the living room window. When I knew they could no longer see me, I turned the corner onto Flaxman Road and headed to the party on Pomfret Road.

The party was fun, with lots of food and drink – I didn't want it to end. When it did finish, Harold's dad asked if I wanted him to walk me home. I said no. I took my bag and left. As I got to the top of my street, I became scared of what would happen to me when I got in. I decided not to go back that night. I found a comfortable hedge outside someone's house on Flaxman Road, used my bag as a pillow, and went to sleep. The following morning, I was awake by five o'clock. I wasn't sure what to do. As I sat on the pavement considering what my next move would be, I saw my dad walking along the street towards an area at the end of the road where people normally dump unwanted furniture and other bits of rubbish. He later told me he had gone there to see if my dead body was there. After looking over the wall, he turned round to head home and spotted me sitting on the pavement. He came over to me, took my hand, and squeezed it very hard. He was surprised to see me alive. He asked me whether I was okay. When we got home, he told my mum to give me some breakfast. They never did ask me where I had been, or where I slept. I think they were emotionally drained.

That incident prompted my parents to start the process of arranging for my extended holiday in Nigeria. The following Saturday, my parents went shopping but didn't lock me in my room; I'm unsure whether they forgot or just couldn't be bothered. Immediately after they had left, I put the door on the latch, hopped on a bus and headed to central London. My sisters were upstairs and unaware that I had left. I wandered around Oxford Street and Trafalgar Square for over three hours before deciding to go back home. When I got back, the door was off the latch; I expected that, as I had been out for too long. I rang the doorbell and my mum opened it for me. I walked in, expecting a flogging from my dad – but when I went into the sitting room, he was on the phone, shouting at someone in Igbo about flights to Nigeria and dates. He wasn't aware I was in the room, so I stood there eavesdropping on his conversation and trying to use my limited knowledge of the language to draw an inference from the discussion and the heated voices.

I was able to decipher that he wanted to buy another ticket to Nigeria, on the same flight as the one that had already been purchased, but he was being offered one at a much higher price than the first one he had purchased. Although I sensed what that meant, I wasn't absolutely sure. After he put the phone down, he asked me to help him get some things from his car. While I was helping him, I kept on waiting for the slap to land on my face. It never did. Sometime in June, my dad sat me down and told me that I would be going to Nigeria with my mum in July, and that I would not be coming back to London. I took in the information very calmly; we were both surprised at my reaction. He asked whether I had any questions. I asked him who I'd be staying with, to which he replied, "your uncle". That obviously meant nothing to me, as I didn't know anyone in Nigeria.

Inwardly, I was quite happy to be going to Nigeria; I had never been on a plane before, never left the UK before, and never stayed with an uncle before. We were due to fly to Nigeria by Nigerian Airways on the evening of the 1st July 1976. As the day drew closer, I began to carry out more audacious acts of rebellion, literally daring my parents to beat me. Most of the time, I got a feeble telling-off. I think they were thinking, "you wait till you get to Nigeria; you'll renounce all your bad ways without being told". I thought so too and began to plan my new changed life in a foreign country. My mum eventually informed the school that I was going away on a holiday; it was before the official school holidays started, so they needed to make up an excuse for my absence.

The day before we left, I decided to carry out one last goodbye act. I waited for Mr Brown to leave for work and then went into his room and rummaged through all his things until I found a ten-pound note. I hadn't taken anything from him since my mum held my hands over the cooker, but this time I had no fear of what anyone might do to me. I would be in Nigeria, over 5,000 kilometres away from a beating. The feeling was sublime.

My dad drove the entire family to the airport. My sisters showed mixed emotions; on the surface, Onyemachi didn't appear to be bothered by my departure. Ugo, on the other hand, looked betrayed. I felt guilty to be leaving her, but I had no choice. We said our goodbyes. They weren't grand departure goodbyes, just a "be a good boy in Nigeria, and listen to your uncle" from my dad, and a goodbye wave from my sisters. I was finally off to my country.

A Rude Awakening
(1976–1979)

I don't remember much about the overnight flight from London to Nigeria, except that I was very excited, this being my first time on a plane. We landed in Lagos, the Nigerian capital, around 4am, and were welcomed by the sweltering blast of Lagos heat which hit my face as soon as we left the plane. It got hotter as we walked through the air bridge, and by the time we got into the Murtala Muhammed airport terminal, we were both sweating like pigs – and it was only 4.30am. We cleared customs and immigration very quickly, although not before one of the uniformed men stooped down and shouted something in my face. I didn't understand a word he had said. My mum responded on my behalf, saying, "He doesn't understand broken". I was thinking, "I haven't broken anything". Eventually, whilst we were waiting in the airport lounge for our delayed connecting Nigerian Airways flight, my mum explained what the man had said, and also told me what broken (or "pidgin") English was.

Our connecting flight was to the Rivers State capital, Port Harcourt, which is also referred to as the Garden City because the houses are built in beautiful, well-planned layouts, and there are open greens spaces all over the city. Our plane finally arrived in Lagos around 6pm, but by the time we took off for Port Harcourt, it was past 7pm. On getting to Port Harcourt, my mum collected our luggage and hoisted it onto a trolley, and we made for the exit. When we left the airport terminal and went outside, I couldn't hide my excitement. I was walking on Nigerian soil for the very first time in my life.

The heat was tremendous, and the sea of black faces speaking hurriedly in many different languages had me staring in awe. I had never seen so many black people in my entire nine-year life. The area was bustling; everyone appeared to be animated and busy doing something or going somewhere. The date was 1ˢᵗ July 1976: my official arrival date in my beloved country. As we stood under a shade waiting for a taxi, I was deciding whether I was elated or disappointed with what I had seen so far of the country. I was worried about the heat; it had been extremely hot during the day in Lagos, and even though it was evening time, the temperature hadn't abated. I was boiling.

My mum looked both nervous and anxious; this was her first visit home since she left nine years earlier, aged sixteen, to join her husband in the UK – the land of milk and honey. She did tell me she was looking forward to seeing her brothers and sisters and the other close relatives that she had left behind. When she had left for London, she hadn't had the opportunity to say her farewells to everyone, only to those relatives living in Calabar. Her parents were able to send her off, whilst relatives living elsewhere got to hear some time later she had left for London. I remembered when we were in London in 1969 and the news of my mother's dad's death reached us. She was understandably distraught at the news. This had occurred during, and as a result of, the Nigerian Civil War, and it was probably from then on that she began to miss her family, having already lost her mother only a year earlier.

As different thoughts flowed through my head, a taxi pulled up and my mum hailed it down; after haggling for over ten minutes, the man got out and loaded our luggage into the car. Once we got in, the car pulled off into the night and across the rugged terrain that led from Port to Aba, also popularly called "Little London". The one-hour journey to Aba was very frightening for me. The roads looked like they had been bombed by tanks; the driver was driving too fast for my liking, zig-zagging across most of the road to avoid the big holes the tanks had left. I was so drained, however, that the terror didn't keep me awake for long, and I eventually fell asleep.

When we got to Aba, the driver wasn't able to find 15 Onyembi Street, which was the address my mum had given him, so he ended up taking us to an uncle's house on Ugorji Street, in an area of town known as 'Over Rail' because, depending on what side of Aba you were coming from, you had to cross a railway track to get there.

Uncle O.O. was very surprised to see us, as my parents had not told anyone we were coming to Nigeria. "Welcome to Nigeria!" Uncle O.O. said. He told me that Aba was the trading centre of the south-east part of Nigeria and was known for being very industrious. The potholes in the roads in Aba were worse than the ones we had already encountered. I made a mental note to find out what those holes were.

The first full night in Nigeria passed with any incident. My mum spent a lot of time talking to O.O. and his wife Bridget, whilst a lot of the young children who lived in the yard kept putting their heads round the curtains to look at me. I felt very shy, but I was also very tired and soon asked my mum where I could sleep. Bridget led me to an adjoining room where there were two beds, and I was told to sleep on the smaller bed. I fell asleep instantly. When I woke up, everyone else was awake, and this surprised me as it was only 5.30am. I soon got used to waking up early, as it was difficult to try and sleep through the different noises from all the yard animals, people getting ready for work, preparing breakfast, and other things.

Another of my uncles, Mr Okoro Ikpo Uzor, had arrived from Onyembi Street – the place the taxi driver couldn't find. He had a very stern look on his face, which I eventually found out was just his look; in fact, most of the men and some of the women from my dad's family had stern-looking faces. Okoro Ikpo Uzor (who all of the people around him called papa Imo, because his first son was called Imo) engaged in a long discussion with my mum, Bridget and O.O. They spoke in Igbo, so I couldn't understand what was being said. It looked and sounded like a fierce conversation. After what seemed like hours, my mum told me we were leaving Ugorji Street and going to stay with papa Imo at Onyembi Street. I didn't know why at the time, but I later discovered that 15 Onyembi Street was my dad's house, which he had bought a year earlier, and so it made sense for us to stay there so we didn't inconvenience anyone.

We got in a taxi which took us across town to Onyembi Street. As we drove through Aba town, I was amazed by the environment; the sea of people carrying nearly everything on their heads and hawking it to anyone, or to people in cars that bothered to slow down or stop. There were no traffic lights, and cars zig-zagged across the brown, untarred and dusty roads, beeping relentlessly for no reason. It just seemed like chaos to me. This was not the Nigeria I was expecting – although to be fair, I hadn't really thought of what to expect from my country. I think the fact I didn't have any preconceived ideas or expectations helped me settle down and acknowledge the country for what it was.

As we got closer to our destination, the roads got a bit rougher, with more water-filled potholes and more hawkers. As a youngster, I was simply intrigued by everything around me. When we go to Onyembi Street, there seemed to be a lot of kids playing on the streets. I was immediately drawn to how relaxed they looked as they engaged in their games; I made a mental note to find time to venture out onto the streets and discover more.

When we arrived at our destination, we were again surrounded by lots of adults and children, who all appeared to be very interested in us – especially me. Most of them said hello, but some just stared at me as if I were an alien. I wasn't scared, although I think I was shy – shy of the children, not the adults. My mum later explained to me that it was a rare occurrence for them to see a child from "abroad" or "overseas" – that was why the children were staring at me. Also, on the odd occasion when I understood the greetings thrown at me in proper English, I responded in English, which the children found funny; it was my accent. I was introduced to all my cousins, papa Imo's children, and the oldest one, Imo, who was thirteen, asked me if I wanted to come outside and play with him.

I said yes and jumped up immediately to go with him. My mum said something to him in Igbo before we left the room to go and play in the front yard. As soon as I got outside, I felt at home. All the children followed us outside, and other children from the surrounding houses also joined us. They all started asking me questions at once: "you eat rice?", "you speak Igbo?", "you come from abroad?" They kept asking different questions until my cousin shouted at them to stop. We started a game of football. At around 11am it was hot, but fun.

We must have been playing for over two hours before my

mum came outside and called me in. In that short time playing outside, I quickly realised that I was going to have a huge communication problem. Even though most of the children I had played with were older than me, most of them couldn't speak English, let alone string together a meaningful English sentence. All they could manage was to cobble a few words together at a time, hoping that I understood. For example, when we were playing football, they kept on saying "pass ball, pass ball" or "catch am, catch am". At times they spoke to me in Igbo, as if to force me to understand the language, or they would embark on the use of 'hand and head movement' language, trying to indicate what they meant. I'd always reply back in English, which they had problems understanding, mainly because I spoke with my English accent. This accent very quickly earned me the very first of many nicknames; "Chima supiri, supiri" or "Chima London". Supiri, supiri was how my English accent sounded to them. I didn't mind the name.

As it was the summer holidays, I got to play a lot, most of the time with Imo and the kids who lived on the same street as us. We also visited a lot of relatives, to whom I was introduced – but I had no clue as to who they were, or how they were related to me. Sometimes they would try telling me who they were, but I couldn't understand them, so my mum would sometimes translate for them. After a while, I lost count – there were just so many. I soon discovered that Sunday after church was a time set out each week to visit friends and relatives, eat rice, and drink.

As we moved around the town of Aba, I decided it was a good time to ask about the dilapidated state of the roads and about the haunted and traumatised look I had noticed on the faces of many of the adults. I soon learnt that the dilapidated roads and potholes were due to the Nigerian Civil War, which had ended just over six years ago. The federal government led by Yakubu Gowon had bombarded most of Eastern Nigeria with bombs, killing thousands of innocent civilians and rendering that part of the country effectively roadless. Although the war had been expected to last no longer than a couple of weeks, it lasted over two and a half years. It claimed the lives of over 100,000 soldiers and over a million civilians, who died mainly of starvation and disease. The haunted looks were an effect of the war, with most people losing loved ones, houses and businesses. Although I did not notice it at the time, the country was also under a lot of tension due to the huge ethnic mix and the after-effects of the war; the conflict did not end in the favour of the Igbos, who live in the south-east of the country. What made matters even worse was the amount of hatred and lack of trust between the different tribes.

My early days in Nigeria were full of shocks, surprises, history, and learning. One of my earlier shocks was when we travelled to my town, Edda, and discovered that there was no electricity there. By 6pm, everywhere was pitch dark and all the night insects and animals came out. For the first time in my life, I saw what I initially thought were shooting stars – they turned out to be fireflies and to say I was scared would be a huge understatement.

Our first stop in the village was Ebunwana Edda, the place where my dad grew up and which I was eventually to call home for many years. I sat there in one of the corners of a mud hut which belonged to my uncle, Chief Ogbonnaya Oko Nnachi, O.O.'s dad, with just one small lantern for light, whilst droves of people streamed in to see my mum and me. In those days, it was quite a ceremony when anyone visited from abroad, so people always flocked to see who the guest was, say hello, and accept any gifts given to them.

Chief Ogbonnaya was a well-known figure within the Edda community; he was a moderator, peacemaker and one to go to if advice or words of wisdom were needed. He had about five wives and over thirty children – thirty-three, to be exact. He had an intimidating figure to go with his understanding of people, which made him a very fearsome character. His wives lived in the different mud huts which surrounded his, and they took turns to cook for him and his guests. They also took turns to spend the nights with him – a tradition quite rife amongst the Igbos and one that usually bred contempt amongst the wives. Living in the same compound as Chief Ogbonnaya was an elderly woman who at first I assumed was one of his wives. I later found out she his older sister, and she became known to me as Nne (grand mum) although most people called her Nne Agbai. Her real name was Mrs Ugo Okoro. She wasn't my real grand mum – she was the older sister of my dad's mum (who was called Ogbonne) – but she had looked after my dad when his mum died a couple of days after giving birth to him. She took care of him until he grew up and left home for better pastures. It took me many years to find out all this information, but I was an inquisitive kid. She was eventually to have a huge influence on me during my stay in the Nigeria.

Ebunwana was a medium-sized village, one of seventy-two situated along the hilly terrain of Edda, known for their farming, fishing, and trading. Edda is probably most widely known for great warriors and mercenaries, who were often hired by other Igbo towns to fight wars for them throughout most of the twentieth century. The incentive for them to go to war was the loot they got after defeating the enemy. The fact that they were always involved in wars had a huge impact on where they lived; they chose to live near impregnable terrains as a defensive strategy against any potential aggressors. The difficult terrain in which they lived meant that their roads were either non-existent or very difficult to travel; this obviously had an impact on their economy and development. The Edda people were also very superstitious and invested a lot in their tradition and culture. I will explain this further later on.

My first whole day in Ebunwana was quite eventful. One

of my uncles, Uncle Meme, took me out to the bush. We took the very narrow bush paths as we explored the natural terrain, something that excited me as there was such a stark difference in environment compared to England. The exploration reminded me of some of the films about Africa that I used to watch. We saw lots of different animals, from monkeys, squirrels, bush rats and snakes, to eagles, hawks, kites, and guinea fowl. It was like a lesson in Zoology. The evening ended very quickly because of the lack of electricity – by 6pm we were back in the compound. Some people were telling stories by moonlight, which I could not understand as they were in Igbo. Other people stared at me as if I'd just landed from Mars. I was still quite scared, as it was pitch black, and all the night animals and insects that you could think of were making themselves heard.

The following day, my mum told me we were going on a three-and-a-half-mile walk to her village, Owutu Edda. We were going to see her brothers and sisters, uncles, aunties, cousins and nephews, half-brothers and half-sisters. When we got to Owutu, an entourage fit for a king greeted us at the house of my mum's younger sister, Ola. People gathered round and began talking excitedly to my mum and her sisters and brothers. Unable to understand what they were saying, I began to get frustrated – this is one factor that prompted me to learn the language quickly. Every now and again, someone would say something to me in pidgin and I'd politely smile and nod, pretending to understand and appreciate what he or she had said.

To my utter horror, some of the older women began rubbing powder on their faces and bare breasts. I had no idea why these ladies wore no bras, nor why they only had on funny-coloured skirts which they kept on opening and closing. How was I supposed to know that what they had on were wrappers, and they didn't wear bras for a variety of reasons, including the fact that it was usually too hot? Nobody in the village stared at women's breasts – except me, of course. These women then proceeded to sing and dance around in circles, clapping their hands and making funny noises. I thought that this was some kind of ceremony they were performing before they killed me and used my body for some sort of black voodoo – that's what watching too much television does to your mental stability.

Anyway, I was scared shitless and began plotting how to escape this horrid ritual before I was dead meat. Where was I going to run to? Things were made especially difficult because I was sitting next to my mum, who was in on the whole thing – she had encouraged me to come to Owutu and meet her family. It took me less than two minutes to conjure up a plan. I very calmly excused myself, saying I had to go to the toilet. I then swiftly made for the street and headed for the nearest foliage that I could see. I ended up in a place called Otitaki. Even though I thought I had run very far away from the impending ritual, Otitaki was just sixty or so yards from my auntie's house.

Once in the forest, I had a huge task ahead of me. How was I going to avoid all the snakes, lions and tigers that lived in the forest I usually saw on television? How was I going to keep myself from being captured by the native bushmen, who ate people? I had made a grave mistake coming into the forest, but there was no turning back now. I barely had enough time to gather my thoughts before I heard shouts behind me – it was the search party that had been sent out to find me. I quickly jumped into the nearest cluster of bushes and crouched down low as the party went past. Where was I to go now? I didn't have enough time to think beyond that because the party had back-tracked and were heading straight in my direction. I made a bolt for it, but I must have underestimated the speed of some of the men involved, and my capture was swift. I thought to myself, I've only been in Nigeria for a week, and they're going to kill me and eat me; and my mum was the master plotter. That made me cry.

When we got back to the house, my mum was furious with me. "Why did you run away?" she asked. "You've started your stupid behaviour here in Nigeria." I asked her why she of all people would want to kill me. Was this payback for the wrong I had done in London? Was my dad in on this plot? She asked me if I was mad. I asked her what was going on, and she explained that the family was celebrating; putting powder on their faces and chests was an Igbo tradition, carried out when a new-born baby arrives. I was the new-born baby. Although I wasn't a baby, they hadn't seen me before, and this was the first time my mum and I had come home to Nigeria. With me now under strict supervision, the family celebrations continued way into the night. I ate and drank until I fell asleep.

My mum had spent most of her early years living with her parents – my grandparents – at Calabar and had only visited Owutu during the school holidays. She was then sent to the village aged eleven to live with her auntie and younger sister, where she would sell cigarettes and alcohol in order to get pocket money. Eventually, she moved back to Calabar. Her engagement to my dad had been quite swift, as had her departure to the UK in 1965, when she was only 16, so she had only managed to spend a couple of days with her siblings and other members of the extended family before she left. During the eleven years that my mum had been in the UK, so much had happened – there had been the Nigerian Civil War, which claimed over a million Igbo lives between 1967 and 1970, and the Igbo pogrom of 1966 in the north of the country, which had claimed over 600,000 Igbo lives.

My mum's own mother had died following childbirth shortly after my mum left, and Oko Elekwa, one of my mum's younger brothers, was nearly a victim of the war when he fell ill with kwashiorkor (a form of severe protein malnutrition) and was abandoned out of necessity. So many of my mum's other relatives had passed away too whilst she was in this foreign country called England.

Probably the one loss that forever left its mark with my mum was that of her dad, who passed away in 1969. The circumstances of his death are still unclear to me. Rumour has it that he had lost the will to live when he lost his wife a few years earlier.

My mum spent much of her time in Owutu catching up with her siblings and everyone else, and we also went to visit many other relatives. One thing they all had in common was how nice and genuine they all were towards me. This is something I revisited later in life; it inspired me to gravitate towards my mum's side of the family as I grew older and wiser. That is still the case to this day. After a few lovely days in the village, it was time for us to head back to Aba. Even though most of the people in the village were very nice, I missed the electricity, clean water, and some of the children who spoke some English.

Throughout the remainder of the time my mum spent in Nigeria, we stayed at 15 Onyembi Street. My dad's younger brother, Mr Okoro Ikpo, who lived there with his first wife Rosaline and their five children, looked after the house. When we arrived in Nigeria unannounced, space became a bit of an issue; although the house had about eight rooms, most of them were rented out, except the three in which Okoro Ikpo. However, out of respect, we were given a room to share whilst the rest of the family shared two rooms and a storage room near the back of the house, usually referred to as the kitchen line.

Before my mum left me to go back to the UK, we did have a falling out. I had asked my mum if I could go outside and play with the other children, but she said no because it was raining and she didn't want me to catch a cold. We started arguing, and after a few minutes of this I got up and kicked her in the stomach. It must have hurt because she doubled over in pain. I did not wait to see if she was alright. I ran off into the rain and didn't come back until it was very late, by which time a search party was already looking for me. I was lucky not to get beaten for that stunt, and I think it left my mum in no doubt that I had to stay in Nigeria. What I didn't know at the time was that she was pregnant with my younger brother, Olugh.

A day or so before my mum left for England, she took me to 7 Ugorji Street. She said my dad had insisted that I stay there and start my schooling. Okoro Ikpo was furious, as he did not understand the sudden change of plan. "Isn't my house good enough for you to leave your son in? Do you think I can't feed him? I have many children of my own – one more is not going to make a difference!" My dad's instructions were final. I did find out many years later that Okoro Ikpo was angry because he was hoping to collect the allowance that my dad would be sending to look after me; he was unhappy that he had lost out on that deal and that O.O. was going to be the beneficiary.

My mum left for England in the first week of August 1976. I was either in denial or too stubborn to admit that

I was being left behind. Even when my mum's taxi arrived and she got in, I just waved to her briefly – as if she was going on a two-hour trip to the local market and not leaving her only son alone in a foreign country and travelling over 5,000 kilometres back to England.

Immediately after she left, I went into the sitting room and sat down in a chair that was facing the wall clock, as if to say, "I'm watching the time to see how long it takes you to come back and get me". That chair became my favourite spot. After two days of waiting, I finally understood what was happening to me: I had been left in Nigeria – a country that was alien to me; a country whose language I didn't understand; a country where I knew nobody; a country too far away from my two sisters, especially my little sister Ugo. It was a country that had no hope or future for itself, let alone for a stranger who had left a country which was full of hope and which had a future – a country that I understood, and that understood me.

For days and nights, I sat in front on the clock and cried. I thought of ways to end my torment but couldn't bring myself to do anything. I wept so much that O.O. and his wife Ugo Bridget got scared I would die of a broken heart – as if there was such a thing. They told me stories of people who had lost dear ones during the war and gave up the will to live; they just wept and wept until their hearts couldn't take it anymore and they died. They were trying to scare me, but little did they know that these stories drove me even closer to despair. I did try to cry myself to death. I wouldn't eat anything, and I only drank water.

After about three weeks or so of crying and eating very little, I had lost three stones in weight. One day, I heard laughter outside my window; for the first time, I listened to what the people were saying, although I could not understand a word. I decided to take a peek at what all the hearty laughter was about, and through a small gap in my drawn curtains I saw a group of barefoot boys playing football in the yard. I watched them play until dusk, and for the first time when I sat down opposite the clock, I did not cry. I believe this was the beginning of my transformation; maybe O.O. and Ugo Bridget's prayers were finally heard by the almighty Lord after all.

The next day, I was up for morning prayers before my cousin Gabriel could come and call me. He was surprised and asked whether I'd had problems sleeping. I went and had my bath, and when Ugo Agwu Chukwu, one of my aunties, asked me if I would eat black eye beans and plantain, I nodded my head. She rushed to the kitchen to start cooking. As I ate, my aunties, uncle, and cousins gathered round me to watch me eat what I think was one of my first meals since my mum had left me. I ate so many beans that my stomach hurt, and I started letting out wind. Later on in the afternoon, I asked for more beans, which I finished. I then went into the yard and watched the boys play football until Ude, one of my cousins, asked me to come and join in. It was just what I was waiting for. It was time to experiment and play football – ten toes, barefooted, skin; time for a test. I was ready, the weeks I had spent inside the house crying had prepared me for this, and I needed to release the anger. Surprisingly, I actually enjoyed myself, although I nearly lost a toe after scraping the top of my foot on the concrete floor that made up the yard. I did not know it then, but it was a push from God; after scraping my foot on the concrete floor, I could not wait for the wound to heal so that I could go back out and show that I could give as much as I could take.

Scrape after scrape, scar after scar, I got used to playing football on the concrete floor with no football boots. That's how they did it in Nigeria, and I began to wonder whether I was becoming a Nigerian. From playing football in the back yard, I started to play football in the front yard, then on the streets, and finally on the football pitch, which was about quarter of a mile away. A lot of people still stared at me. They thought I had gone back with my mum and had been unaware that I was hiding inside. A lot of the younger children followed me wherever I went. The walks to the football pitch were a breath of fresh air for me; Ude would buy me cakes, sweets and drinks, Fanta especially. The kids asked me question after question about England: "Is it true that everyone there is white and speaks English?", "Do all the kids over there go to school?".

One day, on our way back from playing football, we decided to take a different route home. We cut through the back of Golf Course Primary School and took the more scenic route along Ekenna Avenue, which was situated in the GRA (Government Reserved Area) of Aba. It was mainly occupied by British, American and Portuguese people, and some rich Nigerian families lived there as well. Ekenna Avenue was such a contrast to the middle-class Okigwe Road, which ran parallel to it. On the avenue, I met a few other kids who had been born in the UK and now lived in Nigeria. When we realised that we were all from England, the chemistry was instant. My circle of friends was starting to grow, and with it, my confidence.

One day, my uncle O.O. called me and said that we had to go and look for a primary school for me, as the summer holidays were coming to an end. I can't remember whether I was happy or not, but what I do remember is thinking of all the new friends I would make, the time I would have to myself whilst there, and how I could explore the town of Aba. After three days of searching for a suitable school, we found one that was specifically for kids from abroad. It was called Santa Maria Primary School, and it was three miles away on the other side of town, tucked away on Constitutional Crescent, a scenic part of Aba where the rich folk lived. My uncle spoke with the head teacher for quite a while; we then went to the bursary to pay my school fees. My dad had sent enough money to pay for the whole year.

For some strange reason, I was put in Year 6 instead of Year 5. The three-mile walk every day to school did not impress me at all. I had to leave the house at 7am in order to get to school before classes started at 8am. The kids were stuck up and very unfriendly, mainly because they all came from rich families, had lived abroad, or had just had a bad upbringing; the teaching methods were different to what I was used to in London, and it did not help that I had been put up a year; I found it very hard to keep up with anything, often daydreaming or doing something totally abstract instead of paying attention to the lessons. I didn't make any friends and was always picked on by a group of spoilt brats in my class who appeared to know nearly everyone in the school. My long walk home was boring too; I was the only one who walked that far, as all the other kids either lived nearby or their parents picked them up in luxurious, air-conditioned cars. It came as no surprise to me when I failed the end-of-year exams; I didn't take half of them anyway.

My uncle O.O. was very upset with me. He was also concerned about what my parents would say and whether they would blame him for my failure. I explained to him the difficulties I was experiencing – the long walk and the different teaching methods – and he relayed this information to my parents. They told him I should repeat the year. I agreed that I would, but said it had to be in a different school – one closer to home and where it would be easier for me to make friends. To my delight, he chose Golf Course Primary School, where we played football on a daily basis. The school was located on Okigwe Road, very close to the railway track where Overail started. It was about fifteen minutes away from our house, and most of the kids on our street went there. It was co-located with another school, Okigwe Road Primary, although it had a better reputation, and was academically sound. The school was perfect for me.

So, in September 1977, just over a year since I had arrived in Nigeria, I was making another fresh start. I soon made many more friends. One day I got into a fight with the class bully – a girl called Agu, which means "lion". She was in the middle of giving me an arse-kicking when one of the boys, Emeka Kalu Agbai, jumped in and stopped the punishment. Later, he pulled me aside and asked me whether I would be interested in learning Shaolin Kung Fu, which I could use to defend myself if I got into trouble. That was the beginning of our friendship. Emeka was a couple of years older than me and started to look after me at school.

Emeka was from a place called Abiriba, which is very close to Edda. We had met a couple of times at the Assemblies of God church, which O.O. and his family attended. Okigwe Road Primary School served as the church premises on Sundays, and on other evenings for choir practice and bible studies. Emeka was a Shaolin Kung Fu pupil, and I had seen him learning some Sundays when I was at church. It didn't take long for him to convince me to sign up to Shaolin. We trained twice a week; three hours on a Sunday, and an hour on a weekday. Our master was an ex-police office called "Kill and Bury". He was deadly, but a very efficient master to learn the art from. After my induction, Kill and Bury told me I would not need to pay for my sessions because I was too young. My uncle did not like the fact that I was learning this deadly art and that lessons took place on Sundays, but he saw that I enjoyed it, so he let me be, so long as I also went to Sunday School and stayed till the end.

On my way to school each morning, I would pass by Emeka's house on Owerri Road. He would join me, and we'd walk the rest of the way together. After school, I would go back to his house with him to either play or learn Shaolin. It didn't take long for the entire family to get to know who I was; they accepted me as one their own. I would eat meals with them, and some weekends I would sleep over. I was having a great time; I was enjoying my education, was getting very good grades in assessments, and excelled in school. I had a lot of friends, and I wasn't getting into any trouble. Emeka would sometimes take me to see the cinema to see martial arts films; he also used every opportunity to teach me. When I got into trouble with my auntie or uncle, I'd run and stay at Emeka's house until they begged me to come back. In return, I helped Emeka with his homework and other academic work, and he excelled in most of his classwork.

On most Saturdays, I would go to Ekeoha Market with my uncle and cousins to learn about the business that they were involved in. They sold a variety of materials used for sewing trousers, dresses and shirts. It was petty trade, but it brought in enough money to sustain the whole family. I used the opportunity to explore Aba, make more friends, and learn more about the history of Aba and Igboland. Generally, Aba was a bustling market town full of pothole-riddled streets which were equally full of snarling traffic, pushcarts, wheelbarrows, street hawkers, and tyre repair shops. It was an unforgettable, decrepit mix of a postcolonial metropolis, shaped by over seventy years of British rule and British ideas, a decade of military misrule, and thirty-two months of war. There was egregious theft everywhere because people were hungry and still suffering the after-effects of the war and of the ruthless Gowon policy of "no victor, no vanquished", whereby some Igbos who'd had bank accounts before the war were all given twenty pounds, regardless of the amount they'd had in their accounts.

The market soon burned down for what was a third time, and the authorities finally decided to close it and open a brand new one called Ariaria International Market. This market operated just like any other international market – any kind of product for human consumption and usage can be found there.

My uncle O.O. and his family were very religious; we all went to church regularly, including to evening bible classes. O.O. also enrolled me into the church choir, where I sang treble. I enjoyed going to church on Sundays; it was another opportunity to meet my friends, and singing in the choir always gave me great joy – I immersed myself in the songs, learning most of them at home. I stayed in the choir until I went off to secondary school. It also meant I got some illegal spending money – money I was supposed to use for donation at church.

It was at church that I met Mr Anderson, a regular churchgoer and a friend of the family. Mr Anderson was a businessman of some sort who always dressed up very smartly. One day, he approached me in church and said he liked me. He said he liked me because I was very intelligent and also helpful. On some Sundays he gave me money to buy cake and drinks; that used to make my day, as he often gave me enough to last me weeks. Our relationship seemed like a very good one; he was in his late thirties, so was like an uncle to me. When I eventually went to secondary school, our relationship grew, privately and intimately; then it took an awful twist. I'll come back to that shortly.

The months went by very quickly, and it was soon time for our end-of-year exams (common entrance exams), which guaranteed entrance into secondary school. Most children passed the exams, which was great; however, this meant we would be going to separate secondary schools, which was quite sad, considering the relationship we were all beginning to build. I passed the entrance exams with thirty-one marks (the highest achievable mark was thirty-six) and was accepted into National High School, Aba, popularly known as IBONACO. It was a school of high class and great expectations, and it was arguably the best school in Aba. The school was noted for its discipline, high morals and academic excellence, so it was always the first choice for parents and guardians who wanted their boys to have a proper academic and moral upbringing. It is therefore not surprising that today, many alumni of the school occupy key positions in government and business. Emeka was accepted into Eziama High School, Aba, whilst my cousin, Imo, was admitted into Iheorji Secondary School, situated at the end of Ohanku Road. We would all be going our different ways as we tried to pave the way to a better life for ourselves.

By now, I had managed to get a very good understanding of Igbo language. Although I wasn't fluent, I understood nearly everything. The fact that most of my friends who were my own age nearly always spoke Igbo made it harder for me to always speak English, which helped me learn quicker. However, an inadvertent result of my first language being English was that I gained a lot of friends who were a lot older than me – usually five to eight years older. This was because they were able to speak better English, simply because they had studied the subject for longer, so we understood each other very well. Having older friends served me well in the future.

The summer of 1978 was a particularly busy one, as everyone was preparing to go off to secondary school. It was during this summer holiday that an incident occurred between the O.O. family and me which led to me packing my stuff and moving out. One morning, Bridget woke me from my sleep and asked me why I had gone into her soup pot and eaten most of the meat. I told her it wasn't me, but she insisted it was because I was the only one in the house who stole things. I told her that this wasn't exactly true, as Gabriel had been caught stealing a few times, but she insisted I had taught Gabriel how to be a thief. We argued about the missing meat for a long time before she walked off in a huff saying that if I attempted a stunt like that again, she would kick me out of the house. I told her she wouldn't have to wait for another time. "I've had enough of being shouted at and lied to," I said. "You can keep your house, and when your meat goes missing again, you'll have nobody to blame."

Bridget must have thought I was bluffing because she didn't reply; she simply walked out. I waited till everyone had gone to work, or the market, and quietly packed my things, which only filled half a suitcase. I put the suitcase on my head and headed for Okigwe Road, where I jumped on a bus to Ngwa Road by East. From there, I caught another bus to the top of Ohanku Road just by Onyembi Street. When I walked into Number 15 Onyembi Street, everyone was shocked to see me; Okoro Ikpo was at the market, but my cousins were all in. When they asked me what had happened, I told them. I wasn't quite sure whether they were glad to see me or not, but I didn't care; this was my dad's house, and I was staying. When Okoro Ikpo got back, he was surprisingly calm for someone who had an awful temper. Unknown to me, he already knew what had happened. I think he was also happy that I had come by my own free will; he would now collect the maintenance money that my parents sent for my upkeep. He was a greedy man.

I remember there was a lot of fuss about what to buy for Imo – he needed books, clothes, sandals, pens and pencils for secondary school. I accompanied Imo and his dad to buy all his things, but nothing was bought for me. I wasn't quite sure why my dad hadn't yet sent any money for me to prepare for this new exciting stage of my life. I wrote a couple of letters explaining that everyone except me was getting all they needed for secondary school. Just when I was beginning to suspect that maybe he had sent the money to O.O., who had withheld it out of spite, I received a pleasant surprise. After weeks of silence, my dad suddenly arrived in Nigeria – without any notice (and without the bike he'd promised he'd buy me). I was happy to see him because I knew I would get everything I needed to prepare me for secondary school.

My dad decided I would have to stay in the school dormitory because the journey was more than five miles from Onyembi Street to Port Harcourt Road; a journey I wasn't keen on at all. We went to the school to meet the principal, but because my dad had left it very late to enrol me in the school and sort out my boarding facilities, we had missed the registration deadline. He had to pay a bribe to the principal to ensure that I could register and that he could pay my entire year's school and boarding fees.

My dad then took me to the market and we bought most of the things that I would need at school. Everything was a blur to me; I was crying all the time, and I could not work out whether I was happy to get away from Imo's dad and his family or not. It was also an emotional time, as it was the first time I had seen anyone from my immediate family since my mum had left in 1976. I spent a lot of time with my dad, going around Aba, visiting friends and relatives. We went to the village to see relatives there too. I felt like a king for a change.

The feeling didn't last very long. My dad only stayed for three weeks, and just as I was getting used to this homely style of life, he started packing his stuff for his return trip to London. I tried to convince him to take me back with him, but it didn't work. The day he left, I moved into the dormitory of my new school.

My introduction to Nigerian boarding school was a very harsh eye-opener and a shock to the system. Everything was so different to life at home. The rules were very strict, the regimen was gruelling; there was a lot of shouting, bullying and intimidation. Everyone seemed to be older than me. During my brief stint in the dormitory, I did have some new experiences, though. I joined the boxing club for training and practice, which met on Mondays, Wednesdays and Fridays at 5.30am. I managed one session, which I hastily left after being floored with the very first punch of my first bout.

It was a Friday when I arrived, and the first activity of the Saturday was a general inspection of beds and uniforms, together with a detailed briefing on what dormitory life was all about, like it or not. It was like the first day at a military training camp. The head prefect at the time, Mr Mbakwe, shouted at us frightened Johnny Just Comes (JJCs), telling us all the rules and regulations and what happened when they were not obeyed. "The morning wake up-bell goes off at 5am, you get up, make your bed and get ready for morning prayers. After prayers, you go outside for your thirty-minute chosen sporting activity. After sports, there is a rota call for everyone in Years 1 to 4. Anyone who is late or missing will be dealt with accordingly, and you had better not have any excuses," he said.

Mr Mbakwe was a big guy for someone in Year 5, but I soon learnt that people generally started school late, usually because parents had to save enough money to send them there. They were either forced to stay at home and help with looking after their siblings or would go to the market or farm and help bring some form of income in. The Nigerian Civil War (1967–1970) also had a knockback effect on education; many people from the east of Nigeria could not go to school for fear of being targeted by bomber aircrafts, and many of them fled and became refugees. Older boys signed up either to join the Biafran army or the younger guerrilla unit that supported the soldiers. After the war, most of these boys returned to education, so many of the boys in Years 4 and 5 were either ex-soldiers or had had some involvement in the war.

On the evening of that first Saturday, after we had all gone to bed (the lights went out at 9.30pm), I found it felt strange to be in a dormitory full of strangers, most snoring away after the labours of the day. The darkness frightened me to the extent that I couldn't sleep. Around midnight, I was overcome by an unbearable urge to go to the toilet; a Number Two. It was then that it dawned on me I had no idea where the toilets were. During the day, we had used the bushes or grass as a makeshift toilet to relieve ourselves, so I was stuck.

I reached into my bag, which was underneath my bed, and grabbed some paper. I crumpled it up and stealthily made for the dormitory exit door. After spending a couple of minutes hastily looking for a toilet, unsuccessfully, I found what looked like a quiet, slightly bushy area, just behind the dormitory building, and relieved myself. I slipped back into the dormitory and into my bed. Around 4.30am, a very loud bell started ringing. The prefects started shouting "Everyone get up now!" and "Get up and come outside!". We all begrudgingly got up and filed outside. As we began to line up, I froze when I spotted my handiwork from the previous night, in full view of all the students. As I was wondering whether anyone had spotted the mess, I was jolted to my senses when Mr Mbakwe shouted: "Right – who in the hell left this disgusting pile of shit right here for all of us to see?". There was a deafening silence. "Are you impudent boys' deaf?" he bellowed out, "or do you want me to order the flogging of the entire school?".

I shuddered with fear as I weighed up my options. Reluctantly, I put my hand up so he could see me. He walked over to me and shouted, "Was it you that left this shit here?"

"Yes," I responded, as quietly as I could.

"Speak up, you buffoon!" he said.

"It was me."

He looked me up and down scornfully. I nearly did another shit in my shorts as he looked at me. After what felt like hours, he dismissed everybody and told me to come with him. He took me into a classroom and gave me twelve lashes of his belt on my behind. It didn't hurt as much as I had imagined it would, but I was shocked that a total stranger had the power to flog me. After my flogging, he told me to go and clean up the mess I'd left, then report back to him. When I went to clear up my shit, there was a congregation of flies helping themselves to the pile. There was also a small congregation of students standing nearby, sniggering at me. When I reported back to the senior prefect, he told me that he felt somewhat sorry for me and was going to give me a mild form of punishment. He told me I had to sleep under the bed of a

Year 5 student. He pointed to the student, who was sitting on his bed, reading. "What are you doing still standing here? Go and report to him, now, now" the prefect said.

I went over to the senior student, who looked up at me from his bed and said, "So you're the one who shits all over the school compound". I tried to explain, but he told me to shut up. He stood up and introduced himself – his name was Buddy. I told him my name, but he looked at me with no interest. "You will be sleeping under my bed for the next three days. I also expect you to make sure I have water to bathe with and to drink. Is that clear?" he said. I said that it was.

As I was about to walk away, Buddy said, "You can be my junior server, and I will look after you in this school". All Year 1 and 2 students living in the dormitory had a master they did things for, including washing their plates, collecting their food from the canteen, washing their clothes, looking after their water supplies etc. In return, the junior student got protection from the Year 5 student. I didn't spend any time thinking about it; I agreed immediately. For the little time I spent in the dormitory, all the students called me 'Buddy Junior'. Even after I left the dormitory, the name still stuck; Buddy effectively became my nickname.

After about five months at boarding school, I'd had enough of all the authoritarian methods – the shouting, the sleeping underneath beds, and the constant ringing of bells and standing in line for everything. I simply packed my bags one Friday afternoon after classes and went back to Onyembi Street. When Okoro Ikpo got back from the market and saw me with all my bags, he asked what had happened. I told him I couldn't take it there and would be walking from home. He was furious, but I couldn't have cared less. He shouted at me for days. When he got fed up of shouting at me, I told him that nothing would make me go back to the dormitory. I think that from the resolute tone of my voice he knew I wasn't going to budge. He said, "Your dad's not going to be happy with you, after he paid your boarding fees for the entire year". I shrugged my shoulders. When my dad found out about me moving out, he wrote me a very angry letter, commanding me to return to the dormitory. I ignored it, and several other letters. Finally, the letters stopped.

During my time living in the dormitory, I had lots of experiences – some good, but mostly bad. However, the worst experience of my entire time in Nigeria happened three or so months after I started school. One Friday afternoon after classes, I had left the dormitory to go home to Onyembi Street for the weekend. On my way home, I bumped into Mr Anderson from the Assemblies of God church I had attended when I lived with uncle O.O. We started talking; he asked me about my studies and how I was adapting to life in Nigeria. He asked me where I was going, and when I told him I was going home for the weekend he suggested I stay with him at his flat that weekend. He promised me a good time, as well as money.

Stupidly, I agreed and went with him to his house. That night, he asked me whether I wanted to sleep on the floor, with a mat, or on the bed. I said I would like to sleep on the bed, so we agreed to share it. I must have dozed off almost immediately. I was woken up by the heavy breathing of Mr Anderson in my ear. When I tried to move my head to see what was going on, he pinned me to the bed and started to take my trousers off. I tried to wriggle out of his grasp, but I couldn't – he was a strong man. After a couple of seconds, he told me it would be easier if I relaxed, and that it wouldn't hurt. I didn't know what else to do, so I laid back whilst he took off my trousers and pants and proceeded to rape me. I was eleven years old. It was very painful. I tried to scream, but he covered my mouth with his hand. When he had finished, he got off me and disappeared into the bathroom, which was down the corridor. I should have run out of the house then, but I didn't – I was in shock and couldn't get my brain or my body to respond to my thoughts. When he came back from the bathroom, he did look somewhat surprised; he was probably expecting me to have run off. He sat on the edge of the bed, looking at me from the corner of his eye. Eventually he asked me if I was okay. When I didn't respond, he told me that he would give me lots of money if I didn't tell anyone about what had happened. During that weekend, he raped me on three occasions. On Sunday afternoon, I told him I needed to leave. He gave me twenty naira and saw me to the door. The incident scarred me for life. I never did tell anyone about it. I was afraid I would be blamed. I did so many other bad things that I couldn't see how anyone would ever believe me. I never saw Mr Anderson again.

Chima Oko

6, Luxor Street,
London, S.E5 9QN,
18th April,1979

My dear Chima,
     I have been receiving reports of your every day activities. I then seize this opportunity to write you and for your information. When I came to Nigeria last Sept1978 I made every possible effort to see you remain in the boarding. I was successful in seeing you remain there. But now I had a report that you are neither there nor going to school at all. A part from that you have staying where none of my brothers at home knows. They asked you do not want to tell them. Remember Nigeria is wide and you can't lodge all houses in Nigeria. You can only go where my brother tells you to go. Also you oftern go to water side to swim remember that water is extreemly dangerous. People are missing there every day of the week.

     Now listen, you have to obey me being your father. If you do not do what I say well you should as from now bear your responsibilities. So go back to your school today. Obey your uncle. And if I hear a futher bad report from them as I said when we come back you are not going to stay with us you find your own house. Niki is now also in the secondary school, and Eja will be going this Sept,1979. All of them are good boys. Now Onyemachi is going to her econdary school this Sept. So the family will not be prepared to have you if you do not want to go to school. When you will be 15years old or 20years it will be late for you and I was struggling when you are 22years old you would be enjoying your employment. When you do bad at Over-rail you come back at Onyembi. You think you know better than your seniors? NO? So this letter is a warning to you and you should keep this letter safe hence in future if you are suffering you will always read back this letter then you will say I had all chances but failed to make good use of it.

     Remember I have paid your school fee for the whole year. I was sending you pocket money. What again do you want. I was told you have sold all your shirts, books,bocket etc. Anything you do Within a day I know. So do not think you are doing me. The first term you failed to take your examinations. You have to change good or from bad to good before we can accept you Chima.

```
                            - 2 -

     You will have to count your age and if you are above
12yeats you will never be accepted in to the Secondary.
This is your only chance to study.     There are many things
I have heard about you but I am giving a chance to change
from bad to good boy.   Return your school no that I have
paid your school fee including boarding. All these things
am writing your mother is not happy, your sisters are not
happy and they are doing well. So what am saying now is
a word is sufficient to a wise. If you thm think to be
good go back to your school.   Papa Imo has also written
me he has done all he could for you to go back to school
yet to no avail. Ama has written me and the rest.

     I will then wish to hear from Papa Imo you gone back
to your school and your now a good boy.
May God be with you always.


                                    Yours father,


                                    O.O. Chukwu
```

Dad's angry letter to me

Leaving boarding school and living with my uncle Okoro Ikpo turned out to be a blessing and a punishment. My cousin Imo taught me so many different things, including how to play football. He encouraged me to learn the Igbo language, and he taught me how to play a lot of Nigerian games. We were the kings of draughts, ball u, okwe, nails, koso and other games that most Nigerian kids indulged in as pastimes. I learnt so much, I had a lot of fun, and I made more friends.

On the other hand, Okoro Ikpo beat the shit out of me nearly every day, or whenever he got the opportunity to. I was certainly no angel, but he would start beating me for the smallest mistakes, or if I forgot to do something. Unlike my dad's beatings, Okoro Ikpo's beatings carried a lot of force and venom, and they hurt.

Because my school was a very long way away from the house, I had to leave around 6.30am in order to get there by 8am. I always walked to school, as nobody gave me any money for transport or pocket money. Rosaline would make me go to school hungry every morning. When I asked for breakfast, she always said that there was no breakfast available, and that I could have a big lunch when I came back later in the afternoon. One day, however, ten minutes or so into my journey to school I realised I had forgotten something, so I turned back towards home. To my dismay, when I got to the house Imo was sitting down eating breakfast; I had been told there was none. I was furious, but couldn't do anything. This was just one of the many evils she used to do to me. She used to send me to fetch water whilst all her other children stayed at home and played. She always gave me less food than anyone else. She sometimes made me sleep underneath the bed that Imo slept in. I had nowhere to keep my clothes or other belongings. She made me feel like an orphan, and to be honest I felt like an orphan, with no real parents or siblings. It was depressing and sad. When I was alone, I cried a lot because I was lonely. I had nobody to talk to and nowhere to go, and I just couldn't see where my future was heading.

The daily eight-mile round trip, walking to and from

school, proved to be a gruelling task too far for me, and I eventually gave up going to school and skived.

Every day, I'd pack my school bag with books and clothes that I could change into as soon as I left the house. My favourite visiting place was Waterside – a river that runs round the entire circumference of Aba. It is famously known as a place of deliberate sacrificial drownings of people to feed the thirst of the lake goddess, known as 'Mummy Water', and a place of prayers of many barren women, who prayed to the goddess for fertility and children.

Picture of my cousin, Imo

I would go to the waterside near our house, which was called Nepa Waterside. It was so named because to get there you had to go down a road which had huge overhead electric National Electric and Power Authority (NEPA) cables. I would normally get there around 8am. It was quite spooky being there alone, but I got used to it with time. The more I went there, the better my swimming became, and after a while I started swimming longer lengths, and in deeper areas. Most of the time, I would stay there until 2pm, which was when school finished. I would then go home, dump my bag, and go back out to play football.

The few times I did go to school, I always managed to convince the teachers that I would change my ways and start going regularly. They always seemed to believe me. I think they believed me because I was very good at most of the subjects, including Literature, which was taught by an Asian lady who was a great friend of the principal. My English was also very good, and I still managed to put on an English accent when I needed to. When I was in class, my Literature teacher always asked me to read to the class.

Sometimes when I visited Waterside I contemplated drowning myself so I could be rid of the burden of sorrow and cruelty I had suffered. Sometimes it got so bad that I would run away from home and stay with friends, most of who lived on the same street as us. They always felt sorry for me. They would often tell me that I looked like some of the children who suffered kwashiorkor during the civil war. The treatment I received made me rebel a lot. I made a conscious decision to be as naughty as I could be just to piss my uncle and aunty off.

Because I was naughty most of the time, I got blamed for everything. One of my aunties even came all the way from the village to Aba to tell my uncle that she had been informed I was part of an armed gang which robbed people at gun point along the Aba to Port Harcourt express road. These allegations were obviously false, but they were very damaging. My uncle and my grandma, who was in Aba for a brief holiday, both believed her, and there was nothing I say that would convince them I was telling the truth. On another occasion, my uncle beat the living daylights out of me, and he had locked the door beforehand so that the neighbours could not come in and stop him. He literally picked me up and kept on throwing me from one end of the room to the other hitting me against the wall every time. When he was tired of beating the shit out of me, he told his son to go to the bed room and get a razor blade so he could cut off one of my ears, since I did not use them to listen to advice. Fortunately, Imo knew his dad very well and did not get the razor. I was spared, and still have both ears. What had I done wrong? My aunty had told me to go and fetch some water that evening, and when I told her I had already been twice, she called me a liar and slapped me. When I asked her why she never sent her own kids to go and fetch water, she slapped me again and said I had no right asking questions in her house. I told her that the house belonged to my dad, not her husband. When Okoro Ikpo got back she told him, and he descended on me.

Okoro Ikpo used to drink a lot; he would finish his business in the day then go from the market to numerous beer parlours, drinking himself into a stupor nearly every day. You could hear him coming back home, as he was always shouting and cursing people as he approached. When we heard him coming, we would all cower in a corner so that he had nobody to pick on when he got in. It was his wife who was mostly on the receiving end. She always had to get his food for him and try and calm him down.

The abuse and cruelty that was dished out to me continued throughout 1978 and most of 1979. There were times when I wanted to have a go at studying and passing my exams, but I found it incredibly difficult to focus in the face of all the things going on at home. At the end of the school year, in July 1979, I either did not take my exams or the ones I did take I failed woefully, because I'd never had time to focus and study. The head teacher wrote my uncle a letter saying that my results were so bad he wasn't going to allow me to retake the exams; he said I had to repeat the year. The idea of repeating my first year of secondary school didn't bother me; it was the extreme cruelty dished out by my aunty and uncle that scared the living daylights out of me.

Luck, however, was on my side. I was given a lifeline when one of my uncles, Oko Ukpai, came on holiday to Aba from his secondary school in Ohafia. When he arrived and witnessed what my uncle and aunty were doing to me, he was appalled. Unknown to me, he wrote to my dad to ask if he could take me back to Ohafia, where he believed I would be able to focus and study. Surprisingly, my dad agreed for me to go back with him. A family meeting was called, and Oko Ukpai told Okoro Ikpo and his wife that he was taking me to Ohafia. My aunty was happy to see the back of me, but Okoro Ikpo wasn't as happy because he was going to lose whatever allowance my dad sent for my upkeep, which he had been using for himself.

Oko Ukpai taking me with him to Ohafia was an opportunity for a completely new life away from my wicked uncle and his wife. Oko Ukpai said to me that if I stayed in Aba any longer, sooner or later someone would have to write to my parents and tell them that their son was dead. I grabbed the opportunity to move to Ohafia with both hands.

Secondary School Life
(1979–1984)

The September of 1979 was the beginning of a new chapter in my life, and I was looking forward to my resurrection. My new school was Boys' Secondary School, Asaga, Ohafia. It was famously known as "Coronata". At the time, Ohafia was a fairly well-developed town situated in the far south of what was then Imo state. It was fairly close to my town – about thirty miles – and was a lot more peaceful than the bustling and dangerous melee of Aba. My uncle Oko Ukpai was a lot younger than Okoro Ikpo, and he seemed to understand me a lot better. We shared a single room in a small house in a small village called Amuke, near to the school. Everything was small, but comfortable, and my uncle was very nice to me. I had to start secondary school from scratch again, but I did not mind. Our landlady was slightly weird; she didn't say much to us, and sometimes when I said hello to her she'd ignore me, or just grunt – but when she did respond, she was quite nice, sometimes asking about my studies and welfare. Oko Ukpai brought a lot of stability to my life by taking me out of the environment I had endured at Aba. He made me understand the advantages of studying, applying myself in life and trying to achieve my dreams. He completed my school registration for me, and as soon as my dad sent him my maintenance money, he paid all my fees and told me how much was left over, and how he was going to spend it on me. It was mainly for books, clothes and food.

I began to enjoy going to school, studying, taking part in debates in class, tests and exams. I also soon began to form good relationships with some of the more intelligent boys in the school across all the classes. Immediately after I came back from school in the afternoons, I would have my lunch and start studying. I'd study from about 3pm till 6pm, have dinner, and continue studying till about 1am before going to bed, to wake up at 6am. This was a daily routine, which I kept up for one year.

Oko Ukpai and I routinely visited Ebunwana, our village, at weekends, probably every other month. This enabled us to have a short break, get fed very well by my grandma, and collect as many yams, garri, and other food items as we could carry to take back to Amuke. These supplies helped us supplement what we had to buy with our own money. Usually when we left Ebunwana on Sundays after our visits, we would walk for seven or so miles before taking a taxi or bus the rest of the way. We did this to save money so as to use it for food.

Strange Incidents

After the summer holidays of 1980, when I went back to school to start my second year at school, a series of strange, unexplained incidents occurred. These events not only scared the living daylights out of me, they caused a lot disruption and distraction. They were so bad that Oko Ukpai finally resolved to move me into the boarding school where he felt I would be safer.

The first strange incident occurred immediately after the summer holidays. Whilst I was studying in the earlier hours of the morning, NEPA, the authority in charge of the supply of electricity, decided to cut the electricity – something that happened at least three times a week. I decided to go to the toilet and then to bed. On my way to the toilet, which was outside the house, I saw what I thought was a huge tree trunk a few metres away from me. I thought to myself, I do not remember that tree trunk being there earlier in the afternoon. When I took a couple of steps forward to take a closer look, I realised that it was a not a tree trunk but a huge snake, which turned around and slithered into the bushes. I was slightly unnerved by this and told Oko Ukpai, who did not think much of it. After a while, neither did I; snakes were everywhere in Ohafia, so I soon forgot the incident.

The second and third strange incidents occurred a couple of weeks later, both on the same night, and they really shook me up. One night after I finished studying, one of my neighbours, Agwu, who was deaf and dumb, asked if I wanted to go up the hill to the Amuke barn where there were lots of udara (African cherry fruit) trees. The udara fruit is common in the southern part of Nigeria, especially between December and April. The fruits are not usually harvested from the trees but are left to drop naturally to the ground, from where they are picked. They tend to fall at night when it is cool. We walked the short distance up Amangwu road to the barn and settled down patiently to wait for them to start falling. We did not have to wait long, and as they started falling, we started scrambling to pick them up. I realised that Agwu was getting more than me, so I hatched a cunning plan. I decided I was not going to tell him when the udara fell, as he would not be able to hear them. The plan worked. When an udara fell, I would pretend to ignore it. Then, sometime after, I would casually get up, as if I was stretching my legs, and go to pick it up. I kept on with this tactic for a while. Then, all of a sudden, Agwu got up and started running and pointing back towards the bushes. I realised he was running home, but it was something we all did when we were tired and wanted to go; we would scare everyone into running home. I decided I had picked enough udara fruits anyway, so I casually jogged down the hill behind him.

Suddenly, I felt the hairs on the back of my neck stand up, and my instincts told me to look behind me. When turned and looked, I nearly collapsed with fright. About twenty metres behind me was a white, hazy, human-like figure with its arms stretched out sideways. The figure did not appear to have any legs, but each time it moved its outstretched arms, it glided closer and closer to me.

I was seized by fear and panic and started screaming. I dashed past Agwu, down the hill and into our house, where my uncle could not get me to stop my hysterical screaming. By this time, some of the neighbours had gathered around me to find out what was going on. When I finally stopped screaming and explained what I had seen, nobody believed me. Some of the neighbours quickly ran across to Agwu's house to get his version of what had happened. He was older than me and was able to narrate the same story a lot more cohesively. My uncle and the neighbours realised that we must have seen a ghost; they explained that there had always been rumours of a barn ghost, but not many people had seen it.

Later that same night, I woke up at 1.25am to go to the toilet. I opened the door quietly and looked across the street. Opposite our house, right in front of the Jehovah's Witness church, was the same ghost; it was gliding round the building. I watched it circle the church building once, and then I quietly crept back inside, woke my uncle up, and explained what I had seen. When we went back out to take a look, the gliding ghost had disappeared. My uncle said he believed what I had told him, and we'd discuss it in the morning. A couple of days after that, I started to get weird scratches all over my body at night. I also began to feel as if something was either following me or watching me all the time. The final straw came when I got up in the middle of the night to go to the toilet. Just as I got outside, I saw a hazy, transparent figure gliding slowly past me. The figure had a sullen look on its face and was looking in my direction as it glided towards the back of the house. I started screaming and then fainted. When I came to, I was lying on the floor in our room and Oko Ukpai was asking me what had happened. I explained what I had seen. He went off and told our landlady.

The following day, our landlady came to our room and confessed that she had been investigating some of the things that had been happening to me, including the odd things that had been occurring. She was convinced that something or somebody was out to get me. She advised me to move away from the area and renew my faith in God. My uncle took her advice, literally, and decided to move me into the dormitory of the school. Moving me to the dormitory was the beginning of another change I had no control over. In October 1980, after spending the weekend with my grandma in the village, I moved into the dormitory.

Boarding School Life

It felt like a whole new world in the dormitory; everything was so different to life as a day student. I made some great friends with boys like Daniel Ochonma, Godwin Eni and Eke Onyekwere – all from Arochukwu. There was also Kalu Kalu Osonwa from Ezi Afor, who was popularly known as papa KK Runson (a literal translation of his name), Hilary Ofor, and many others. I also had friends from the years above me: Santos, who I served as a junior; Nnachi Azu Agwu, aka Jomoh, who was the son of our village chief. I also made friends with a guy called Okoro Uduma, aka Professor, and Idika Agwu, aka Some Guy.

In those days, having a nickname was a must. I kept the nickname given to me during my short stint at National High School in Aba – Buddy. A lot of my friends called me Buddy Case, because I was always in trouble, or in 'cases', as it was referred to in those days. Getting up to mischief was the normal order of the day for me, and for some of my friends. This was nearly always paired with getting very serious with our studies and making sure we did well in our exams. We called it survival. During exam time, Godwin, Daniel and I always competed against each other for the top position in our year. This brought out the best in all of us, with the three top places in our year always rotating between us. This approach encouraged us to work studiously together, always challenging and pushing one another's boundaries. After studying together, we also used to sneak away and study privately. In the dormitory, our studying time was restricted, so if we wanted to do more, it had to be done in secret.

Living in the dormitory introduced me to independence, thoughtfulness, and studiousness. I also relished the fact that nobody from my family knew what I was up to. This was helped by my world of comfort and confidence created by the friends I had around me, all of whom had varying levels of life experience, which I drew upon. Being from the UK, there was just so much learning to do, and the more I learned and gained confidence, the more I explored to find out things I didn't know, or things I knew existed but which I hadn't had the opportunity to look into until now. I began to realise that my learning would probably never end – from learning about language, culture, thinking fast and being smart to understanding the desperation, isolation, loneliness, cruelty and jealousy that existed in many Nigerians I met.

I loved the rigid and systematic life of boarding school; something I felt was odd, considering that the pattern was similar to that of National High School, which I did not like. Either I wasn't meant to attend that school, or I was just too much of a novice at that time. I enjoyed having a master to serve and having meals at specific times of the day; having three meals a day was something of a luxury for me. In the past, I had only had breakfast and dinner. Waking up at 5am every day and going to the stream once in the morning and at least twice in the afternoons was all new to me. All these things came as a surprise, a challenge, and an opportunity to me, and made my life very exciting. However, I was miserable at times because I still missed my real family when my friends would talk lovingly about their parents.

After a while, I began to develop confidence and courage. This enabled me to challenge people when I felt they were wrong. I also challenged ideas; this became a nice hobby for me, and it didn't take long for me to join the school debating society. I became more outgoing, joining in conversations and offering my opinions when I could. I still suffered rejection and despair at times. The fact that every so often I would wet my bed had quite a lot to do with the challenges I faced, as both friends and enemies would tease me about it. The senior students also had a huge role to play in victimising me and anyone else who had the misfortune of wetting their bed. On one occasion when I wet the bed, I was made to strip naked and stand on top of the bunk bed. I was given a script to read for all to listen to and laugh at. The script read: My name is Chima and I have a small willy – one of the things my small willy does for me is wet the bed. As you can imagine, the entire dormitory would erupt into laughter. On confidence-shattering days like these, I would crawl into my shell and avoid everyone, sometimes missing classes to avoid the stares and sniggers from my classmates. As the days went by and a bed-wetting episode was gradually forgotten, I would slowly re-integrate myself with school and society – until I wet my bed again. This was the regular rollercoaster pattern for me throughout Year 2, and it wasn't until sometime in Year 3 that my bed-wetting episodes reduced considerably and only occurred if I was stressed or unhappy.

My experiences – even the negative ones – offered me opportunities, which I always tried to take. I used them to learn anything I could, as quickly as possible. My first opportunity in boarding school came in September 1981, when I had just started Year 3. Oko Ukpai had left Oha-fia in July 1981 after finishing his exams. I was sad to see him go but there wasn't anything I could do about it. I had to get used to my newfound independence. The water prefect, Abuma, also known as Abu Shirt (because he had a habit of wearing his shirts with the collar up) told me he was going to make me the junior water-marker. He had decided to give me this position because he had realised that I struggled to go to the stream and get water. I just found it such a gruelling task carrying buckets of water on my head. So, when the junior students were asked to fetch three or four buckets of water, I usually managed one trip, after which I would give up. The water-fetching rota was always called before dinner; anyone who hadn't completed their task was normally flogged before being allowed to have dinner. Most times, I simply didn't attend dinner. I would hide in the bushes behind the refectory and listen to the names being called. Abuma always sensed I was nearby and would call me, even though I hadn't completed my task. "Buddy Case, Buddy Case, I know you're hiding – come out now and your punishment will not be severe", he would call. Usually I would relent and come out of the bushes and accept my punishment; not all the time, though, and when I didn't, I had to go without dinner.

Being made me junior water-marker meant that I no longer had to go to the stream three or four times a day to fetch water – I would have the privilege of staying behind in the dormitory and accounting for every bucket of water that the students in Years 1 to 3 had to fetch. Abuma must have felt sorry for me. This was one of the most coveted positions for a junior or senior student to occupy;

it brought untold pleasures and benefits. I did not have to go to the stream myself as often as I had before, and in addition the juniors approached me for concessions – if I let them fetch two buckets instead of three, I would sometimes get cash donations, food, snacks or other forms of gifts. The senior students also approached me for favours; those seniors who didn't have anyone to serve them usually had to go to the stream themselves, or borrow from their friends, so they would sometimes ask me to divert a bucket or two to their corner. These favours were normally rewarded with cash or food, and sometimes protection from other senior students.

Believe it or not, being a water-marker had its downfalls at times too. While most junior students were at the stream, the senior students had the opportunity to bully any juniors left behind. I was constantly reminded that being a water-marker did not shield me from carrying out other chores. While everyone else was at the stream, I was constantly barraged with chore after chore, shouted at, and even abused at times. One gruelling chore that the senior prefect had me performing at any opportunity was writing up his notes from all his lessons; unfortunately for me, my writing was immaculate. So once I started writing for the senior prefect, other seniors got to see my writing and subsequently got me writing their notes too. Before I knew what was happening, I was writing notes for six or seven different seniors. This meant that I did not have to carry out most of the normal chores that others did on a daily basis, but it made my friends and peers jealous and spiteful towards me. It also meant I had very little time to do anything for myself, including studying. Being in Year 3, where I was studying up to fifteen subjects, this meant that I did struggle; I often had to wake up in the middle of the night to sneak out into the classroom and do some of my own studying.

Year 3 was a sort of mid-point in secondary education; if you had got that far, then the chances of finishing secondary school were high. Being in Year 3 brought with it many challenges, including studying fifteen subjects while trying to focus on particular subjects that were going to be the mainstay of one's career, and at the same time maintaining a regular student life; playing, doing the daily dormitory chores, water-marking, or water-fetching. Students in Year 3 earned a lot of respect from those in the year groups below due to the sheer number of different subjects they had to study.

Halfway through my time in Year 3, I was promoted to the position of senior water-marker, which meant I was entirely in charge of the water supplies for Years 3 and 4. I was also very lucky to be given the unique position of food-sharer. Talk about opportunities. Food-sharers distributed the food just before meal times; this exercise was carried out in the dining hall whilst all the other students went on about their routine chores. It was quite obvious how this position helped win me many friends, but it also won me many enemies. I normally tried to be as fair as possible when sharing the food, although this was not always possible, sometimes due to unforeseen peer pressure from classmates and other seniors, who always wanted me to help them get more food. Sometimes, students who were in my bad books and on the wrong side of my goodwill would get noticeably reduced portions.

Whilst in Year 3, I went back to taking Shaolin lessons, continuing from where I had left off when I was at Aba. By the time I left Ohafia in 1984, aged seventeen, I had achieved my black belt. Year 3 was a dream for me. I started to realise that I could eventually graduate from secondary school, something that had seemed impossible when I was living in Aba. That alone was inspiration enough for me to continue to do well and prove my uncles and aunties wrong. Studying hard increasingly became a joy and a hobby for me, I worked very hard with Daniel Ochonma and Godwin Eni, my Arochukwu friends. We constantly pushed each other, always trying to be better than one another, and in the process being better than everyone else in Year 3.

The only subject I never did understand at secondary school was mathematics. The grasp of basic maths eluded me throughout my secondary school career, and it did not help when I joined forces with others who also felt maths was just too hard and started missing classes. It started off with missing one or two maths lessons a month, and then I stopped attending maths classes completely. I still worked very hard at all the other subjects, including ones

I did not particularly like, but maths was just too much for me. During the exams, I either failed maths or found intelligent ways to not take the paper and get awarded an average pass mark. I never looked suspicious because I was excellent in most of the other subjects. I managed this way till my final-year exams. I did, however, get to grips with basic mathematics after leaving school, mastered it, and got good grades.

As young boys, we were always looking for adventure, and we looked nearly everywhere. Around 1982, Daniel, Kalu Kalu and I hatched one of many plans for how to get more food during meal times. I was no longer a food-sharer. In order to make sure we were kept well-fed most of the time (a rarity in boarding school), we began to pass double plates. Having been a sharer myself, I had inside knowledge as to how this system worked. During dinner time, when it was time to take plates to the dining hall and leave them for the sharers to get to work, we each left two plates. Anyone who has lived in a boarding school will know this is a cardinal sin. We had a variety of strategies for making sure all our plates either disappeared or that we ate all the food in the hall without being caught.

Strategy 1: When the food bell went and we all sat at the table (tables were arranged according to class order), we would each take our first plate very quickly and balance it on our lap, under the dining table, whilst eating casually from our second plate. When we finished, we would swap plates and continue as if we were eating from the same plate. In order to pull off this feat we had to be very fast eaters, and we had to be very quick with our hands when swapping plates. It had to be done when nobody was looking – especially the seniors. Sometimes one of us would cause a distraction in order to give the others time to make the swap. We also always used similar-looking plates so that after the swap nobody would notice. After eating and praying, everyone would usually rush off to do their chores, so this gave us enough cover to take all our plates out.

Strategy 2: When the food bell went, we would sit at the table; all but one of us. One person would hang back and go around the back of the dining hall and hide near one of the windows. When we were using this strategy we always made sure we sat near the window. Once the students inside were seated, we would immediately pass the extra plates through the window to the person waiting outside. These plates of food would then be quickly taken to our special hiding place in the bushes. We had an immaculate hideout in the bushes where we did all manner of things, including drinking garri if we were hungry, roasting cashew nuts, chilling out, and meeting when we needed to plan covert operations. The ones who had been in the dining hall would meet the other person at our hideout to share the food. This method of getting more food worked for us up to our fourth year, when I came up with a grand plan to get even more food – food we could eat for days on end.

The Grand Plan

Having worked in the kitchen for some time, and also having helped out as a food-sharer, I had discovered a couple of things about kitchen operations and the cooks that most people didn't know. The kitchen, although a finished building was not wholly complete; it did not have a ceiling because firewood was used in the kitchen and this blackens and ruins ceilings. I noticed there was a small gap between the wood that supported the roof beams and the actual zinc roof itself, and discovered that I could actually fit through this small space and get into the kitchen without having to use the door. I had also noticed that the cooks left and went home very soon after preparing our dinner at about 3.30 in the afternoon. They would lock up the kitchen with all the food in it, and when it was time for our dinner to be served, the refectorian would use his own key to open the kitchen for the sharers to take the food to the dining hall. The fact that the kitchen stood in an isolated area of the school, about thirty to fifty yards away from the main dormitory, was very useful. We hatched our plan.

Immediately after the cooks locked up and left, which coincided with our afternoon reading time, the three of us would go to our secret hiding place in the bushes and collect a large pot. Sometimes we would take two, depending on the food that was available that evening. I would climb through the gap between the roof and the wall and into the kitchen, unlock the back doors from the inside, and let my colleagues in with their utensils. If the menu for the evening was rice and stew, we would use one pot to take as much rice as we possibly could. We would use the other for the stew and for as much meat or fish, or both, that we could take without arousing suspicion. I would let my friends back out through the back door, lock it, and climb back out through the gap. We would usually take our haul to a friend's house somewhere in Asaga, where we could keep it in a fridge and visit as and when we needed to eat it. This plan carried on for almost six months, and we made the most of it; eating to our hearts' content and selling our paltry plates of food in the dining hall for as much as we could. We even promised some of our classmate's additional food. We would sometimes go to our secret outlet in town and bring in container-loads of food, which we would sell to unsuspecting students.

As with all things covert, we did have a couple of near-misses where we nearly got caught either by the cooks, our colleagues, or our seniors. One very close call came when I had just climbed into the kitchen. I was about to open the back door for Daniel and Kalu Kalu when one of the male cooks opened the main front door and walked in. He froze when he saw me, and I froze too.

Eventually, we both managed to get over the initial shock; he was the first to respond. "What the hell are you doing in my kitchen?" he asked.

My ability to come up with ideas on the spur of the moment was something me friends marvelled at, and in this delicate situation, my mind came alive. "You cooks are always eager to rush off home after cooking our horrible food," I said, "and you don't even check to make sure everyone is out of the kitchen".

He looked at me, puzzled. "What do you mean?" he asked.

Quick with my response, I replied, "I came in to check the water level in the water tank in order to know if the students needed to go to the stream to fetch water – you saw me walk past you but you still forgot me and locked the door, trapping me in here for over twenty minutes". His puzzled look turned to trepidation as it began to dawn on him that I could actually get him into trouble for his obvious lapse in security and in health and safety. "Don't worry, I won't tell anyone if you give me some food to quash my hunger pangs that I've been carrying around for hours now" I said.

Quick to please me and get me out of the kitchen, he made me a small plate of rice and beans, piled on some large chunks of fried fish, and ushered me out of the kitchen. When I got back to our hideout, Daniel and Kalu Kalu stared at me, astounded. I explained how I had gotten out of that mess, and we laughed about it for a while. Then we decided it was time to call it quits before we did get caught and were expelled from school.

School Holidays – Village Life

Living in Ohafia, and in the dormitory in particular, presented me with another opportunity. This was the opportunity to visit my village, Edda, more often than I would have been able if I had stayed in Aba. Although I was told by my uncle Okoro Ikpo to go down to Aba sometimes during holidays, I ignored these instructions, as I knew they wanted me to go so they could use me as their slave. Instead, I went to Edda for some weekends and during all holidays. Most of my time in the village was spent with my grandma, who I loved and respected dearly. Nne meant the world to me; she was the only person in the world I would ever listen to and respect, and she knew it. She took good care of me whilst teaching me how to cook various local dishes. She also told me stories about her father, my great grandad, and about life before the English missionaries came to Nigeria. She remembered things being harmonious and friendly; everyone talked to each other, and people did not steal, kill or even argue much. All her stories reminded me of the history books we read at school.

Apart from learning how to cook and listening to stories, I also went to the farm a lot, either with my grandma or with Nna, who was her younger brother. Whilst grandma was the head of the family, Nna was the paternal head, so it was his job to ensure all the boys in the extended family were taught how to be men. Nna resolved all family and village issues. Warring families would visit his house with gifts, asking him to help them resolve their problems. As young men, we sometimes sat outside and listened to the issues. Whilst we waited for a resolution, we were sometimes given some of the food brought as part of the gifts. This was good, old-time conflict resolution, which the Igbo tribe were well-known for in those days. Courts were not used much, as people saw them as too aggressive and too expensive.

Whenever I was in the village, I played a lot of football. In fact, I played football all morning, from 7am till 11am. Then I would go to the stream to have a bath and also to fetch water that grandma would use. I would then go hunting with my friends for guinea fowls, squirrels, bush rats, snakes, and anything else we could find. Whatever we caught was shared equally amongst all of us. I would take mine home to my grandma, and she would use it in her cooking. I also went fishing a lot, catching all types of fish, big and small. I took these home to my grandma too. When it got slightly cooler in the evenings, I would go back to the football pitch and resume playing football again until dusk.

The time I spent in the village was so exciting and enjoyable for me. Immediately after getting to the village from boarding school and spending some quality time with Nne, I would head for the football pitch, popularly known as Mission because it was at the site of the village primary school, built by missionaries in the early 1930s. Mission was also the site of the girls-only secondary school and of the local Presbyterian church – one of the earliest in the town and where the missionaries resided when they first came to Edda. We would play football for as long as there was daylight, after which we would head to the iyi nde teacher (stream for teachers) for a bath; most people used soap when having a bath, but we never applied cream to ourselves afterwards because the temperature was too hot.

After having a bath in the stream, we would head for the village square, which was where most youngsters met to play, talk or fight. The village square was a place to relax and meet old and new friends. It was normally well-lit by lanterns – there was no electricity in those days. We would look for various errands we could do for the adults so as to get rewarded with cash or other gifts. As each evening came to an end, we would all agree the meeting time for the next day and then say our goodnights and go home. As much as I enjoyed my playtime with my friends, I equally enjoyed the late evenings I spent with Nne.

First of all, she would cook our dinner. I loved watching her cook. After we had eaten, I would wash the plates, and then we would sit outside in the moonlight on a palm frond mat and she would tell me stories. Her stories were about the village and how things had been in the 1920s and 1930s, and about her dad, my great granddad, who was a warrior and often went to war.

In those days, the disputes and wars were normally over

land, women, honour and respect. The mark of a great warrior was how many human heads he came home with at the end of a war. My grandma also told me stories about village politics and governance, family arguments and feuds, places and people to avoid. She told me a lot about my dad – his early days, school, and business ventures; how he set up a technical school in Cameroon, West Africa; how he married my mum; and how he left Nigeria for England. She told me late-night fables which always had a maxim at the end. I found these stories amazing and intellectually stimulating. I did other things with my grandma too, such as shopping at the small village market and sometimes at the bigger Afo market in my mum's village of Owutu. I also went to the farm with her, where we would spend most of the day weeding, cleaning, eating and talking. Life in the village taught me many things; things I would never had learnt had I stayed in Aba.

On some days, I went fishing with my friends, and on other days we went hunting for bush rats and other small rodents. When hunting for rodents, we always split ourselves into two teams; one team concentrated on digging any burrows we found, whilst the other team were on standby at all potential escape routes, waiting to pounce and kill. We also always had one person who was the expert searcher. This person would put their hand in the burrows to determine if anything actually lived there, and could tell what type of rodent lived there from the fur and smell – sometimes they could even tell how many.

There were times when the burrows were empty because the rodent had left or had been eaten by a predator, and there were even times when we would find a snake that had devoured the rodent still resting in the burrow. When we caught something, we would share it equally amongst ourselves. Some of my friends would roast and eat their share there in the bushes, but I always took my share home to Nne, who would praise me for being a good hunter. She would then roast my spoils and keep them for a day, when she would cook a soup and add them.

I learnt a lot about the seventy-two villages that make up Edda. I visited many of them too, for one reason or another – mainly to see relatives. I visited Owutu Edda frequently; I spent time there with my aunties and uncles and sometimes spent entire weekends there. I also learnt a lot about the culture, including the age grade formations and how they work. The age grades featured prominently in the village and town politics and governance. They tended to cut across other ties such as family, compounds and lineage.

Ukejiogo is the most prominent age grade and has strong managerial duties in the village community. All the policies, rules and laws of the land are enforced by this group. In principle, they are a group of men in their late fifties and early sixties whose patriotism is without question. Having been drilled from childhood on the dos and don'ts of the community, by experience, exposure and age they are qualified to teach the younger age grades how things are done. People in the under fifty-five age grade were often used by the Council of Elders to implement its decisions. The elementary lesson of being your brother's keeper is learnt, practised and ingrained in the psyche.

In August 1982, after having watched the yearly Ipu Ogo (initiation into manhood or puberty) rite a couple of times in the past, I decided it was time to get initiated. Anyone would tell you that the road to initiation is not one taken lightly. Neither was it generally a decision taken by the boy who wanted to be initiated – but as usual, I didn't care for rules or protocol; this was demonstrated again a couple of years later – in 1984, after years of being silent bystanders to the affairs of the village, I and my friend Ama Oji Okoro (who was also known as Nobles) set up the age grade for boys our age.

This initiation is usually for adolescent boys and is both extensive and expensive. It separates the boys from the young men. The initiation is meant to bring adolescent boys into adult life and is at the heart of the Edda tradition. It is a cultivated and well-guided path for a boy who comes out a man on the other side of the initiation. In Edda, the ceremony takes place during the rainy season. Normally, the father or a representative leads the candidate to the Ogo (village square) at a time when non-initiates and women are not expected to be around. This act of leading them to the Ogo is known as Ipu Ogo, or Iba Igo. They go to the Obi Ogo, a gathering place where men, especially elders, congregate to talk, relax and make decisions. There, they stay and receive training into the Egbela cult.

Candidates retreat into the eko ndishina, a special place where only those who have completed the initiation rites are allowed. There, they receive instructions and advanced endurance training. Such training includes guerrilla warfare that prepares them for the effective defence of the village. They emerge from such training as potential soldiers. In addition, candidates take up some community roles like cleaning the village square and general toilets. They also learn traditional medicine – the use of certain potent herbs for healings. The ceremony reaches its peak with the initiation proper, which takes place on Nkwo Offia. Nkwo is a day of the Igbo week (the days are Eke, Orie, Afor and Nkwo). Offia means forest. Nkwo Offia means the going to the forest on Nkwo. A cane fight is declared to usher in the initiation proper, and the candidates go into the bush, where the rituals are conducted. The village is closed for non-initiates and women, whose freedom of movement is restricted. Those being initiated are taken into a very dense forest, far away, for the final rites, and then they have to run back to the village. During the run back, initiates can encounter ambushes by enemies, who will beat them. People who have an old score to settle will often wait for that day to try and harm someone, because anything that happens on that day is more or less allowed as part of the tradition. In the olden days, some people never made it back from the forest.

Instead of going through the normal process of getting initiated, I decided to do it differently. I asked Nne if I could get initiated, but she told me it wasn't a decision for her to take, and that Nna would be the best person to ask. When I asked Nna, he told me to wait until the following year, as the ceremony was already halfway through. In my infinite wisdom, I decided I couldn't wait till the following year, so I concocted a plan to get my way.

Ukpo is the name of the masquerade that the young men 'become' and dance as, as part of the initiation. After the ukpos had finished dancing for the afternoon, they retired to the eko in Amaorji (one of the communities in Ebunwana) to get some rest. When I thought nobody was paying any attention, I went in and joined all the other initiated boys and men who had flocked around the candidates to wish them well and to eat some of the food and drink. But before I had time to get comfortable, some of the young men recognised me and started shouting "Ipule Ogo?", "Ipuru Ogo ole afa?", and a whole load of other questions to try and verify whether I had been initiated in the past. They quickly realised that I wasn't initiated, and most of the young boys and men jumped on me and started beating me up.

After what felt like hours, some of the older men intervened and stopped the beatings. When they asked me who my dad was, I said Nna Oko Nnachi, hoping to buy some immunity. Without waiting to hear anything else from me they proceeded to drag me through the streets to

Amaeke, where Nna lived. When we got there he asked what I had done and they explained. They then asked him what he wanted to do about the situation. He told them that since I had already seen what went on behind the scenes, they might as well complete the entire process by initiating me. Despite the beating I had received, that was good news for me. I had achieved what I set out to do. As the Ipu Ogo process is a male-orientated affair, I had to move into Nna's house. I had to stay there for the entire Ipu Ogo period. For me, as much as being a cultural process, it was a unique experience which helped me understand the law of the land, the tradition and culture of the land, and the meaning of being a man. I enjoyed every bit of it.

When I went to the village for weekends or holidays, I also got involved in farming activities. These included clearing the bush (during February and March) and making the yam moulds and planting the yam seeds (in April). This was followed by the weeding season, also referred to as the Unwu season (time of little) because there was hardly any food to eat; most of it had been planted. The weeding was done manually using hoes and machetes. Harvesting the yams (August and September) was the most exciting time, as there was great anticipation about the size and success of the harvest. Sometimes there was so many yams that a huge range of different dishes were prepared. Food was plentiful at this time. The harvested yams were stored in the barns and were mainly sold at the Afor market in Owutu. The new yam festival was held every year to mark the harvesting of the yam crop. The village chiefs and traditional title-holders made it a religious practice by not consuming yam till it had been offered to the gods. During this festival, villagers offered prayers, thanking their ancestral gods for the blessings of the land and the women's fertility. There was a parade of traditional dances, and a variety of delicious yam dishes were cooked.

My experiences of the village did not, however, always create fond memories; in fact, as often as I had times of joy and fun, I also went through awful times of hardship, frustration, despair and hunger. During some of my holidays in the village, when Nne was not around, her grandchildren, Eleya and Ucha – Ucha especially – took joy in making my life hell. Eleya, Ugo and Ucha were sisters whose mum had died a long time ago, before I arrived in Nigeria. Eleya and Ucha lived with Nne, whilst Ugo lived with O.O. in Aba. Ugo showed nothing but love towards me when I saw her and pampered me at any opportunity. However, her sisters despised me and treated me with aggression. Ucha would wake me up every morning and drag me to the farm with her to help her do the weeding, even though this was primarily a woman's job. (I would go sometimes with Nne because I enjoyed her company, and she always asked me, but it was different being dragged there). After spending the entire day at the farm, when we got back home, Ucha would send me to the stream to fetch water for her to bathe and cook with. I always struggled to go to the stream after walking five miles from the farm. When she had finished cooking, she made sure I got as little food as possible, always swearing at me and telling me that if I wanted more food, I should write to my parents to send more money for my upkeep. She always did this when Nne was absent, daring me to tell Nne and saying that if I ever did tell, she would make sure I suffered even more.

In order to get through the day, I would sometimes wake up very early, go onto the streets and collect dry palm kernels that had been left in piles by their owners. I would crack as many kernels as I could and eat them, then wash them down with water. This would not fill me up, but it sustained me through most of the morning. One day, my friend Nobles saw me cracking the kernels and asked what I was doing. When I told him that this was what I normally had for breakfast, he was gobsmacked. Even poor people did not eat those sorts of kernels off the streets. He invited me back to his mum's house for lunch. From then on, I went to Nobles' mum's house for lunch quite regularly. After eating, Noble and I would go to his sitting room to talk and study. We discussed what we wanted to be when we grew up. I wanted to be a doctor, while Nobel wanted to be a lawyer.

As the holidays drew to an end, Nne and I would start getting food items ready for me to take back to school. This was normally garri – lots of it – which was the mainstay of what most people who lived in the dormitory survived on. We would soak the garri in water, add some sugar and sometimes powdered milk, and drink it. Garri was also a popular food product used to pay off favours with and bargain with. I also took coconut, peanuts, yam and cabin biscuits, and was also given a small amount of pocket money, which I used to buy provisions such as Nido, Bournvita, sugar and Milo. These things were never enough, but we had to make do with the little that was available. In those days, finding transport to certain towns was not very easy, and Ohafia was one of them. Most of the time, after packing all my things together, I would begin my journey back early on a Sunday afternoon by walking from Ebunwana up Ugwu Lyere (Lyere Hill) to Ekoli, from where it was much easier to get a taxi to Ohafia.

Before I left for Ohafia, Nne always sat me down and explained the fact that I had to grow up now. At fifteen years old, I felt scared. That feeling always dissipated as soon as I got to the school gate on Sunday evenings amidst the shouts from the senior students. "Oya, everyone in Years 1, 2, 3 and 4, kneel down now … everyone in Years 3 and 4 bring out five cabin biscuits each." The Year 1 and 2 students were told to go to the dormitory and make themselves comfortable, but Years 3 and 4 would always have to open their neatly packed suitcases and bags and fork out the compulsory cabin biscuit levy before being ushered through to the dormitory. This always meant that even before I had time to unpack my bags, a valuable proportion of my provisions had been taken from me. This always made me feel unhappy because I wasn't good at begging for things – due to my pride, I guess – so when I ran out of provisions, I normally had to make do until my next visit to the village, and even then I was not guaranteed anything. Other students would beg for provisions throughout the term after they ran out. That was the way of life, I guess.

The Riots of 1983

One more serious incident occurred in secondary school before I left. On Friday 28th January 1983, just before the Year 5 students (who were preparing for their final General Certificate of Education (GCE) O-Level exams, also referred to as WAEC) handed over the running of the school to us students in Year 4, they decided to go on a rampage and make things difficult for Year 4. This was an annual ritual, so nobody thought much of it. Year 4 students were punished or beaten up for the slightest of reasons. In previous years, as this ritual only took place in the dormitory, many Year 4 students would leave the school compound and seek refuge in the neighbouring villages of Asaga or Amuke for a couple of days.

Unfortunately, in 1983, the Year 5 students decided to take the ritual to a whole new level. They decided to go into the village of Asaga and look for any Year 4 students; once identified, these students were given a thorough beating, just for being in Year 4. This continued for most of the afternoon, until they came across one student, who they beat up very badly before throwing him over a bridge and into a shallow stream below. The boy survived the fall but was seriously injured. This caused a small mob to gather around the Year 5 students, and fighting broke out. The Year 5 students were able to escape the mob and make it back to the dormitory that evening, but I think they sensed that what they had done would lead to further trouble, so they called all Year 4 students and asked us to join them and prepare for any reprisals from the Asaga villagers. We decided not to support them. They were furious but were unable to convince anyone to join them.

As the junior students gathered into the classrooms to ponder on what to do, stones started to rain down on the roofs of the surrounding buildings. The revenge attacks had started. The Year 5 students started throwing stones and rocks back in the general direction of where the onslaught seemed to be coming from. This went on for half an hour. As we all stood around in the classroom and discussed the possibilities of trouble, one of the Year 4 boys, Uduma Uduma, popularly known as U.U., said he'd heard a scary noise which sounded like a whistle but could easily have been a prompt for an attack. We barely had time to digest U.U.'s words when a group of about thirty men came running out of the bushes, where the stones had been coming from, armed with sticks and machetes. Everyone headed for the dormitory, including the Year 5s, with the mob hot on our heels. We locked ourselves inside and waited. When the mob arrived, they began to break the doors down with anything they could lay their hands on. It wasn't long before they were inside beating people up. It was chaotic, with people running everywhere, crying and screaming. The fact that it was very dark, as there was no electricity, made it even scarier. I thought to myself, is this how I'm going to die?

As I got up to join in the pandemonium, I saw U.U. sitting quietly on a bed, watching the drama unfold. I thought, if anyone knows how to protect themselves, it's U.U., so I went over to him and asked if I could stick with him. He said that was fine, so I sat down beside him, and we watched as people were beaten up one by one. The mob had about ten or so men guarding the doors, whilst the rest were inside, beating people up as they ushered them outside. Once students were outside, they were given severe beatings – especially Year 5 students.

After a while, U.U. told me it was time to move; we edged slowly towards one of the exit doors. As we got closer to the door, a huge figure appeared from nowhere and stood in front of us. The figure peered at us for a brief second. I think he tried to stare U.U. down, but U.U. didn't relent. U.U. was a Shaolin expert and was over six feet tall; anyone would think twice about getting into any sort of altercation with him. We moved on, got to the door, and walked out very slowly. We were watched by a couple of people from the mob, but nobody made a move to stop us or do anything to us. When we got outside, we found an area in front of the dining hall and stood to watch what was going on. It was very pitiful to watch people being shepherded out of the dormitory and then being beaten with sticks as they tried to run to safety. There was blood everywhere. One Year 5 student, Ajah Nwunta, the refectorian, had been chased out of the dormitory. As he began to run away towards the bushes in his bid to escape, someone hit him in the face with a chair. He continued running for a couple of feet, then collapsed onto the floor in a pool of blood; his entire face was covered in blood. It was at that moment that U.U. told me it was time for us to get off the school premises. We walked slowly to the back of the dining hall and headed for the bushes that led to Amuke. As soon as we got into the bushes, we ran for our lives.

When we got to Amuke, we found refuge in a friend's house and stayed there, too afraid to venture out and find out what had happened. Later that night, news began to filter in that there had been lots of students who had been injured, and some had been taken to hospital. There was also a rumour that several students had been abducted and taken to the Asaga chief's house. It later transpired that one of the students, Peter Ume Maduka, had been beaten up with an iron bar and died in hospital a week or so later.

The next morning, Saturday 29th January, most of the

boarding students returned to the dormitory to discover that it had been totally destroyed, with most of our belongings looted. The entire place was a mess. As we roamed around looking for friends and exchanging stories, the dormitory bell started ringing, which we found odd, as we were not in the normal dormitory mode of life; we were trying to figure out what had happened the night before. We gathered slowly and cautiously in front of the dining hall, as per normal procedure. To our surprise, it was the principal, Mr Ulu Awa, ringing the bell. This was a very rare occurrence. In the past when I had seen the principal ringing the bell, there was normally bad, or sad, news to be delivered.

Once we had all gathered round, he began to speak solemnly. "As you know, there was some trouble here yesterday which eventually led to a riot." I would not have called it a riot. It was more like a carefully planned attack on the students living in the dormitory by armed Asaga local men. "A lot of students were injured during the riot," he continued. No shit, I thought. It was a surprise that there was no news of any fatalities (yet; Peter Ume was still alive in hospital at this point) considering what I had seen the night before. "It is with a sad heart," the principal went on, "that I have to tell you that Boys' Secondary School, Asaga, will be closed temporarily while the police carry out a thorough investigation into what happened. I urge you to take your time, collect all your belongings, return to your homes, and await further information from the school."

That was a shocker. The penny dropped; we all realised the magnitude of his speech. Go home. No school. What now? As if to answer my question, cars started to pull into the school compound; worried parents who had received the news of what had happened were starting to arrive. That was the prompt for students to disperse and start collecting their belongings – or what was left of them. As we were packing our stuff, more parents arrived to collect their children. When I had finished getting my things together, it suddenly dawned on me that nobody would be coming to pick me up. How was I going to get home?

As I stood in front of the dining hall and pondered what to do, I heard someone bellowing out my name. When I looked around, I didn't see anyone I recognised. The voice called again, "Chima! Are you still here?" Eventually, I was able to see who was calling me. It was an uncle of mine called Francis Kalu Okoro, popularly known as F.K.

F.K. lived in Ebem Ohafia, where he worked as a civil servant. He was the father of the now-popular and renowned gospel singer Sinach, and he was a very generous man who I often spent time with when he came to the village for the weekend or holidays. He also, however, had a very fierce temper at times, which I had witnessed on a few occasions. I was very happy to see him; at least I knew I would be able to get back to the village. He took me to his house, where I stayed the night before he took me to the village the next day. The riot was all over the news; everyone was talking about it. My family were very happy to see me that Sunday. I think they were relieved I had not been killed.

I spent the first week playing around whilst everyone else in the village was at school. It felt good not to have to study whilst others did. However, by the beginning of the second week word reached the village that our school would be closed for quite a while. My uncle, Oko Elekwa, suggested I register temporarily with the school he attended at the time – Government Secondary School, Owutu, Edda – which was a good school and relatively new, having opened in 1978. In order to register with the school, I had to get a temporary transfer certificate, so I went back to my school in Ohafia to see whether the principal would oblige. He signed one for me, although unknown to him, I had other plans. My intention was to register temporarily at Government Secondary School but then apply to stay there permanently. With this plan on my mind, once the principal had given me the transfer certificate I went into the main school compound, which was largely empty apart from a handful of students collecting some of their stuff. I proceeded to write my nickname on every wall in the school. "Buddy Case", "Buddy Case in town", "Buddy Case on tour", "Buddy the case man", "Buddy Case in trouble", and so on. I was going to make sure my name wasn't forgotten. When I had finished, I left.

I was at Government Secondary School for nearly three

months. While I was studying there, I had a very demoralising showdown with one of my uncles from my mum's side of the family – Pastor Orji Abia Onyike. He was a pastor of the Brotherhood of the Cross and Star church. He had previously lived in Suleja, Abuja, where he was some kind of contractor. However, when the decision was made to make Abuja the country's capital and its development started, he very quickly lost much of his business and property. He went back to his home town, Owutu, where he launched a series of legal battles against the Nigerian government.

He had a small, modest house in Akanu Owutu. I used to spend a lot of time there with his nephew, Nnanna. Just before the Easter of 1983, he told me he was going to Calabar to celebrate with the church. He trusted me, and left the keys to his personal room with me. I opened the room every morning to dust it down and keep it clean as he had instructed. When he came back about five days later, I handed him his keys and went off to play football at Ejike Ewu Primary School, the usual place for footballers.

When I got back from football, I could tell something was wrong. Orji was shouting at the top of his voice. "That thief Chima stole my money and thinks he can get away with it! When I get my hands on him, his parents will come from London and pay me back!" He saw me coming towards him and started to shout at me. "You ungrateful thief! Where is my money that you stole? You are a well-known thief – and for me to be so stupid to trust you, and you repay me in this manner!"

I was shocked, and my brain started ticking. I had not taken any money; in fact I did not remember seeing any money in the room. Before I could transfer my thoughts to words, I was hit with two dazzling slaps. I tried to explain I had not seen or taken any money, but Orji would have none of it. He told me to take all my clothes off; he was going to treat me like the thief that I was. I started to beg, but he hit me twice in quick succession and tore my t-shirt off. He then grabbed my shorts and pulled them until they ripped and came off. He then took hold of my pants and ripped them off. I was left standing naked, ashamed, humiliated and crying as people watched. How could my uncle do this to me? He was a man I had thought understood me. He had recently travelled to London and spent time with my parents and had agreed to keep an eye on me when he came back to Nigeria.

He held me firmly and asked where the money was. I asked him how much was missing; he told me twenty naira. I thought, so I am being humiliated because of twenty naira? That, I did not take. I continued to beg him, and after what felt like hours, some members of the crowd begged him to let me go. He eventually relented and let me go. I gathered my clothes and went to see my mum's younger sister, where I explained what had happened. She didn't say much. After having dinner at her house, I told her I needed some fresh air and left for a long walk to clear my head. That incident scarred me.

In May 1983, I received a letter from Principal Ulu Awa explaining that the police had completed their investigation into the riot and that all students were needed back immediately. I wrote a reply explaining that I no longer wanted to go back, that I was comfortable at Government Secondary School, Owutu, and that I needed a transfer certificate to enable me register permanently. A couple of days later I received a huge shock; it was another letter from the principal explaining that he would never let me leave his school. The letter made it very clear that he intended to keep his good students, and although I was a stubborn, mischievous boy, he had great plans for me. I was happy that he thought highly of me and that he had plans for me, but I had started getting used to life in the village. After dragging my feet over the return to Ohafia, I eventually packed my things on Sunday 29th May and went back. They had carried out a lot of repair work to the damaged buildings, and the burnt beds and chairs had been replaced. The place looked very clean, apart from the ghastly sight of Buddy Case scribbled on every wall in the school. It was embarrassing, actually; everywhere I looked, Buddy Case was staring at me from a wall. Students who knew me shouted out "Buddy Case!" every time I walked past them. Even though the principal thought highly of me and had plans for my future, he also wanted to set a certain standard after what had happened—and I had given him the perfect opportunity to do just that.

On Monday morning, at the general assembly, the first to be held since the riots, we sang the principal's favourite hymn – Hymn Number 1: Holy, Holy, Holy. Afterwards, he gave a very brief speech about maintaining law, order and respect. Then he called me up to the platform where he was standing. "This young man took it upon himself to try and repaint the entire school compound with his nickname, Buddy Case, and as I did not give him the authority to do so, nor will I entertain any such behaviour here at Coronata, I am going to exact my harshest punishment as a deterrent to other students." He sentenced me to twelve lashes of his cane, in front of the entire school. The embarrassment hurt me more than the physical pain. He also ordered me to find a way of removing my name from all the walls in the school, banning me from classes until I completed the task; and I wasn't allowed to get any help from friends or junior students. It took me an entire week to clean my name off all the walls, and the principal came and inspected my work in case I had missed anything or was lying to him. I eventually got the all-clear. The punishment helped make me even more popular – Buddy Case became a household name.

When the principal made me the chief refectorian, most people who lived in the dormitory started calling me Buddy Mama because I was in charge of the food; mother of the students. Being made refectorian brought huge responsibilities: I had to estimate the amount of food needed for the students for the week, put together a budget for the food, and go to the principal's house – usually on a Friday evening – to present the budget. Once the budget was agreed and signed off, he would give me the food money. I would then go to the main market in Asaga with some junior students and we would buy what we needed for the week. If there was an underspend, I sometimes kept it for the following week and told the principal, who would deduct it from the next budget. Every now and again, if there was money left over, I would give some to the juniors who had come with me to the market and keep the rest for myself.

I was in demand. Senior students who wanted their food rations increased came to me. People who wanted me to buy food for them from the market came to me – if I bought their stuff with the rest of the school stuff, for which I got wholesale discounts, it was cheaper. Even students who lived in Asaga village rather than the dormitory came to me and asked me to buy food for them. Basically, I made a lot of money. I also made quite a few enemies, who were jealous of my achievements. I didn't care, though. And I enjoyed my reign.

During the summer holidays of 1983, I spent my time in the village as normal. I also spent a lot of time thinking how I could improve the running of the school refectory and its associated affairs. I really wanted to make a difference. When I went back to school in September, I implemented a student survey through which the students got to decide what dinners they ate by majority decision. I encouraged some of the students to come with me to the market so they could better understand the method of haggling for items – something very common in Nigeria. I also wanted them to have a better idea of what being a refectorian involved, and some of the difficult choices I was faced with.

In December, I went to Enugu for my first time; my mum's younger brother, Onyike lived there, so I decided to go and pay him a visit. I hadn't told him I was coming, so he was surprised to see me but welcoming all the same. I was in Enugu about two weeks after a fatal plane crash. A passenger jet carrying sixty-six passengers from Lagos to Enugu had crashed just before landing on the 28th November, killing fifty-three people. Enugu looked very gloomy and sad. The crash had actually occurred about 500 metres from where Onyike lived, a place called Aviation Point. People were still coming to visit the site of the crash when I arrived. After a week or so in Enugu, I went to the village for the Christmas holidays; my final Christmas as a secondary school student.

I was glad I had tried to make the most out of my position in school because time went by very quickly; it was soon time to hand over the running of the school to the Year 4 students and get back to the real world of studying for the final WAEC exams. Come to think of it, I was quite focused when going into the exams – some of my friends used to tease me about my total dedication to education, although their perception wasn't entirely accurate. I didn't have a girlfriend throughout my secondary school career, didn't smoke, and didn't drink. So, with no vices to spend any time or money on, I spent a lot of time just studying. I did go to a couple of parties in my fourth and final year, but that was it.

Before I sat my exams, I knew which subjects I would do well in. I had ambitions of studying law, so I had focused a lot on the arts subjects – I totally ignored physics and maths.

Lost
(1984–1986)

After the exams in June 1984, I decided to go and spend some time in the village with my grandma whilst I waited for the results. By this time, my bed-wetting had stopped. Because we had finished our exams early, most students were still in school when I arrived in the village. This was slightly unusual for me because school was normally closed by the time I came to the village on holidays.

The fact that our village had the only all-girls school in the whole of Edda meant Ebunwana always attracted a lot of people. During the first week of my holidays, an odd incident occurred that led to an interesting couple of weeks. One evening, I was walking down the street when I passed a group of three girls. As I passed them, they burst into laughter. It appeared as if they were laughing at me, although I wasn't entirely sure. An hour or so later, on my way back to my grandma's house, I came across the same group of girls; again, when I walked past, they burst into laughter. I was now convinced they were laughing at me. After thinking through what I would do, I came back out of my grandma's house and walked towards the main village square, where I had passed them on the two previous occasions. As I had expected, they were there. My intention was to confront them for laughing at me.

As I got closer to them, one of the girls shouted out, "Excuse me, can I speak with you for a minute?" I agreed, feeling nervous and shy. She introduced herself as Julie and jumped straight to the point. "My friend, Benedicta," she said, pointing to one of the other two girls, "really likes you and wants to invite you to our house for dinner." By this time, my heart was beating so hard it hurt. Somehow, I mustered the courage to respond. I asked her why her friend couldn't ask me herself; she said that Benedicta thought if she asked me herself I might feel too shy and say no. She was probably right. I told Julie that I would like to come over for dinner. We walked over to the other two, and Julie introduced me to Benedicta and Comfort. I asked Benedicta when she wanted me to go over for dinner. When she told me she wanted me to go round the same night, I almost fainted. I finally gathered my wits and told her that this was fine.

After leaving them, I immediately rushed off to see a friend of mine, Oluchi, to tell him about my chance encounter. Being a novice when it came to girls, I really needed a crash course on what to do and say. Oluchi quickly rushed through his limited tips on what to do and say to a girl, and how to try and win her over. When we had finished, I went to the stream to have a bath, went back home, and got ready. Eventually, as I made my way to Benedicta's house, the fear that had gripped me all evening suddenly evaporated. All of a sudden, I was full of courage.

Before I could knock on the door, Julie opened it and let

me in. She told me Benny was in the kitchen, preparing dinner. I sat down and we delved into some small talk before Benny finally appeared, looking very pretty and different to the person I had seen a couple of hours ago. She sat down and joined in the conversation. All four of us had dinner, and then Julie and Comfort announced that they were going out to visit a friend. When they had gone, Benny and I settled down and tried to learn more about each other. It appeared she knew quite a lot about me; she said she had seen me on numerous occasions when I came to the village for weekends and holidays. Her full name was Benedicta Abagha, and she was from Afikpo. She was in Year 4, and she was twenty-one years old – four years older than me. We continued talking until around midnight, when I decided it was time for me to go home. Before I left, she invited me to her school's interhouse sports competition, which was taking place the next day, Saturday. I readily agreed. The next day, I met up with Oluchi and brought him up to speed about my date before we headed for Ebunwana Girl's Secondary School for the interhouse sports competition.

The next couple of days were spent in the company of Benny, talking, playing and relaxing. Benny was surprised I actually liked life in Nigeria. She said she would have run back to the UK at the slightest opportunity if she was in my shoes. I began to wonder whether this was how holidays should be – had I really been missing out on all this? The time flew by, and just as I was getting into our relationship, Benny finished her end-of-year exams and had to go back to Afikpo. We said our goodbyes. A day after she left, I decided to go to Enugu and stay with Uncle Onyike whilst I waited for my results; although he was very strict, he was young compared to the other uncles I had stayed with.

A couple of weeks into my stay with Onyike, he asked me whether I had taken the Joint Admissions & Matriculation Board (JAMB) exams. I lied and told him I had. I actually had intended to take the exams, which normally took place in February each year, but I had been unable to get an application form because none of my relatives would give me the money for the form, which cost thirty naira at the time. One weekend, while staying at the village, I had walked five miles from Ebunwana to Ogbu to beg my Auntie Eleya (who was a teacher there) for the money. I had gone there with my friend Uche, who was very shocked when Eleya refused to give me the money, saying she didn't have it. When I asked for transport money back to Ohafia, she refused that too.

By the time we left, it was quite late in the evening, so we jogged all the way back to Ebunwana. I was in tears, as I knew my chance to register for the exam would disappear. The deadline for registration was the coming Wednesday – four days away. On the Sunday, to get back to Ohafia with the little money I had, I had to walk from Ebunwana to Nguzu junction, a distance of about eight or more miles. I contemplated walking from Nguzu junction to Ohafia – probably another nineteen or so miles. However, the road leading to Okagwe Ohafia had always been rumoured to be dangerous, so I got a taxi to Ebem Motor Park and then walked the rest of the way to Asaga. In total, I must have walked up to twenty-six miles that weekend in order to try and get thirty naira for the JAMB exam. The irony was, though, that a day after the JAMB deadline, Eleya arrived at my school and gave me forty naira to get the application form. I knew I'd missed the deadline, but I took the money. So, when anyone asked me about the JAMB exam, I would say it went well. My plan was to tell my relatives I had not got the required pass mark to study law and that I would retake it the following year. This fitted with my having told Onyike that I had taken the exams. I thought the issue would be forgotten by Onyike. However, after getting to know a bit more about him during my stay, I should have known he would not let the matter go so easily.

When the results were released, he asked me which university my results would be published at; I told him it was the University of Benin. He called his older brother, Oko, who lived in Benin City at the time, and told him to go and find out what my score was. A couple of days later, Oko rang back and told him my name wasn't on any published list. When Onyike came back from work and told me this, I tried to explain it away, saying I had probably failed so miserably they hadn't bothered to publish my results. He didn't buy it. He called Oko again and told him to take the day off work and go and have a thorough look. Oko did take a day off work. He went to the university and bribed the vice chancellor to let him look through all the records himself. My name wasn't there. He informed Onyike that there was no way I had taken the exams. When Onyike came home from work that evening, I noticed a certain look about him. He had brought his policeman friend, who we called Agha Police. They both came into the sitting room. Agha stood his police rifle by the door, locked the door, turned round, and called me "Good Morning". When I asked him why he called me that name, he said it was because those words were the only truth that came from my mouth. I thought that was a huge exaggeration. It didn't matter, though. Onyike turned around and faced me. "Chima, did you truly take the JAMB exam?" he said.

"Yes!" I responded. I'm not really sure why. That was my chance to tell the truth.

When he explained the thoroughness with which his brother Oko had searched for my name and my results, but to no avail, he asked me again – and this time, there was a dark look on his face. "Chima, did you truly take the JAMB exam?" he said gravely.

After a long pause, I told him I hadn't. I began to explain my reasons, but before I could get the first sentence out, Onyike pounced on me like a leopard. He started punching me in the face and stomach. I did try to defend myself, but I guess his anger and frustration outweighed my defensive mechanisms. After a while, I started moving around the coffee table, making sure it stayed between us, making it difficult for him to get to me. After a few seconds, he drew his belt from his waist. Agha Police swiped the table out of the way as Onyike began to land his belt all over my body. I had been beaten with belts before, at school, but they were probably conservative with their flogging, not wanting to do too much damage and scar me, which would have spelt trouble. Onyike, however, spared no thought to the damage he could do to me; he was my uncle, and he was mad. After what felt like hours of beating, Agha jumped in and told Onyike it was enough. Onyike put his belt back on, and he and Agha left the house. I was asleep when he came back. I believe it was after that incident that Onyike decided he was going to have a go at making something out of me. He never did ask me for an explanation of why I hadn't registered for the JAMB exam.

When the WAEC results were finally released in March 1985, instead of August or September of the previous year, I found out to my joy that I had passed all the subjects that would help me gain entrance to university to study law. I was now in a position to apply for the 1985 JAMB exams, and if I passed them with a high enough score, I would be going to university in September or October 1985. I was proud of my achievements, and wrote to my dad to tell him.

His response turned my whole life upside down. He said that there was no way a child of his would study law, because all lawyers were liars, and he would not have me lying for a living. He wanted me to study medicine or pharmacy. I was totally lost. What was I going to do? I had planned my whole secondary school life around my future law career. I was good in the right subjects. I had literally ignored the sciences; I was good at arguing cases, with credible facts. I was a lawyer in the making, so to be told I couldn't study law … well! I was totally thrown off the rails by this decision. I was angry, confused and dazed. What was I going to do now? If I disobeyed my dad and applied to study law, he would probably refuse to pay my university fees. This meant I had to find a way of studying and retaking my O-Level Chemistry, Physics and Maths subjects.

When Onyike realised the problem I had, he tried to convince me to register at the Institute of Management and Technology (IMT), Enugu, where they held courses for students who wanted to obtain their O- or A-Level qualifications. IMT also held other technological, managerial and engineering higher-level courses, up to OND and HND. It took me a very long time to get my head around my drastic, abrupt career change. I rebelled and refused to visit IMT. Onyike tried to enrol me into St Patrick's Secondary School, Emene, Enugu, where I could retake my sciences; again, I refused. He even brought a work colleague whose younger brother was studying at IMT to explain how wonderful the institute was. To get him off my back, I told him I would visit the institute to see what it was like. I didn't go. In fact, I spent an entire year sulking and squandering my time in Enugu. My only good deed that year was enrolling to take Taekwondo lessons at Gym 35, which was based in Emene. I had wanted to go back to Shaolin, even though I had graduated, but I could not find anywhere that taught the art. Taking Taekwondo classes gave some form of outlet. It gave me thinking space, and space to vent my frustration. Because I already had a black belt in Shaolin, I was allowed to start as a green belt. It took me less than two years to get my Taekwondo black belt. I trained and sparred with very inspirational colleagues, including Ali Baba, Emeka Ida, Obinna (Emeka's younger brother), and many other people.

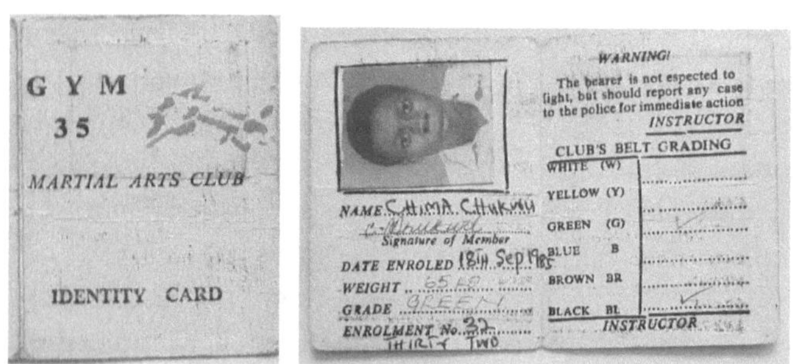

Taekwondo identity card

When I went to the village for the 1985 Christmas holidays, I vented my anger by being very stubborn, rebellious, ignorant and naughty. During this time, my grandma bore the brunt of most of my silly actions. I partied for three or four non-stop, hopping from one village to the other every day without bothering to return home. My relatives worried about me because most of the time they didn't know where I was. If I was sighted somewhere, the news would be quickly fed back to my grandma and uncles, and they would come looking for me. They were always too late. My cousin Nnanna Azu (aka "Bouncing") and I had gotten into the habit of going to parties, entering dancing competitions, winning, takings our spoils and moving off to find another party in another village. My first village-hopping stint was fun for me; we always managed to find a relative who would let us stay the night, then feed us during the day before we left. My second stint was not planned. It must have been around the 26th or 27th December. I had been invited to a thanksgiving and survival party which was being hosted by Ndukwe Oji Nnachi (popularly known as Ndukwe nwa Mma Grace – Ndukwe, the son of mama Grace), now Dr Ndukwe Oji Nnachi, a senior lecturer at Ebonyi State University. Dr Ndukwe was older than me, but as I explained before, I did have a lot of friends who were a lot older than me due to the fact that they could speak the English I understood when I originally went to Nigeria. I had kept in touch with all of them. The party attracted the "who's who" of Edda and the surrounding towns. The MC of the occasion, Irem Ibom, now Honourable Irem Ibom, told me to leave just as the party was about to get started. When I told him I had been invited, he simply didn't believe me. He started shouting at me to leave immediately, otherwise he would be forced to physically drag me out. As he moved towards me, Ndukwe walked in and intervened, explaining that he had invited me to the party. Irem left me alone.

During the party, I was dancing with a girl. I thought I knew her from somewhere, but I couldn't recollect where. Midway through our dance, the generator cut off and all the lights went off. In that instant, she pulled me closer to her and kissed me on the lips. I barely had time to process what had happened and savour the moment before the lights came back on and we continued dancing as if nothing had happened. Before I left, she asked if we could see each other the next day, and we agreed to meet. The following day, I went to see her at the house she had described to me. When I saw her, I once again thought to myself, I've seen this girl somewhere before. As we were sitting down, talking, a friend of one of my older cousins walked in. That's when it dawned on me who the girl was. She was his girlfriend – her name was Ugo. On a previous occasion, he had asked me to make sure she got home safely to Owutu. Without saying anything to us, he walked straight back out of the house.

That evening, whilst I was at a party with my cousin Nnanna, one of my friends came and told me that someone was looking for me with a group of three or four other boys. I knew exactly who it was. My older cousin's friend wanted to teach me a lesson for talking to his girl-friend. I didn't wait around till they arrived; Nnanna and I disappeared into the bushes. Eventually locating the bush path, we made our way to Owutu, where we knew we would be safe. In order to be doubly sure I didn't get caught, I village-hopped again, spending a maximum of one day in a village before taking the bush roads to move onto a different one. As this venture wasn't planned, and I didn't necessarily want anyone to know where I was, I made sure I stayed in circles of people who didn't know me so that they were not in a position to spread any rumours as to where I was, or where they had last seen me.

Eventually, after about three days, I went back to Ebun-wana. I went straight to my older cousin, Ude, and ex-plained what had happened; he already knew it was a misunderstanding. He had to go and beg his friend to forgive me – thankfully, he did. I couldn't wait to get back to Enugu and out of harm's way. Even though I wanted to go back to Enugu in early January 1986, I ended up spending the entire month in the village, trying to make up for lost time with my grandma. I also had a sense that things were about to change; that I was about to emerge from the dark aura that had descended on me uninvited. Before I left, my grandma blessed me, wished me well, and told me to always listen to my uncle.

Lightbulb Moment (1986–1988)

When I got back to Enugu, I felt as if I had been baptised with intelligence and wisdom. It felt as if all my life experiences, good and bad, had come together and now urged – actually, demanded – that I wake up and fulfil my purpose here on earth. It was as if my experiences had established a unique energy of their own and they were going to make sure I had a positive impact on anything that came my way. I was miraculously full of energy, purpose and hunger to achieve and to inspire anyone and anything I came in contact with.

Without informing Onyike, I made some enquiries and found out that registration for the Junior Basic Studies (which was the equivalent of O-Levels) at IMT started around April. Between February and April, I would sneak off to the IMT library when everyone had gone to work and would bury my head in the science books. I was trying my best to reacquaint myself with the gruelling task of reading and studying before I started in September.

As soon as registration started, I informed Onyike, who was surprised, shocked and happy, all at the same time. He gave me the registration fees immediately. The next day, I went to IMT and registered for the Junior Basic

Studies one-year course. It was a great feeling. I was suddenly back on track to making something out of my life after being derailed for so long and nearly abandoning education and all sense of purpose.

My first day at IMT in September set the tone for the rest of my studying life. As I walked onto the campus and down one of the many roads that led to my class, I saw a guy who was teaching maths informally. As I stopped to watch, I overheard people talking about him; his name was Chuka, and he was a Junior Basic Studies student, like me. Before lectures, and sometimes after lectures, he would find an empty classroom and ask students who didn't understand what had been taught to join him while he went over the maths lectures again, in detail. I thought to myself, I want to be like him. By the end of my first year, in June 1987, I had joined him, and we were both teaching maths and physics in empty classrooms. We didn't charge anything for it, either – something people found odd. Teaching other students helped me understand the subject matter so much better myself, and it also gave me a lot of confidence and reassurance that I knew my stuff.

The 1987 O-Level exams were quite straightforward. The JAMB exam was slightly trickier, although I still felt very confident that I would get enough points to go on and study medicine; I had applied to the universities of Benin and Port Harcourt. I passed all my O-Level sciences with 'A' grades. In the JAMB exams, however, I got 270 points – 10 points short of what was needed to get into university to study medicine. Not having any money or a "godfather" in a high enough position to push my case or help me, I couldn't get any of the universities to change their minds. I wasn't too unhappy about the situation; in fact, it strengthened my resolve to do better the next time.

While I was pondering my next move, my dad decided I should go to England for a holiday; the first since I had left in 1976, eleven years previously. I was elated to be going to visit. Onyike was happy for me – I think he knew it would do me some good to get away for a couple of months and be reunited with my family. He was right.

In July 1987, I left for England. The six-hour flight to London was totally occupied by thoughts of how I would introduce myself to my siblings: "Hi – remember me? I'm the one you write to in Nigeria." "Gosh! You've grown." "Hi – tell me all about England, starting with you, Olugh." Eventually, I decided that I would do no talking. I was the guest; I would let them try and make me feel at home. I thought they must have missed me more than I missed them. Well, we'll soon find out, I thought to myself.

My plane arrived at Heathrow airport at around 8pm; my father was there to meet me. After a rigid handshake and a few rounds of "how are you?" and "how are your uncles and cousins?", we proceeded to the car and made our journey back to South London, my birthplace. The feeling was surreal; I felt as if I was dreaming and had to keep pinching myself. Was I really back in London? When we got to the house, I recognised it straight away – it still looked the same. The only thing that was different was the paint on the outside stairs. There was nobody in sight apart from my mum, who was in the kitchen cooking and singing. We exchanged greetings casually, almost as if I'd just come back from work after leaving in the morning.

As I sat down, I began to wonder where everyone was. Surely they couldn't all have gone to bed? It was only ten o'clock. Surely they were as excited as me and had stayed up to see me come home? As I sat there, still taking in my surroundings, my younger brother, Olugh came bounding down the stairs, into the kitchen, and into my arms. We hugged for what seemed like hours, swaying from side to side. He was ten years old at the time, and I had never seen him before, so it was an emotional moment for both of us. We had written to each other regularly, sent pictures of each other and spoke occasionally on the phone, but that was not the same.

Whilst in Nigeria, I had begun to wonder what I had done that was so bad that my parents did not want me to meet my younger brother. Did they think I'd be a bad influence on him – show him all the bad things that I knew? The thought made me quite bitter. As his older brother, I believed it was my job to show him the ropes, look after him through his school days, and do all the other things older brothers do for their younger brothers.

Olugh began to tell me about everything in his life, all at once: his school, his friends, homework, how to work the gas cooker, and where the cornflakes were kept. As he was doing this, Onyemachi came in. We shook hands, strangers to one another, not exactly sure of which form of greeting to use. Ugo was the last to come downstairs and say hello. To me, that day was symbolic; it was the first day that the entire family was together. For me, it was a moment of happiness.

The next day, Olugh brought his friends round after school. He had told them that his older brother from Nigeria was in town and was a grand master in Shaolin. They were mesmerised, and I was shy. Conscious of my deep Nigerian accent and afraid I would not understand everything they said, I tried not to say too much. Instead, I either nodded or shook my head in response to their many questions.

During my eight-week stay, I learned to love my siblings. We did a lot together, trying to catch up on the lost eleven years. They helped me with the English language and the English way of doing things, from movies, jokes, and food to the currency, where to get the bus, and how not to talk to or say hello to everyone I met. This last one was something I found quite odd, as it was exactly the opposite in Nigeria. I explained the Nigerian way of doing things, the different tribes, languages and cultures, the camaraderie, the lack of food and other resources, the superstitious beliefs, the educational system, the judicial system and the fact that without money you were nobody going nowhere – and if you did have a lot of money, you were regarded as a god. They were both perplexed and confused by my stories, but there was no other way to explain Nigeria. By the end of my stay, I was very sad to leave my "newfound" siblings. I was concerned that the relationship we had built up might crumble once I was back in Nigeria. At the same time, I was happy to be going back to continue with my studies and to start building my life as I wanted it to be. Spending time with my parents and siblings and hearing how dedicated my siblings were to their studies really gave me all the inspiration I needed. Onyemachi was already doing her A-Levels, and Ugo was making progress. I needed to raise my game. I relished what lay ahead, and left for Nigeria on near the end of September 1987.

Back in Nigeria, I directed all my attention to studying. I went back to IMT and registered for my A-Levels. I also registered for the JAMB exams again. My plan was to use the A-Level studies to build on my O-Level knowledge, which would better prepare me for the JAMB. Onyike rented out an extra room in the house we lived in so that I could have it specifically for my studies. It helped a lot.

When the JAMB exams came out in June 1988, I was three points short of what I needed to study medicine at University of Nigeria Nsukka. I was absolutely devastated. I was offered a place to study pharmacy at Nsukka. One of my friends, Phillip, who wanted to study pharmacy at Nsukka but was offered pharmacology, tried to convince me to take the pharmacy offer and join him at Nsukka. I refused; I believed I was good enough to study medicine at Nsukka. I travelled to the JAMB office at Ogbo Hill, Aba, to see if I could get some assistance, even though I was unsure of how this would happen, as I didn't know anyone at the offices, and neither did I know anyone I could approach for help. Sad memories of my experience the previous year began to surface.

I spent three days begging at the JAMB offices for them to have mercy on me and grant me a medical place at Nsukka. On the third and final day, I went there feeling despondent, knowing all would be in vain. The fact that nobody from my extended family cared enough to even come with me to the offices made me feel even more hopeless. By 1pm on that last day, I had made up my mind that my fate had been decided for me. If I couldn't study medicine at Nsukka, then I wasn't going to stay in Nigeria any longer. I still had a burning desire to achieve many things, but Nigeria was stifling my innovation.

With that final thought stamped in my mind, I left the JAMB offices with a new incentive. I was going to leave the country. I was going to go back to England and continue my quest to succeed in life. In fact, I was quietly happy to be leaving the shores of Nigeria for good. From 1986 through to 1988, Nigeria had gradually gone from a booming African economic powerhouse to a catastrophic nightmare. To underline some of the country's problems, the World Bank had reclassified Nigeria from a middle-income country to a low-income country. Falling oil prices had affected Nigeria's per capita income, which fell to $380 in 1988, down from a high of $800 in 1985. Due to unpaid bills, Nigeria Airways was grounded in Copenhagen, two of its Airbus jets were grounded in France, and the company was barred from the International Air Travel Association. Nigeria as a country was at the start of a disastrous downward spiral. This was exactly the right time to leave before I got swallowed up and lost in a country whose future looked as bleak as mine had a couple of years ago.

When I got back to Enugu, Onyike didn't ask whether I had been successful or not. He was already upset with me and my parents. He was upset that they sent me huge amounts of money to purchase a return ticket to London. He did not see the point of me going there again. He believed the money would have been better spent on trying to secure a university spot. I had agreed with him initially, but when we were unable to find someone reliable to help us, I lost interest in the idea. If we did find someone to bribe, what were the assurances that it would work out? The day after the money my dad had sent for my ticket arrived, I asked him for it, and he begrudgingly gave it to me – 80,000 naira. Little did he know what my plans were. I said my goodbyes and headed to the village to tell my grandma that I would soon be going to England and wouldn't be coming back. Surprisingly, she was very happy for me – she probably knew I had a better future there than in Nigeria. She said that I should continue to focus on my education, and when I finished, I should come back to Nigeria so she could find me a good wife. I also told my cousin Ude. He too was happy I was leaving.

After a couple of days in the village, I left for Aba. When I got there, I spent a couple of days refining my escape plan. I had to keep reminding myself that I was leaving in order to have a chance of living a successful life. When I was ready, I went to the Nigeria Airways offices on Azikiwe Road to find out about the cost of buying a one-way ticket to London. I was flabbergasted to find the cost was nearly the same as buying a return ticket. I did not have quite enough for a return ticket, nor for a one-way ticket. The man at the desk said the only way I could get a cheaper one-way ticket was to pay in pounds sterling. I knew that if I changed my naira to pounds sterling, I would be able to afford the ticket, but I wouldn't have enough to also get to Murtala Mohamed airport from Aba. I begged, cried, and begged some more, but the man was adamant that I had to change my naira to pounds sterling before purchasing my one-way ticket. I left the offices in tears and beside myself, not knowing where to turn. How could my excellently crafted plan have collapsed so easily? The thought of not being able to go to England hurt too much.

As I was walking home, a thought crossed my mind. My dad had a business partner, Mr Onuoha, who I had met a few times before when my dad had come to Nigeria. I thought to myself that he might be able to help me. He sold electrical equipment such as fridges, air conditioning units, fans and TVs at his shop on Hospital Road by East. I headed straight for his shop, but when I got there, I was told he had gone home for the day, so I continued on to his house, which was somewhere along Ngwa Road by East. Thankfully, he was in. He was surprised to see me, as I had never been to see him before; I always went with my dad to visit him at his shop. When he asked me how he could help me, I was unable to control my emotions – I burst out crying and explained my situation. I told him I needed to buy a one-way ticket to London but couldn't get Nigerian Airways to sell me one. When I explained the reason why, he reached for the telephone beside him, without getting up from his armchair, and dialled a number. I overheard a voice say, "Nigerian Airways", and stood by whilst he explained to the person on the other end of the line who he was and asked to speak with someone else – some top guy, I believe. When the top guy came to the phone, Mr Onuoha had a brief conversation before he put the phone down and told me to come with him.

We went downstairs to his car and he drove to Azikiwe Road, parked outside the Nigerian Airways offices, and marched in and up to the front desk. He asked for a one-way ticket to London in my name. When the guy at the desk asked who he was, he explained. Within five minutes,

I had my ticket. When we got outside, Mr Onuoha said he was going to a meeting and wished me a safe journey before driving off. I stood there for a while before bursting into tears of joy and relief. My dream was alive again.

When I got home, I told Okoro Ikpo that I had bought the return ticket and was relieved that he didn't ask to see it. My flight to London was booked for the 11th August, which meant I had lots of time to kill. I decided I would try and use the time wisely. The next day, I went off to see my good friend Ama Oji. I needed to tell him that I would be going to London for good. When I got to his house at School Road, Aba, I was told by his niece that he was not in. She asked whether I wanted to leave a message, but I said no. As I turned to leave, she said she wanted to talk to me. She told me that her name was Ego and that she was sixteen. I told her that I already knew who she was as I had seen her a couple of times in the village when she came back for the Christmas holidays. Their house was behind Nna's house in Amaeke Ebunwana. Then she took me by surprise; she told me that she had seen me a couple of times, both in the village and in Aba, and that she liked me a lot. I was dumbfounded and speechless. When I recovered my composure, I told her I was flattered to be told such a nice thing by such a beautiful young girl. I also told her I was going to England and was not sure when I'd be back, which was why I was looking for Ama so I could tell him. She said that going to England should not stop us from having a relationship;

she said we could have a long-distance relationship and see how it went. I didn't spend much time thinking about it. I was still flattered and probably would have agreed to almost anything she asked.

We met up the following day and went out for a stroll, followed by a drink and a long discussion about our lives, school, likes and dislikes. On the third day, we met up again and continued where we'd left off. After a long discussion, I walked home with her to see if Ama was in. He was. I told him about my impending journey to England. He was sad to hear I wouldn't be coming back, but knew it was the best thing for me. Ama had seen me suffer endlessly at the hands of Okoro Ikpo, Eleya and others. We said our farewells, and I left.

On the 6th August, I headed off to Lagos. It was only the second time I'd been there since landing at the airport over twelve years earlier. I had resisted going to Lagos because I had heard how busy and rowdy it was. I also had an awful premonition that something terrible would happen to me if I went there, so I had avoided it up until then. I went to Owerri airport, where I got a flight to Lagos; it was a smooth and uneventful journey. When I got to Lagos, I had to find where my friend Uche Agwu Uche lived in Itire, Surulere. As somebody who had never been to Lagos city before, I felt overwhelmed by the sheer number of people and cars moving in every direction, the noise, the heat and the vast look of the place. I took a taxi straight into the heart of Surulere; a residential and commercial area bustling with energy and life. Although it was a bit congested, the area was reasonably clean, and most of the roads were tarred and driveable – I was impressed. I planned to spend the last couple of days enjoying Lagos and visiting friends and family.

Everything went to plan, although I had one frightening incident. Uche, Emmanuel, a few other friends and I went to a night club to celebrate my last days in Nigeria. We were sitting at a table, drinking and listening to the soulful music being played by the DJ. Someone behind us was smoking. This didn't bother me at first, but when I turned around to see what was going on behind me, I got a full blast of the cigarette smoke in my face. This immediately triggered off an acute asthma attack, and I began to find it difficult to breathe.

At first I thought I couldn't breathe due to the stuffiness of the place. I got up and went to the gents' toilet to try and get some fresh air. When I got to the toilet, the attack gradually got worse, and I remember thinking to myself, I need to get out of this toilet, otherwise I am going to collapse and die, and nobody will even know what has happened. I made my way back to where my friends were, sat down, and quietly whispered to Uche to call me an ambulance as I couldn't breathe. He thought I was pulling some sort of prank. I then told him I was dead serious and would bite off his ear if he didn't get me to the hospital fast. He realised the seriousness of the situation and raised the alarm.

My friends said that it would be quicker to walk or run to the hospital than call and wait for an ambulance. My friends lifted me onto their shoulders, shouted for people to get out of their way, and jogged the two miles or so to the nearest hospital. On arriving at the hospital, my friends asked to see the doctor in charge. We were told there was only one doctor available as it was past 7pm, and he would be out to see me as soon as possible. Around twenty minutes later, the doctor emerged from a room behind us and asked whether we had paid any money to be attended to. Uche said that we had not yet been asked to pay anything. The doctor said that if we didn't pay, he could not attend to me. Uche immediately gave him around 3,000 naira, explaining that money was not an issue. The doctor ushered me into a room. Uche came inside with me whilst the others waited in the reception. The doctor disappeared into a smaller room, emerging a short while later with a syringe. He asked me to straighten my arm and administered what I now know to be a corticosteroid injection. The attack subsided almost immediately. He kept me under observation for about an hour before discharging me.

Immediately after we left the hospital, I suggested to my friends that we return to the night club and continue where we left off, but I got the feeling they thought we had lost our momentum – not to mention the fact that the dash to the hospital had left them exhausted. We all went home, and the rest of my stay in Lagos was uneventful.

I finally left for England on the 11th August 1988. I saw this date as an end to one chapter of my life and the beginning of another. It was an emotional and sad time for me, as I knew I was not coming back and there would be people I'd never see again; the dynamics of my relationships with my friends and family in Nigeria would change. I was going to miss my grandma, and I didn't know what to expect in England, which was now a foreign country to me. At the same time, I was full of anticipation for the future that lay ahead of me. I was excited at the thought of delving into the unknown, and I was proud because I was returning to my country of birth, from which I had once been banished, as a changed, young, resilient and purposeful young man.

Back to My Roots
(1988–1990)

When I got to Heathrow airport, I was able to find my way home to Brixton, South London, from the airport without any assistance – something I considered a huge accomplishment at the time. It did help that I had very little to carry; I had decided to leave most of my belongings behind in Nigeria so as not to raise suspicion of my intended plans and to keep up the pretence of coming to England on a holiday.

When I got home, the welcomes were a bit more relaxed and understanding compared to those of 1987. I put this down to some of the bonding time I'd spent with my family when I had visited the previous year. I think it was also due to the fact that we had written to each other more over the past year in an effort to capture some lost time and maintain a closer relationship.

That evening, my dad suggested I should try and get a job as soon as possible so as to make some money during the short period I was in England on holiday. I agreed. The following day, my parents went to a church service, something they did quite regularly. When they came back later that night, my dad informed me that a member of his church might be able to help me get a job in a hotel in Kensington. I was overjoyed; I would get my first opportunity to earn some money.

The following day, the entire family got ready and accompanied me to my hotel job interview. It wasn't a formal interview, as Lin, the Chinese lady who interviewed me, explained. She said the fact that I came by recommendation was good enough for her. She just needed to ascertain whether I was entitled to work in England and whether I could start on Monday 15th August. I answered in the affirmative to both questions, and I was overjoyed when she told me I would be paid £5 an hour in cash. She also told me I would be working a shift pattern. At this point, I had no idea what a shift pattern was, nor what the job entailed – and I did not think to ask. When I got home and Onyemachi asked me what I would be doing, I realised I had no clue.

On the Monday, I turned up for work nice and early, taking the same route we had taken to get there on the Saturday. The London Tara Hotel was located on Scarsdale Place, Kensington, not far from Kensington High Street Tube station, in a quiet residential corner of the Royal Borough of Kensington and Chelsea. I reported at the reception desk and asked for Lin. Ten minutes later, Lin appeared from downstairs and welcomed me with a wide smile. She led me downstairs and into her office where she offered me a seat. I sat down, and she explained that I would be working in the laundry section of the hotel in the basement. My main job would be to load dirty towels into the large industrial washing machines. Although this was not a career-building job, it seemed very easy and stress-free. In the basement, we worked in teams which were organised by shift. Everyone working in that section was black, mainly from Sierra Leone and Ghana. I was the only Nigerian there, and I was by far the youngest. All the other men there were married with children, and all looked over the age of forty. They moaned constantly about how hard the work was and how little money they got paid.

The weeks seemed to fly by, and as we got to the second week of September, my dad started to fuss over what he needed to give me to distribute to his extended family and relatives when I got back to Nigeria. After a couple of days of playing along with his idea that I was soon going back to Nigeria, I knew I had to tell him I wasn't going back. I just didn't know how. I thought the opportunity had come when my mum asked me what my plans were when I got back to Nigeria. I braced myself and told her that I wasn't going back this time around. She appeared shocked and confused. She asked me what I was going to do, why I hadn't told my dad, and where I was going to stay. I thought she'd be happier that I was staying, seeing as she had tried to persuade me to stay the last time I came. I think the news that her first son, who had been living away from home for more than twelve years, was now coming back to stay was all a bit unexpected and overwhelming for her. She must have wondered whether I was still as stubborn as people in Nigeria said I was, and whether I held a grudge against her for allowing me to be sent to Nigeria and suffer as I had.

The next evening after work, whilst we were all sitting around in the living room, I plucked up the courage. I told my dad I had something important I wanted to tell him. "I'm not going back to Nigeria," I said.

He took his glasses off and looked me straight in the eye. "I beg your pardon?" he said. I repeated myself, a lot louder this time. "Oh yes you are!" he said. He asked me what date my flight back to Nigeria was. When I told him I had bought a one-way ticket, I thought he was going burst an artery. I could tell he was shocked that I had planned the whole affair before coming to England and had kept quiet about it throughout my stay. "Well," he said, "if you are not going back, you will have to find somewhere to live and hope you can afford to pay the rent. What's going to happen with your education? Have you really thought this through?"

I told him I had thought it through thoroughly and believed it was the best thing for me at this time. I explained the difficulties I had experienced getting into university, and didn't want to continue repeating the JAMB exams. At this stage, my mother joined in the conversation and was naturally on my side, begging my dad to let me stay in England and finish my education. She said she was tired of hearing conflicting news about how I was doing back home. She was also worried for my welfare, as

I was a lot older now. After what seemed to be hours of discussion, begging and shouting, my dad finally agreed for me to stay in England. He instructed me to write to all my relatives back home and inform them of my decision not to come back to Nigeria. I agreed I would write the letters, knowing full well I would never do such a thing. Why should I? Most of them didn't care about me anyway. The exception was Onyike, who I did write to with an explanation of my decision; I felt I owed that to him. I told him I would continue to work hard to achieve my educational goals. With all immediate important decisions about my future made, I didn't have to wait long to register for college.

The college of my choice was South London College in Knights Hill, West Norwood. My sister Ugo had applied to go there, so I decided it would be a good place to go too, especially as it was known to be a good college for those interested in the sciences. The registration and enrolment process was straightforward, although I had to register to start my A-Levels all over again, as I didn't have any documentation to prove I had already completed a year in Nigeria. I was also not entitled to a grant or any form of government funds; I did not qualify, due to my short time in the country. Despite all this, I was looking forward to starting a new life in England, closer to my family and far away from some cruel relatives and many unhappy memories.

When college started, I was ecstatic. I was on the way to

achieving my dreams of becoming a medical doctor. I continued working at the Tara Hotel over the weekends whilst I went to college, hoping something else closer to home would come soon. The journey from Brixton to West Norwood was quite straightforward. I could catch a bus to Camberwell and get the No. 68 bus to college, or I could catch a bus to Brixton then catch the No. 2 or 3 bus to college. Sometimes I went in with my sister, but our timetables were different, so this was not a regular thing for us.

I soon got myself into a routine; going to college for my morning classes and spending most of my free time at the library in Battersea. I normally stayed in the library until 9pm, after which I would go home, eat, and go to bed by 11pm. I would normally wake up very early in the morning, around 3am, to study before heading off to college. At the weekends, I always went to the library to study. Life at college soon became busy as I started to make friends, and we would hang out, tell stories, spend time talking in the canteen, go out to restaurants, and sometimes study together. My main friends were Kishore, Rosie, Tayo and Michael. Through these friends I made numerous acquaintances, although I was quite happy to keep the number of friends I had quite small. Sometimes I would hang out with my sister and her friends in the canteen, and I soon became good friends with some of her friends too, including Charity and Esther.

Apart from going to college to learn (which was fairly

straightforward, as I had covered most of the topic areas in Nigeria), I also had to get to grips with the English culture and accent. It was like relearning how to live life from scratch. I tried very hard to get rid of my Nigerian accent, and although I was successful, every now and again it would find its way into my conversations without warning. That was quite embarrassing.

At some stage in my first year, I met Evelyn Abordo on the No. 2 bus on my way home one day. She was a beautiful, petite, charming Ghanaian girl. We started talking and found out that we had quite a lot in common, including our tastes in music and books. We soon started meeting in the canteen, and the library, and anywhere else we could find. I had tried to avoid getting into any relationships, because I felt Ego and I had unexplored ground to cover, and until I spoke with her face to face to decide where we were headed, I did not want to date anyone else. We did write to each other all the time, and we had even declared our feelings for each other in our letters. However, it wasn't long before Evelyn and I started dating; I only had a long-distance relationship with Blessing, and she was a long way away. My relationship with Evelyn was slow to develop, probably because we were both very studious people and were keen to do well in our education; we didn't have much time for each other initially. The relationship did develop over time and we became quite close, doing a lot of things together. I often went to her flat in Tulse Hill, where she lived with her mother and older brother. Neither liked me much because I was Nigerian. I took her home and introduced her to my parents, who were welcoming, to my surprise. I wasn't quite sure why it came as a surprise that they liked her, given her humble and well-mannered nature.

Every once in a while, I would bring her home in the afternoon when nobody was at home so we could spend some quiet time together. On one occasion, we went to my house in the middle of the afternoon, but whilst we were there my mother decided to come back home from work earlier than I had anticipated. We were in the living room, which was situated at the very top of the house. We waited until I heard her go into the kitchen, then we slipped downstairs, past the kitchen, into the ground floor flat, and out through the back window into the garden. We jumped over our garden fence into someone else's garden, where we cowered as she peered through the window; she must have heard something. We must have been in the garden for just over five minutes when we were startled by the approach of two huge police dogs accompanied by three burly policemen. They had come out from one of the neighbouring houses. We were told to turn around and get on our knees which we promptly did, not quite sure why we were being placed under arrest. One of the policemen said that somebody had seen us cowering in the garden and had reported us, so we were arrested for trespassing. We were handcuffed and led out onto a busy Coldharbour Lane in Camberwell where we were placed in separate police vans and driven off to Brixton police Station.

At the station, we were questioned in different rooms, and thankfully we shamelessly told the truth as to how we came to be in someone else's garden. We were eventually released without charge and went our respective ways that evening. That was my first encounter with the police as an adult, and it would not be my last. I obviously didn't tell my parents what had happened, although my mother did say she thought she heard noises in the house when she came home early that Friday afternoon. My dad put it down to "the Father" working on her ears (meaning God was making her hear things).

My relationship with Evelyn seemed to be on a moderate path; we were doing all the things we wanted to, including studying very hard. Some evenings we would finish studying and then go to Ruskin Park in Camberwell and spend time talking and romanticising about our future together. Just before our first summer together, the summer of 1989, one of her former secondary school teachers asked if Evelyn would be able to look after her house for her whilst she went on a three-week holiday with her husband. Evelyn told me about it and said she would only do it if I agreed to stay with her over the three weeks. We both went to see Mrs and Mr Simmonds at their house on Fawnbrake Avenue, Herne, South London. The place was a quiet, spacious, clean, five-bedroom house with a lovely garden. I immediately agreed to stay with Evelyn at the house. They agreed to give us spending money which would last the three weeks for most things we needed. Without informing my parents, I one day quietly collected some of my belongings in a small bag, pretended I was going to college, and disappeared to Fawnbrake Avenue.

Apart from brief periods spent at her mum's house or at my parents' house, this was the first time Evelyn and I had ever been together on our own, so we were very excited. We actually felt like grown-ups, finishing college and going home together to the same house. It gave us abundant time to talk about our future and to find out things we didn't know about each other. I said that even though she was a beautiful girl, her main ambitions were to study and achieve excellent academic qualifications, which probably meant she was a focused individual – something I had definitely observed in her. Her mother and brother were also very strict, and that sort of upbringing made it difficult to stray from the values already set. We spent close to three weeks at Fawnbrake Avenue, and whilst Evelyn had an agreement with her mother that allowed her to stay there, I had not been given consent to do so by my parents. I actually had not even asked them; at twenty-two years of age, I didn't feel I needed to get anyone's permission to do anything.

I did occasionally sneak home to get some new clothes and books, and I also did ring home. The first time I attempted ringing home, my dad put the phone down on me. Eventually, my mother answered the phone; I explained where I was and convinced her that the atmosphere was very conducive to studying, which is what I was doing. She conveyed this to my dad.

During my stay, Evelyn convinced me to try hard and get a job closer to home. I eventually quit my job at the London Tara Hotel and found something more local, working for Jackets, a small food restaurant which specialised in potatoes. They had three branches; in Clapham, Clapham Junction and Brixton. The pay was quite good for a job of that type – it paid £9 an hour, and I was in a position to save most of my wages, as I had very few outgoings.

It really did seem like Evelyn and I were mature adults living together and paying our way through life. The three weeks came and went very quickly; a day before the owners of the house were due back, I begrudgingly packed my things and headed home, bracing myself for the arguments that I knew lay ahead with my parents. The argument was huge. My dad wanted me to move out immediately, and for once my mum supported him. I tried to explain that I was an adult and could do as I pleased. I emphasised that they knew I was not far away and that I was not doing anything bad. I felt unwanted. At the slightest opportunity, my parents were eager to get me to move out – to leave the family again. I was tempted, but I kept reminding myself of the reason I had left Nigeria. It was to make a better life for myself and have an impact on people around me. Our dispute went on for over a week. Finally, we came to a truce. I was to behave myself for the rest of the year, and I had to be home every weekday by 9pm. I wasn't too worried; I only came back late when I went to the library, and I worked weekends. I stuck to the deal arrangements and everything seemed to be going well.

Then, on the 3rd October 1989, I came back from college and my dad told me that my cousin Gabby had rung earlier from Nigeria to tell him that my grandma had passed away the previous night. The news, and the realisation that I would never see her again, left me devastated and empty. Less than a week earlier, I had received a letter she had written to me, asking me to buy her a blanket to help keep her warm. I began to think that maybe there was a secret message in her letter to me, telling me that her time on earth was up.

Amemu – New Layout
Ebunwana Edda
Afikpo Local Government Area
17th Sept. 1989.

My dear Son,

How about your studies? I hope you are doing it. Please, Iam here advicing you not to emulate the foolishness of your parents and your sister Onyemachi, because immediately I saw your mum and Onyemachi, I started to prepared pottage for them and after I have finish cooking my food, they totally refused to taste my food. However, if you said that am really your mum do not immediate their bad characters.

Moreover, I was in support of your going back to London again, inorder to finish your Carriers over there. Take note of my advice to you, I do not want you to fail prey like your father and mother, for their refusing to come back to Nigeria again. Immediately you have finish your Carriers over there make a haste to return back to Nigeria, before then you might have reach the age you will engage a wife which I will seek a very nice girl for you to marry.

My lovely Son, I really love you and that is why I reply you, because if it were your parents, I couldn't have reply back to them, because Iam no longer use to write them. You are really more intelligence than your parents.

Furthermore, this is to let you know that I was seriously ill but am now feeling fine. Please, I want you to purchase BLANKET for me which I will be use for covering myself during the cold time. Since your father have determine not to see

... my body at the time of my death when God say it is the day for my departure on this earth, but if only you will see it when you return back at that time, the better for me.

please, tell my lovely son Olughu that I have greeted him. I am also looking forward for his letter. Then also tell him to study hard and to be a good boy too. Let him be emulating your Character. Thanks. Your Heavy mum Ugo Okoro.

Grandma's letter

Much of the improvement in my behaviour had been due to my beloved grandma's influence; I wanted to impress her by doing well for myself and being able to look after her when I finally got a job. Nearly everything I had done since deciding to make something of my life had been to please her. She had promised to find me a good wife back in Nigeria when I finished my studies. I had promised her I would go back to Nigeria once I completed my education. Now that she was dead, everything seemed irrelevant.

I called Gabby that evening to confirm the sad news; unfortunately, it was true. I asked my dad whether he was going to Nigeria for the funeral. He said he wasn't going and that there were enough people back home to take care of the funeral. If I hadn't been studying, I would have gone to Nigeria for the funeral. I felt like my entire world had collapsed and disappeared, and I was left help-less.

Amid all the things that happened that evening, something seemed odd. It wasn't until much later on in the night that we all saw a letter written by Onyemachi, explaining that she'd had enough of living at home and had moved out. That didn't come as a shock to me because she had hinted to me that she might not be staying around for much longer. I had forgotten about that conversation until this point. Initially, there was panic as my parents tried to establish where she had gone. The abrupt manner in which my sister had left the family home only added to my sinking feeling. Situations could change so quickly. We eventually found out where Onyemachi was living; my parents had decided that it was really her choice what she did with her life, so they let her be, surprisingly.

Grandma's funeral came and went without me being able to attend. That was a killer for me; it nearly broke my heart. Life became a bit of a blur for me for many months after the funeral. I still went to college and the library, and I still played football, but I was not doing any of these with any conviction.

On my twenty-third birthday, 11th December 1989, something very surprising happened at college. Tayo and Rosie, two very close friends of mine, bought me a large cake and an even larger birthday card. I found this quite embarrassing, especially as I had a girlfriend who happened to be present when they gave me the items. Evelyn questioned their motives, but I explained that they were good friends who had my best interests at heart – nothing else. The situation created a little bit of tension between the two of us. She kept asking me where I had been whenever she didn't see me for half a day.

In February of 1990, I started to receive some complimentary attention from Tayo. This attention was coupled with a barrage of prompts from Rosie, indicating that Tayo fancied me. As they were friends, I found it quite awkward and under pressure to succumb to the advances. On the other hand, I felt that to do so would be wrong; in my book, it would be as good as cheating on Evelyn. After a few weeks of avoiding Tayo and Rosie, or making sure they didn't catch me alone, I decided to be brave and sit down and discuss the matter with them. I asked them if we could take a stroll and discuss the matter, to which they agreed. I explained that I was already in a relationship with Evelyn, who they knew about, and that we were committed to making the relationship work. Tayo said she understood what I was telling them, but that she could not suppress how she felt. We agreed to remain friends and hoped that it would work out. It did work out, as I avoided them both at all costs, only bumping into them on rare occasions when we were rushing between classes.

The rest of the semester passed relatively quietly, as most of us were settling down to study for our end-of-year exams. I was determined to do well in my A-Level subjects, Biology, Chemistry and Physics, so as to get into a decent university outside London and study pharmacy. The decision to study pharmacy instead of medicine had happened by chance, and it was one that had taken my entire family – including myself – by surprise. It all happened just after the summer of 1989, at a time when a lot of junior doctors were under a lot of stress, working very long hours and not coping well with the pressure on hospitals. It was constantly in the news, and this is how it came to my attention. It played on my mind for weeks. After careful consideration of this issue and of the fact that pharmacy seemed like a less stressful career and one which allowed for a more flexible lifestyle, I decided I was no longer going to study medicine. I had been hell bent on studying medicine while I was in Nigeria; it was the main reason I left the country in the first place. When I told my parents, my dad asked me whether I thought it was a wise choice, considering all the hassle I had been through to ensure I studied medicine. I told him I was happy with my decision, so he let me be.

University Life
(1990–1994)

When the A-Level results came out, there were no surprises for me: I got a B in Chemistry, a B in Biology, and a C in Physics. I actually got a U (unclassified) in my Physics practical's after having a brain freeze, but I still managed a C overall. With these results, I assumed I wouldn't have a problem getting into the university of my choosing. I did, however, encounter problems getting into Leicester School of Pharmacy at De Montfort University. They kept my application on hold for two days before finally offering me a place. The two-day wait was agonising; so many thoughts went through my head. What if they turned me down? I knew that if I got turned down, it would be the end of education for me; I'd had enough of being bashed around by different systems and people. But I remained quite positive, praying, focusing on what I really wanted to do with my life during university and afterwards.

When Leicester granted me the place, I was over the moon to finally be going off to university – and outside London too. I didn't want to study in London, as I knew I would be distracted too much. Somewhere far away would help me concentrate on my studies and get my degree. De Montfort University was very well-regarded in many of its specialist fields. I applied for a government grant to help me through my degree course but was denied on the basis that I had not been resident in the United Kingdom for three years. I could have lied on the grant application form, but my dad advised me not to. I took his advice.

Apart from the fact that I was denied a government grant, I also had to contribute to the costs of my education by paying tuition fees of £390 a semester; over £1,000 a year. That did not give me the type of start to university education I was expecting. However, I was not deterred; if anything, it made me more determined, and throughout my time at Leicester I remained focused and dedicated to doing well. I was going to make it all worth my while. My girlfriend, Evelyn, gained a place at the University of Essex, Colchester, to study biochemistry, and although it seemed fairly far from Leicester, we had agreed that wherever we went, we would remain in our relationship.

As part of my preparation for university, I decided to take my driving test. I had taken nine driving lessons over the summer and my tutor, Big Ron, of the Royal Driving School thought I was ready. I took it and passed first time. I was ecstatic. It also boosted my confidence; I would be able to drive back down from Leicester if I needed to.

When I finally went up to Leicester at the end of September, I had to find a place to live and some roommates. Leicester is a city in the East Midlands, and is one of the most ethnically diverse cities in the United Kingdom, with well-established South Asian and Afro-Caribbean communities.

I eventually met up with three boys – Daniel, Kevin and Obi – and we went house-hunting. We managed to find a decent house on our second day of searching. The house was on East Park Road in the Highfields area of Leicester. We decided on Highfields because it was within walking distance of the university and the city centre and offered many amenities for religious, social, cultural and commercial activities. All four of us got along pretty well and did a lot of things together – walking to university, going shopping, partying and other things.

When I started at Leicester, there were ninety-eight pharmacy students in our year. They were mainly white and Asian students, with four black students: Anna Boto, Anne Chigbu, Stephen Chigundu and me. Although I enjoyed every subject, except pharmacognosy, the part I enjoyed the most was the practical's – be they microbiology, pharmaceutical sciences or biochemistry – for the simple reason that we got to wear our white laboratory coats, which I thought made us look very professional. I made lots of new friends; some from my department and many more from other departments across the campus.

At home, although we all got on as a household it didn't take us long to realise that we were all very different individuals, with different habits and different tastes in music, women and food. We still got along well as friends, but after living together for two semesters we decided to all go our separate ways. Kevin and I moved in with an Igbo girl called Mabel on East Park Road in the same Highfields area, whilst Daniel and Obi found accommodation elsewhere.

The social scene was not entirely what I was used to, coming from London. There were hardly any night clubs that played R&B, soul or hip hop, and most of the places I did end up going to closed at 1am or shortly afterwards. The lack of a social atmosphere was very difficult for me to bear, so I kept travelling down to London every two weeks to get a bit of the fast, colourful city life I was used to. After travelling down to London on a regular basis for many months, I decided I needed to do something about the dire situation of the Leicester night life and become a music promoter and DJ. After thinking through what I could do to rejuvenate my social life and also do something to help some of the people around me, I decided to start a music promotion and entertainment outfit called Downtown Entertainment.

I took my time to visit some of the local night clubs to see if people actually enjoyed the music they listened to or they listened and danced to it because there was nothing else for them to do. I also spent time working out who the local DJs were and how good they were at their job. I found out that a lot of people were interested in having a variety of venues playing different music, and that the main DJs were a young man called School Boy, who played R&B and soul, and was also good at mixing, and his older brother, Black Magic, who mainly played reggae music. I truly believed there was enough room for me in the Leicester music scene. I decided on my DJ name – Mr C. The 'C' was for 'Chima', and I thought it sounded authentic.

I hosted my very first event whilst I was in my first year at university, at a place called Night in Town. The event was called Soul Jam, as a huge percentage of the music billed for the night was soul. The event was a huge success; I managed to get School Boy to join me as a DJ on the night. Having School Boy on the bill meant he was able to influence a lot of local Leicester people to attend. My job was to influence the university students to attend, including people from London who were interested. The plan worked, and the mixture of different people and cultures was a very new offering that everyone enjoyed.

At £3 a head to get in, it was quite affordable, and the synergy of music that School Boy and I supplied had the entire crowd on their feet right till the very end. Downtown Entertainment – the name I gave my music and production company – had been launched. That initial event launched me into the public DJing forum, and I was approached several times a week to DJ at private house parties and night clubs. I was earning something in the range of £150 to £250 a night; some weeks I played out four times a week, earning over £1,000. I saved some of the money I made for my tuition fees, rent, maintenance and food, but I also used a lot of it to buy records, old and new. My quest to build my record collection took me to towns like Nottingham, Birmingham, Coventry and many other towns around Leicester. It actually cost a lot of money, but I saw this as an investment. I bought two turntables, a microphone, speakers, a mixer, a CD player, and a tape player.

The fact that I was now a DJ meant I developed a mini-fan base at the university. This was quite unusual for a pharmacy student, as most were too busy studying micro-biology or pharmaceutical practical's to indulge so deeply in the local social life. I enjoyed all the attention and the money, and it also helped me focus on my studies. I would often come back from playing at a night club or house party, pack away my records, and settle down and study until the morning; I didn't want to be the student who spent most of his time partying his life away while others were studying and passing their exams. I also made sure I set myself small, achievable goals, which helped me fo-cus on some of my short-term reading, assignments and other projects.

Towards the end of the third semester of my first year, a very awkward incident happened.   It was around May of 1991, just before our end-of-year exams. I was in the Hawthorn Building with some friends after finishing my lectures when a friend of mine came running towards me. He told me that he had just bumped into two girls at the library who were looking for me; they said they'd come all the way from London. Initially, I thought it could be my sister Ugo and a friend, as she had visited once be-fore. When the friend explained that one of the girls was

Asian, I panicked – I knew exactly who they were. It was Rosie and Tayo, my friends from South London College. I thought of going home straight away so they wouldn't be able to find me. Not many people knew where I lived, so that would have been the easy option.

After much thought, I decided to go to the library and see if I could find them to ascertain what they wanted. They could have been in Leicester for a different reason, and maybe they had just decided to check in on me as an old friend. I got to the library and found them on the first floor. Although I was glad to see them, I was eager to establish why they were in Leicester. After catching up on news of life in London, I asked whether something was wrong. They said there was nothing wrong; they had simply decided to come up from London to visit me, as they had not heard from me in a long time. My mind started racing; I had no food at home, and I didn't know where they going to sleep or how I was going to entertain them for the evening. I wondered whether Tayo would give me a difficult time.

I asked them if they were hungry, and when they said yes, we headed to a lovely Indian restaurant that I knew of on Belgrave Road. I was lucky, as I had quite a lot of money at the time following a busy and successful weekend of DJing. After dinner, we walked back to where I lived on East Park Road. I introduced them to Mabel, who looked at me quizzically; I stared back at her, blankly. Once they had settled down in my room, I disappeared into Mabel's room. She had a host of questions for me, none of which I could answer: Why were they here? Did I not find it odd that they had turned up to see me unannounced? I told her I was as baffled as she was about the whole situation, but I was going to take everything in good faith and just play it by ear.

After speaking with Mabel for some time, I rediscovered my bravado. I went back to my room and asked them if they wanted to go to a night club. They said yes. But they said that before we headed out, they wanted to discuss something with me – something quite important. I excused myself and went to the kitchen, where I poured myself a big glass of Martini Rossi and downed it quickly. I waited until the mixture of vermouth and gin had made its way to my brain cells before climbing back upstairs to re-join them in my room. Rosie began by saying that they were sorry for turning up unannounced, but that they'd thought if they told me they were coming, I might panic and make myself unavailable. They had probably been right about that.

Rosie went on to explain the problems Tayo had been having with the men she'd been dating. She had turned down most advances from people since I left the college, and the men she had dated complained of her lack of enthusiasm for a relationship – something she said had to do with me. She believed that she was meant to be with me. I turned to Tayo and asked her to explain what Rosie was saying. She broke down in tears, saying that she was finding it very difficult to accept that I did not want to be with her. It had so far prevented her from entering into a serious relationship, as she kept expecting that I would change my mind at some point. I felt sorry for her, and I told her so. I also told her that I was still going out with Evelyn and that although she was studying in Essex, we still had feelings for each other and saw each other regularly. That was actually a lie; I had met up with Evelyn only twice since we'd both left for university. I told Tayo that the distance between Evelyn and me had actually brought us closer together than we had ever been. Another lie.

I told Tayo that we were best friends, which was a wonderful thing for me, and that although I understood her predicament, there was nothing I could do about it. We talked a bit more about our friendship, and Rosie actually tried to help her friend see the reality of the situation, telling Tayo that she should allow herself to date and that she would soon forget about me. We eventually all got ready to head out to a night club in town; we had quite a few drinks before leaving, to get us in the mood. Kevin and Mabel joined us – I think for moral support and my protection.

We actually did have a good night and finally got back around 2am. I took my mattress off the bed and laid it on the floor so that it would be able to accommodate all three of us. We lay there talking for a while until Rosie drifted off to sleep. Tayo then turned to me and began begging me to accept her; she tried to kiss me, but when I refused she burst out crying. I tried to comfort her, and after what seemed like ages, she finally stopped. Through clouded, red eyes, she managed to tell me that Evelyn was a lucky woman and that I should never change the way that I am. We both eventually fell asleep without further incident. Rosie and Tayo left for London the next morning. Although I met up with Rosie in London a few times after that, I never did see Tayo again – her auntie sent her to Nigeria to study. That was the last I heard of her.

The rest of the semester passed nearly without incident. About three weeks before we broke up for the summer holidays, something very drastic happened. One of my friends from the pharmacy course, Stephen Kigundu, who was from Uganda, was found hanging by the neck at Leicester train station. All the pharmacy students were informed by our head of department that the police believed he had committed suicide. This came as a huge shock. Stephen was a fun-loving man who was always smiling – he was always in good spirits and talking during lectures. We often went to restaurants and night clubs together, and he had seemed to be settling into life in Leicester. Like me, he had found it difficult, at first, coming from London. He had actually just returned from London after seeing his dad, who had come all the way from Uganda to see how he was getting on. He had been in high spirits when he returned, so it was very odd that he would then go and hang himself.

I got together with Anna Botho, who was also from Uganda, and together we went around town and asked a couple of questions. We spoke to some of the locals who knew him and had seen him the night before he was found. There was a strong rumour that he had been killed in a racist attack after leaving a night club in the early hours of the morning he was found. We took our concerns to our head of department, who calmly told us that he had received reliable information from the police, and he believed it to be accurate. He also told us to leave the matter as it was and get back to our studies, otherwise we would end up in trouble and would not be able to complete our pharmacy course. Sadly, that effectively put an end to our endeavours, as we decided it would be better not to pursue the matter. At that time, I had not fully developed my sense of resolve; if I had developed a habit of not letting things go so easily without investigating, I would probably have continued to pursue the matter and would have ended up being kicked off the course.

Stephen's death affected a lot of the students; he was very popular. I felt stunned and withdrew from the music scene for a while. I spent a lot of time thinking about what his last moments would have been like. Had he fought? Was he outnumbered and overpowered? If he could be killed, who would be next? Could it be me?

I enjoyed returning to London for the long summer holidays, as most of my friends were also around. We could hang out at the parks or outside my parents' house, and there were loads of house parties to attend – usually two or three on any given Saturday. We normally went as a big group – there would be me, Nnamdi, Joe, Ugo, Agatha, Charity, Esther, Mabowunje (also known as Booms) using two or three cars to drive in a convoy. We would meet at my parents' house, wait till everyone was there, then head out – normally with bottles of wine, which were essential for house parties in those days. We would start by going to the party that was the furthest away and spend some time there; the better the party was, the longer we would stay. Then we would move to the next one, and the next, until we got to the last one. We did not always manage to get to all the parties.

As we spent time together as a group at parties, we decided to give ourselves a name: "The Original Ravers". As Nnamdi and I were DJs, we were at parties most weekends that I went down to London. During the holidays, it was even more fun because we always had a huge following, which was a good ego booster. People also wanted to invite the group to parties because there were quite a lot of us, which helped fill up a party.

This summer break was no different to others, except that on at least two occasions when I spoke to Evelyn to either meet up or go out, she had a reason why she could not come. There was one particular house party that I was playing at in the Tulse Hill area of South London, close to where she lived. I had asked her about it some weeks back, and she had agreed to come with me. When the time came, she told me she had to help her mum with some house chores. I asked what sort of chores she needed to help her mum with at such a late hour. I even offered to come over in the evening before the party to help out so she would have the free time to attend, but she still refused. I felt quite sad and upset about the whole issue, as I had not seen Evelyn since February 1991.

I got to the party with Nnamdi and we set up our DJ equipment. The party started off around 10pm, and very soon afterwards, people started turning up in their droves. The Original Ravers were all there, and everyone was having a good time. I always packed my record box with the music I knew people liked. I always made sure I had the big club hits, just in case the crowd proved hard to get in the right mood; I also packed my own records – those that I used for the special mixes I had perfected and that I knew people would not have heard anywhere else because only I could mix those records in that particular way.

These were the times when the music genre was expanding with the likes of New Jack Swing, En Vogue, Guy, Al B Sure, The Boys, Bobby Brown, The Good Girls, MC Hammer, Heavy D and the Boyz, Today, Troop, Wreckx N Effect, After 7, Basic Black, Boyz II Men, Hi Five, TLC and lots more. The R&B scene was also alight with artists like Cameo, Earth, Wind & Fire, Luther Vandross, Prince, Michael Jackson, Sade, Teddy Pendergrass, Marvin Gaye, Color Me Badd, and Tony! Toni! Toné!. There was so much good music around that it was difficult to choose what to play, and the party people were spoilt for choice.

As the party went on into the night, I decided to go and check on Evelyn. I thought she would have turned up after finishing whatever it was she was helping her mum with, and was surprised she hadn't. When I got to her house, I rang the doorbell. Her mum opened the door almost immediately. I asked her whether I could speak to Evelyn, but she said Evelyn had gone out earlier that evening and she was surprised she was not back home yet. When I asked who she had gone out with, her mum told me it was a guy she had met a couple of weeks ago. I thanked her for the information and went back to the party.

The following day, I tried several times to get hold of Evelyn but was unsuccessful. I didn't think much of it at the time. On the Monday, Ugo, Olugh and I went to visit Onyemachi, who lived in Canning Town. On the way back on the Underground, I saw Evelyn sitting with a man. He had his arms wrapped around her. I made sure she did not see me; we waited for that train to leave and got on the next one. When I got home, I called her to find out how she was and where she had been. She told me she was fine and had been at home all day. When I told her that I had in fact seen her on the Tube with another man, her voice froze. She then changed her story and said she had been to visit a friend, but that whilst she was there, she had developed very painful stomach cramps.

Her friend's brother had volunteered to take her home, and this was the person I had seen her with.

I did not believe her, and I think she knew. At this point I felt angry, vulnerable and betrayed. The following day, she called me in the afternoon and asked if we could meet up to talk. We agreed to meet near her house later that evening. It seemed strange that she wanted us to meet near her house rather than at her house. When I arrived at the meeting place, she was already there waiting for me. She said she did not want to mistreat me and knew I was a good person; that was why she wanted to speak with me before things got complicated and probably worse. She then dropped a bombshell – she was going out with someone else.

I was crushed; although it was what I suspected, it still hurt. When I asked her what had prompted her to make such a decision, she said that the distance between us had become a problem and she was finding it difficult to cope at university without a boyfriend. I spent over two hours begging her to reconsider and take me back. I reminded her of all the things we had done together, good and bad, and the promises we had made to each other. We had promised to weather any storm throughout our university days and then see what the future held for us once we graduated. She wouldn't budge. Eventually, I gave up trying to convince her; she asked if we could at least remain friends, but I told her that I had no interest in staying friends, and it would be to our benefit if we made a clean break from each other. We said our goodbyes and parted company.

On my way home, I bought a couple of bottles of Nigerian Guinness, which I used to drown my sorrows. I tried to look at it from a positive angle; I was going back to university as a single young man. I would also be able to focus even more on my studies and myself. I felt a bit better after a couple of days; the breakup also gave me another opportunity to review what I wanted in life, and what I wanted from any woman who was going to be in my life.

By the time I went back to university after the holidays, I was actually excited about my newfound, purposeful and attractive status. I had shaved off my pony tail; it was something Evelyn had encouraged me to grow, as she said it made me look like a singer. I had a brand new look to go with my brand new status as single. On my first day back at university, I headed to the library to borrow some books to get me started for the year. Whilst standing in the queue, I realised that nobody recognised me. For quite a while, it seemed people just looked straight through me. Finally, my friend Jeffrey called out my name and then looked at me in shock. When I asked him what the problem was, he motioned to my head. "What happened to your hair?" he asked. I told him I'd got tired of washing my shirt collars every day and having to go to bed with a du-rag on. He said I was unrecognisable.

It seemed as if my breakup with Evelyn had done something good to me. I had shed most of the shyness I' had when I first arrived in Leicester, and I now started to network even more widely than before, eager to build my links with as many people and university departments as possible. I joined the African-Caribbean Society and was elected to the position of social secretary; they had been trying to get me to join since my first year. I also joined the Pharmacy football team. I moved into a house with three girls on the other side of town. I was advised by Gavin, a pharmacy colleague, who had lived with the girls the previous year, not to move in – although he did not explain why. I obviously did what I usually do; I went against his advice. I had lived with Mabel the previous year, and she was like a younger sister to me. She was also nice, kind and respectful, and we got on very well. I had also got to know her parents and other family members who lived in London. This situation, however, turned out to be very different.

Two of the three girls I lived with were sisters, and the third girl was a friend of theirs. Although we mainly got on, they were very untidy and dirty. I often found underwear soaking in the kitchen sink, and the bath was always filthy, again with underwear left all over the place. I resorted to going to the gym very regularly so I could use the showers afterwards instead of using our dirty bathroom. I did speak with them on numerous occasions about our living arrangements and how I found it difficult to cope in such an untidy environment. My pleas, however, fell on deaf ears. In order to refrain from going insane, I buried myself in my coursework, assignments, DJing, the gym, and anything else I could find that kept me away from the house. Whilst in my second year, I organised Soul Jam 2 and 3, sequels to my original event; both were a huge success, building on the success of the first one and my newfound popularity. On both occasions, I organised, coordinated and advertised the events myself, using the enticement of a clash between two of Leicester's best soul DJs, Simon (Schoolboy) and myself (Mr C). I also used the contacts I had made as social secretary of the African-Caribbean Society. Schoolboy managed to get all the local people to attend. It was useful that he played on the local radio station, whilst I was able to attract all the students to come and support me.

For Soul Jam 3, a coach was organised from London to bring a contingent up to what was billed as the East Midlands versus London 'Rumble in the Jungle'. The event generated a lot of interest and money. Fortunately, organising these events kept me away from the house and the girls most of the time. I mainly came in late at night to sleep and left early in the morning to get to my lectures.

At the end of my second year, I went back to London, eagerly looking forward to the long summer break. I managed to get a job at Boots the Chemist, Brixton, as a healthcare assistant. I enjoyed it quite a lot; it was close to home, the pay was reasonable, and it was very relevant to my degree. During my lunch break and after work, I would walk across the road to Red Records to find out what the latest music releases were and buy them.

Sometime during the holidays, Evelyn contacted me and asked if we could meet up for a chat. When I asked her what it was about, she wouldn't tell me. We met at a McDonald's restaurant in Clapham Junction. After ordering some food, we sat down in a corner. She began by apologising for causing me so much pain the year before and told me that she wanted us to get back together again. I explained that I was no longer interested in her, and although I still had feelings for her, I was not going to risk being hurt by her ever again. She begged and pleaded, but I was insistent. Finally, after what seemed like hours of listening to her begging, I said goodbye to her, wished her luck for the future, and walked out. I bumped into her on occasion at the library in Battersea, but we never spoke to each other again. I preferred it that way. I had done a lot over the past year to make sure my feelings for her were buried and forgotten. I wasn't going to be held back by someone who had no ethics when it came to relationships.

My third and final year was the most exciting and eventful of all. I moved out of the house I had shared with the three girls and moved in with five other boys: Girnik Sanghara from Birmingham, Harry Harron and Steve Corey from Northern Ireland, Noamaan Baig from London and Gavin Taylor from Wales. We were all final-year pharmacy students, and although we didn't know it at the time, we had similar aspirations for the year; we were also very similar in so many other ways.

We lived at 279 Fosse Road South. This ran parallel to the infamous Narborough Road, which was known for its dense student population. We very quickly became known as the Fosse Posse because of our great house parties, to which we invited some of our senior lecturers. We partied quite a lot at the weekends, and sometimes during the week; we were the envy of many of our pharmacy colleagues, who did not understand how we managed to burn the candle at both ends. What most people didn't know was that although we partied hard, we studied even harder. Sometimes we would study throughout an entire weekend without leaving the house. Sometimes we would each take a different assignment and each person would read up on the area they'd been given. After a couple of days, we would all meet in my room, which was the largest, and provide constructive and robust feedback. This was a method of learning that helped us get through the huge workload of projects and assignments we were given.

My no-nonsense approach to the running and upkeep of the house and my attention to detail around the personal affairs of my housemates quickly earned me the notorious nickname "The Landlord". I was renowned for my straight-talking and my integrity. My dad had always told me that integrity is an important attribute to have but that it is rare to find. He used to tell me: "let people know you for what you stand for; do not copy others just for the sake of it; and always do what you think is right – and this applies in public as well as in private". Those wise words have stuck with me.

The Boots pre-registration recruitment experience was one of those occasions that typified the behaviour of the Fosse Posse. The recruitment team of Boots the Chemist had come from Nottingham to our department in a move to attract and recruit new pre-registration students to train with them once they finished studying. They hosted an evening to which all students who had an interest in working for Boots were invited. Around eighty of us attended. We were first asked to take a psychometric test. Most graduate employers used psychometric tests as part of the selection process for their graduate schemes; they were often used as a filtering mechanism at an early stage in the recruitment process.

Even though we had been informed about the test beforehand, none of us bothered to practice or revise for it. After the test, there was a drinks reception. We had decided to have as many drinks as possible and got slightly drunk before we even had dinner. Dinner was set aside for prospective candidates to talk to their potential future employers and find out more about the company. After dinner, we decided we'd had enough of the Boots formalities. We had a couple more guzzles of the wine that was available, then decided to go to a night club instead of staying to discuss future employment opportunities.

The following morning, we all attended the interviews. A few weeks later, when the names of the students Boots had selected for their pre-registration scheme were released, all six of us were on the list of about thirty-three. A lot of people were amazed that we had managed to get placements and asked what we had done to get on the list. Some thought that after we left, we'd had secret meetings with some of the recruitment team. We had simply approached the whole affair in a very relaxed manner, using common sense, wit and frankness – characteristics which would only have shone through if they were natural, which they were. That was the Fosse Posse approach.

The Fosse Posse – left to right (Steve, Gavin, Noamaan, Chima, Nik, Harry)

Another occasion that typified Fosse Posse behaviour was the Pharmacy sports weekend, held by the Leicester Pharmaceutical Students Association (LPSA). The sports weekend was scheduled to take place in the small South Welsh town of Port Talbot, which is built along the eastern rim of Swansea Bay. On the same weekend, Nik was getting married in Birmingham. A dilemma ensured. The LPSA was affiliated to the British Pharmacy Students' Association (BPSA) and was quite a powerful organisation; we wanted to be at the weekender because of this and also because it was going to be fun. It was also our last sports weekender as final-year students. How were we going to go to Wales on the Friday and then attend Nik's wedding on the Saturday?

We decided to hire a car; five of us drove to Port Talbot on Friday evening whilst the rest of the LPSA went by coach. When we arrived in Port Talbot, we attended the introductions to the event and a visit to a restaurant for dinner. When we got back to the hall where all the sports and entertainment activity was taking place, we commenced drinking alcohol in earnest. We ignored nearly everything that went on and drank until the early hours of the following morning. We had to wake up early anyway for our 140-mile drive to Birmingham. By 5.30am we were awake. It took Steve two and a half hours to get to Birmingham, driving whilst recovering from a serious hangover. The rest of us slept all the way there, and by the time we arrived in Birmingham at around 8.30am, we were ready to get down to business.

The entire wedding ceremony was a superb display of Sikh tradition and culture, such as I had never seen before. The first part of the ceremony, which was religious, took place at the Gurdwara. We all had to cover our heads before going inside, where we sat cross-legged on the carpeted floor. After the ceremony, we went to another venue for the more informal part of the celebration, which commenced with lots of bhangra music and colourful dancing. This was followed by some speeches by family members. Our group from Leicester had a separate table to ourselves; we were served plate upon plate of delicious food and pints of beer, followed by bottles of Johnny Walker whisky.

As it had been agreed that I would drive back to Port Talbot, I had to stay sober. I had a pint of beer, then avoided having any more alcohol. The entire occasion was full of fun and entertainment. The bride and groom, Nita and Nik, looked very beautiful and happy. The lads took full advantage of the free alcohol. Harry had so much to drink that he eventually collapsed as he was dancing and passed out. We took him outside and laid him in the snow to see if he would sober up, but this did not work, so we left him in a chair in a corner whilst we continued having fun.

When it was time to drive back, we bundled an unconscious Harry into the car and headed back to Port Talbot. I asked Gavin for directions, and he told me to stick to the M5. After that, all my passengers fell asleep. I stuck to the M5 for what seemed like hours, until I saw a sign indicating that we were about 10 miles from Exeter in

Devon. I woke the lads up and asked them how much longer we had till we got to our destination. When they realised where we were, they were in absolute shock – we were about 130 miles away from Port Talbot. I should have taken one of the junctions leading to South Wales; I had obviously missed it. We pulled into a petrol station, filled the car up and headed back in the opposite direction. We finally arrived in Port Talbot around 9pm; we had missed all the sports but were just in time for the fun part of the evening. We left Harry, still unconscious, in the car and went inside to join the fun. About half an hour later, Harry turned up to join us with a pint of beer in his hand. It was unbelievable – after being unconscious for over five hours, he still had the appetite for more alcohol. It was definitely a weekend to remember – a Fosse Posse weekend.

When I had worked at Boots in Brixton in the summer of my second year, I had met a French woman called Lydia who worked as a beauty consultant at the No. 7 section of the shop. I sometimes used to cover her section when she went on her breaks, so we met quite regularly. We became quite close, as friends, over the summer holidays and met up sometimes after work for drinks and a chat. Just before I went back to university, she asked whether we could ever be in a relationship. I told her that I had not thought about our friendship in that way. I said that I was in my final year and needed to focus on my studies. We agreed to keep in touch. After about three weeks at university, I was at home one Friday afternoon when someone knocked on the door. When I opened it, I was shocked to see Lydia. She had intended her visit to be a surprise. I was chuffed that she had taken the time to visit, but I had a lot planned for that weekend and now had to accommodate her. I changed some of my weekend plans but had to honour the parties I had been booked to play at. Lydia attended both parties, and we did have a good time. She said I did not need to introduce her as my girl-friend. I didn't. After that weekend, she did come to visit a couple more times. However, I eventually asked her to stop visiting me. She did.

I did have several female admirers, especially in my final year. However, I kept thinking it would be stupid of me to mess up my studies now, especially after getting so far. I decided to exercise caution, honesty and willpower. It was not easy, especially being a student and seeing all the shenanigans of student and party life.

The Fosse Posse were quite famous in the pharmacy department, among students and teachers alike, and we were also popular among some of the students from other departments. We had regular visitors to our house – mainly girls. Some came looking for companionship, as it was a well-known fact that some of us were single. Others came to enjoy our company, eat, drink and play. Our favourite visitors were pharmacy colleagues Humera and Sumanjit (Suman). They were housemates who lived on the Narborough Road, and they frequently came round to chat, do classwork, and sometimes cook for us. Suman and I became close friends, sometimes studying together in the library, going to night clubs together, and studying together at home.

I was somewhat surprised when one day Suman came to my room and told me that she and Humera had had a nasty argument and were no longer friends. She did not tell me what the argument was about, and I did not push to find out. She spent a lot more time with me, sometimes studying till late into the night with me. On many occasions she would sleep in my bed after studying and leave to go home in the morning. All my housemates believed that there was something more intimate between us. Even after reassuring them that − contrary to what they suspected − we were just good friends, they didn't believe me. The only person who said he believed me was Noamaan.

As the weeks went by, I did find myself admiring and thinking about Suman quite a lot, and because she was always around me it became difficult to think of much else. After many weeks of distraction and thinking, I decided to speak to one of our mutual friends, Anne Chigbu, about my feelings for Suman. Anne told me that Suman did not feel the same way about me and that I should forget about any relationship between us. I tried to get her out of my mind, but it did not work. I then made a very big mistake. I asked Suman's ex-friend, Humera, for her opinion on the matter. She advised that I should approach her and tell her, but before I could summon enough courage to talk to Suman about my feelings, Humera decided to spite Suman by teasing her about the fact that I was in love with her and was too shy to approach her. Suman was outraged and came storming to our house. She came to my room and asked me whether what Humera had told her about my feelings was true. I told her it was true, but I was too scared of her response and that was why I had not told her. She said she had not expected me to fall for her like that, as we were great friends. I explained that friends do sometimes fall in love; in fact, it happened quite a lot. I thought I might have had a chance if I had approached Suman right at the beginning. Maybe not; either way, that chance had gone. We did stay good friends, but something changed.

The rest of the year passed by fairly quickly, and as our exams drew closer, we all settled down to study and aim for good grades. Unfortunately for me, my final-year research project, which was on the effect of additives in children's cough medicines, meant I had to depend on pharmaceutical companies to write back to me about the ingredients they used in their medicines. Most of them needed chasing, and by the time the exams came around, I had not received all the information I needed to complete it. I had to shelve it and concentrate on the exams. After the exams, I then had to turn my attention back to project, most of which I did over the summer holidays. The fact that I did not complete my project before the final exams meant I could not graduate with the rest of my year. That was very painful, upsetting and demoralising. it also meant that I had to defer my pharmacy pre-registration placement. The pre-registration year is the culmination of many years of study, and it is important to make the most of the training and get as much information and support as possible throughout the training year.

At first, I was in limbo and unsure of what to do. I had finished my final-year exams but could not start my pre-registration because I had not officially graduated. After a couple of days of weighing up my options, I decided to approach the manager of the Boots store in Brixton, where I had worked previously, and ask him for any sort of job.

Mr Hopkinson was a good man and manager and gave me a one-year contract at his Brixton store. I ended up working for Boots as a 'glorified' healthcare assistant for an entire year. Although this was another setback for me (I had by now lost about five years during the course of my education), I used my time at Boots to consolidate my pharmacy sales and business knowledge, my dispensing and my customer service skills and my ICT skills, all of which I knew would be key to my career.

When I finally did get to start my pre-registration training in September 1994, I was absolutely ready and able to concentrate solely on the pharmacy side of my development. I was ready for the real pharmacy world.

I did my pre-registration training with Boots in Catford,

London. I thoroughly enjoyed my experience with my tutor, Mr John Skellett. He was very inspiring and flexible; a great teacher. He always encouraged me to take charge of things, especially when I was in doubt over what to do. He was one of the people who instilled leadership qualities in me. After the one-year training period, Mr Skellett had to complete a competency assessment of my ability to practice as a pharmacist. He did not show me the report, but I was reliably informed that I had made a very good impression. I then had to take the registration exam in order to register to practice as a pharmacist. The exam was introduced in 1992/93, so I was among the third set of students to take it.

I was now well and truly prepared to be unleashed as a pharmacist.

Climbing the Ladder
(1995–1999)

T he exam results came out on the Saturday 15th July. It had been a very nervous wait, but it was worth it – I had passed. Mr Skellett congratulated me and wished me all the best in life.

On passing the exam, my first job as a full-time pharmacist was at Boots the Chemist, Brixton, on Monday 17th July. Having worked in Brixton before, everything seemed the same – apart from the fact that I was now a pharmacist. I could authorise the sale of pharmacy-only medicines, I could authorise the handing out of dispensed medication, and I was on a salary of £23,000. I was also no longer expected to do the menial tasks in the shop. The good thing about working in Brixton was that it was a ten-minute walk from home. It was always very busy; sometimes it was so busy that I didn't get time to take a break. This made the time go past quickly.

Being a pharmacist had been my dream for many years, so I was over the moon. Having fought and worked so hard to earn myself a career, I had finally made it. I wished my grandma was alive to see me – she would have been very proud of me. If she had been alive, I would have gone to Nigeria at the first opportunity just to tell her in person and to give her some of my well-deserved earnings – and to remind her to start the process of finding a beautiful wife for me.

I was living in a small, comfortable flat at my parents' house and was not paying any rent, so I had a lot of spare cash at the end of each month. I spent a lot of it on records, clothes and other things. I deserved it. I did give my parents money, although this was not on a monthly or agreed basis.

I could now go to Nigeria as a qualified pharmacist. This mattered a lot to me because the main reason I had left Nigeria in the first place was to study and get a good job. I had reached a stage in my life where I could take stock. I was happy, I had money, and the future looked bright. I felt it was time for me to set my next targets in life. I did, and they included moving up the rungs of the Boots management ladder, but also joining a Nigerian community organisation where I could get involved in knowledge-sharing and finding solutions to some of the issues Nigerians faced in the UK and back in Nigeria. This was one of my greatest passions. If I was going to go back to Nigeria to live, it had to have a system that worked. I had some great ideas to help fix the now broken and corrupt country. As my grandma was not alive to find me a wife, the task of finding myself a serious girlfriend was also on my list of things to do. At the age of 28, time was definitely moving along quickly, and I was determined to keep up.

After the incident with Suman, I had decided to stay single until I was sure I felt ready to venture out and get into a relationship. Although I had visited Nigeria a couple of times since leaving – in 1992, 1994 and 1995 – and had spent considerable time with Ego on both occasions, the distance was not ideal for our relationship. A defining moment for our relationship was when my older cousin, Ude, sat me down and asked if I ever thought our long-distance relationship would work. He said that no woman would wait for a man who lived that far away unless there was a significant commitment from the man. He asked me whether I had made any commitments. He said that when it was time for me to get married, I should be in a position to choose a partner in a leisurely way rather than feeling compelled to get married. He told me to leave Ego alone and enjoy my young life. Although I truly felt that Ego and I could mould a great future together, his words had a defining effect on me. In 1996, I came back to London and did not continue the lovely letter-writing dialogue I had with Blessing. Our relationship did eventually wither away. It made me quite sad, as I knew we really did suit each other and could have built a future together. I also knew she would be upset. However, my older cousin did have a good point; there was some truth to what he had told me. After a while, I felt I had moved past my memories of ill-fated relationships, and that the time had come for me to find a girlfriend. I was not going to go out and feverishly look for anyone; I was going to take my time and just see what happened. It was at this point in my life that I missed my grandma again. She was not around to see the man I had promised her I would become, nor was she around to find me the wife she had promised me she would find when I grew up.

In my endeavour to use my time wisely outside of work, I sought out a few constructive activities to get involved with that would help me give back to Nigeria; activities that would enable me to have an input into how Nigeria could develop to be best-suited for the twenty-first century, and that would also have a positive influence on other people.

I got myself a regular Sunday evening radio show on the popular South London Community Radio station, Lightning Radio. My airtime slot was between 5pm and 7pm. I named the show the "Good Groves Show", and I played mainly soul and R&B music. My good, long-time friend Nnamdi had introduced me to the management of the station in 1994 following my renowned DJing period in Leicester. In 1994, we had started off as a twosome on his original show, where we played great music and cracked good jokes. Eventually, the management decided I could have my own show, and because of my presentation style I was originally given two prime-time slots: Thursday evenings, 8pm till 10pm, and Sunday evenings, 7pm till 9pm. My Sunday evening show aired immediately after that of veteran self-styled presenter and DJ, Chris Goldfinger. I also brought my friend Tricia (Lady Mystique) to Lightning. She supported me with my show, and eventually got her own show.

After a while, I decided to do just one show a week on Sunday, 5pm till 7pm. I normally had a busy week and felt that keeping it to one show a week would give me enough time to plan and prepare effectively. I went on to become a renowned DJ and presenter, and was well-respected in the music community, operating under the alias of Mr C. I didn't usually play at night clubs, as I felt the crowds were normally too used to mainstream music – and because people had to pay to get in, they were more demanding and always wanted to listen to either the latest or the most popular music at the time; there was rarely a time to play authentic soul music.

The crowds at house parties, on the other hand, were very different. They were open to hearing different and new music. They were more relaxed and were happy to listen to whatever music was played. This gave me the freedom to select a wide range of music which I felt would be educational to the crowd. That was what I liked about the house party scene.

My sister, Ugo, tried to induct me into an Igbo organisation she attended called Young Igbo Social Club (YIBOSC). The organisation met on a Sunday, every other month or so. She had often invited me to attend, but their meeting times always clashed with my Sunday radio shows. I did often wonder what the organisation was all about, but it took me a long time to finally agree to attend a meeting. As opportunity would have it, one Sunday when the radio station was off air after a raid by the Department of Trade and Industry, Ugo invited me to attend with her and I agreed to go. I found the meeting surprisingly engaging and interesting; the topics of discussion were very positive and were about supporting young Igbos here in the UK. I agreed to go back again whenever I was free to.

A few weeks later, my sister told me that she had a party that I might be interested in playing at. A lady from YIBOSC was having a birthday party and had asked if anyone knew of any good DJs – my sister had loyally told her that I was good. She gave me the lady's number so that I could call her and discuss it further. When I did call her, she was impressed with the explanation I gave of my approach to DJing, and with the type of music I played. Her name was Nnenna Anyanwu. We spoke several times on the phone to work out what she needed and whether I could provide it. Eventually, we agreed a price, and I was booked. The party was great; the host was impressed with my approach, and so were the guests.

A couple of weeks after the party, I went out for a drink with Nnenna. I suspected we would meet again because when we had talked over the party plans on the phone, there seemed to be some chemistry, and when we finally met for the first time at her party, there was obviously a connection between us. Our first meeting went well. I found out she was from Mbaise in Imo State, Nigeria.

She had studied accountancy and worked in the film industry. She was intellectual, easy going, laughed a lot, and was very focused on what she wanted to achieve in life. I liked her a lot, and the feeling was mutual. After a couple of dinner dates, we started dating officially, and this eventually led to a serious relationship. I introduced her to my parents, who took a liking to her, and this helped our relationship.

Many months into our relationship, Nnenna and her sister Chika agreed it would be a good idea for me to meet their dad. I thought it was a good idea too, but on the day of the meeting, their older brother rang and said it was not a good idea. The meeting was cancelled. Her brother did not give any reason for the abrupt cancellation, and this concerned me at the time. Nnenna was not happy with the situation, but I told her that it was okay and that when the time was right, I would meet him. Our relationship had very few problems, and after nearly a year together, I began to wonder whether it was time to take it to the next level. For some unknown reason, I felt anxious about what the future might hold for us. This feeling bothered me a lot and sometimes kept me up at night. The thought of actually moving a step closer to marriage, was very scary, even though I knew I was ready for it. But this was what I had been working towards since I left Nigeria; it was the next rung on the ladder I was climbing.

I decided to take a holiday to give myself time and space to think clearly about what should be my next step with my relationship. In August 1996, Ugo and I decided to go on a two-week holiday to Orlando, Florida. The flight gave me lots of thinking time. When we got there, we picked up the hire-car we had arranged earlier. As I drove to our hotel, we were involved in a car crash which was not my fault. We wasted time while we waited for the police to arrive and assess the scene before letting us go. We checked into a decent Best Western Hotel on the popular International Drive, Orlando, which stretches approximately 11 miles and is a corridor for tourists. It is home to the Orange County Convention Centre complex, the Pointe Orlando entertainment complex, major hotels, SeaWorld Orlando, the Wet n Wild Orlando water park, the Orlando Eye, the I-Drive 360 entertainment complex, museums, themed restaurants, bars, outlet malls, and other tourism-related commercial properties and tourist attractions. It was a wonderful place to stay, and we took our time to visit all the available attractions, restaurants and bars.

During our stay, we also visited Miami. The 240-mile drive to Miami through the Florida Turnpike took us about four hours, but it was an amazing experience, with wide roads and masses of land everywhere. The plan was to explore Miami during the day and night, sleep over in a hotel and return the following day. Unfortunately for us, we had left our travellers' cheques in Orlando, so we didn't have money to pay for a hotel. We explored the city very quickly and had to leave to return to Orlando the same day. I was shattered from the drive by the time we got back and needed the whole of the following day to recover.

We also explored Busch Gardens in Tampa, a theme park which had Florida's best roller coasters, rides, attractions, shows, animal encounters and fine dining. We went to the beach quite often too, mainly to chill out and read. This was where I found the space and time I needed to think about my relationship with Nnenna. I thought long and hard about what I wanted, when I wanted it, and how I wanted it. I also took into consideration some of the comments my sisters had made, probably flippantly. I guess it would have helped to have another man to speak to at that time; to get some advice from and bounce ideas around with. I didn't, so I made my decisions on my own, which I thought was what a man was supposed to do anyway. A few days before we left Orlando for London, I decided that I would call off the relationship with Nnenna.

When we got back to London, Nnenna was at the airport to pick us up. My friend Joe was there too, as I had called him and asked him to come and collect us. Joe told me to go with Nnenna, but I had already made up my mind not to. We went in Joe's car, and Nnenna followed behind. When we got home, she came in and asked what she had done wrong. I told her she hadn't done anything wrong and that I had a lot on my mind. Looking back now, I know I should have broadened my mind and thought more thoroughly about my future with Nnenna. I feel guilty for not even consulting her about our relationship. At least I could have explained to her the situation and my thoughts before she came to collect me at the airport. She was a wonderful woman and did not deserve to be treated this way.

The following day, she called so that we could talk. She was shocked when I told her that our relationship was over. She begged me to explain what she had done wrong. It took me a long time before I told her that she hadn't done anything wrong; I was just not in the right place to continue the relationship. She wanted to know if there was another woman involved. I told there was nobody else and that I just wanted to be alone and not in a relationship any more. That is how our relationship ended. I decided that if I kept myself busy, I'd forget about Nnenna and be too busy to think about women for a while.

I plugged myself into my pharmacy work, and I also made a conscious decision to make the effort to attend some of the YIBOSC meetings. I gradually became very active in YIBOSC, getting involved and helping them organise parties, workshops and conferences during 1996 and '97. That is essentially how my service to the Nigerian community started. During this time, I also helped set up the Ebonyi State Union UK & Ireland, following the creation of the new Ebonyi State in Nigeria by the corrupt dictator and military leader, Sani Abacha. I served as the interim secretary in the Union.

Around November of 1996, Michael (aka Mickey Flex), a Jamaican friend I had made during my pre-registration training at Boots, introduced me to an acquaintance of his from St Lucia called Nicholas Webb Edwards – also known as Nicky Dreads because he wore his hair in small dreadlocks. Later in the 2000s, his despicable and criminal behaviour would shock me, my friends, and anyone who knew him or got to read about him.

Nicky was a bit of a wild animal, doing a lot of things that most men would only dream about doing. He would see a beautiful girl in the street, and without thinking what he was going to say, he would approach and start talking with her. This always seemed to work for him; he always had two or three girlfriends at any one time. He was also a crazy car driver, always driving above the speed limit and doing 180-degree car spins whenever he got the opportunity. For an unknown reason, I was somewhat attracted to his insouciance. I started introducing him to my own friends, including Julian (aka Ranks), Joe, and John (aka Big John, because he was very tall; about 6 foot 7 inches). We all became good friends, hanging out together after work and at the weekends. We would go to parties, to bars, or to the park, or just hang out at home and play music. For me it was a good feeling; I was still slightly carefree, and needed to occupy my time, as I was single.

On the 7th December 1996, I organised a big 30th birthday party for myself. It was also a joint party with my two sisters, who had recently qualified as nurses. We decided on a brandy and champagne party, and it was to be held at a community hall in Myatt's Field, Brixton, London.

On the afternoon of the party, my friend Ranks and I had gone with my two sisters to decorate the hall and drop off some drinks, with plans to finish off later in the evening. As Ranks and I headed home, we were stopped by two police cars right in front of his house. We were ordered out of the car and separated. Whilst this was happening, a helicopter arrived and hovered overhead. A huge crowd instantly gathered to watch, which was very embarrassing. As I stood beside my car, hands in my pockets, a policewoman came up to me and told me to take my hands out of my pockets. When I told her I was cold, she said it was for my own safety. At that exact moment, I looked into one of the police cars that had stopped us and saw someone sitting in the back seat with a gun, the red laser dancing up and down my chest area. The sight of the laser scared the life out of me, and even though it was winter, I started sweating.

I slowly removed my hands from my pockets. The policewoman asked me where we were coming from, and whether we had any knives, guns or other weapons on us. I answered all her questions. They had not yet told me why we had been stopped. I began to wonder whether Ranks was involved in some criminal activity that I was unaware of. They finally finished their questions and searches. Then they told us that someone had been stabbed in the Myatt's Field area, and that we matched the description of the two suspects seen fleeing the scene. They apologised for their mistake. Ranks walked slowly towards his flat and all the people who were looking at us. I drove straight home, shocked and scared by the incident. I was speechless for over an hour. I ran myself a warm bath and soaked for a long time, just thinking about what could have happened had I been shot. I was convinced that had the police shot me, or both of us, and then realised they'd made a mistake, they would inevitably have tried to stage some form of cover-up. We would probably be portrayed by the police and media as drug dealers. I could imagine the headlines: Two sophisticated drug dealers were gunned down in Camberwell as they tried to escape the police, who had been following them for months as part of an undercover operation. And some people would have bought the story. Some friends would have said, "I always thought Chima was into something criminal like drugs; he was always partying, his eyes were always bloodshot, he always had money".

I didn't tell anyone what had happened until after the party. The party was a huge success; nearly everyone there managed to get drunk by the end of the night, as the bar was serving brandy with champagne, as planned. I had given my car keys to my younger brother to hold for me in case I got too drunk and lost them. He was helping out on the door with his friend William (Smooth G Wills), monitoring people coming in and out. After the party, when I went to retrieve my keys from him around 5am,

I was shocked to see him lying on the floor, with William, both drunk and totally incoherent. I got them up, retrieved my keys and looked for someone to give me a lift home. Ranks was so drunk that he couldn't remember where he lived. Neither could I. We'd both had a lot to drink following the earlier incident, as it had left us both very shaken. We did eventually find his flat, and I left him there and went home. The rest of that weekend was a blur, full of recuperation and thoughts of what might have happened.

At work with Boots, I continued to apply all the skills I had picked up as part of my pre-registration training, my time as a healthcare assistant, and at university. I applied for a manager's position at the Boots store in Norbury, London. Although I had only been qualified for just over a year, I believed I had enough experience and competencies to get the job. At the time, Boots had an unwritten policy which meant managerial positions were only given to those who had completed at least 18 months as pharmacists. I argued that I had considerable experience, having worked for Boots since my university days. A strongly worded reference from the south-east area manager at the time, Anne Marie Kitchen-Wheeler, who had a lot of confidence in my ability, managed to get me the job. It was October 1996, and barely a year after qualifying as a pharmacist, I had my first pharmacy manager job. I was ecstatic and promised myself that I would do my best. I was going to seize this opportunity with both hands and show the Boots senior management team what type of stuff I was made of.

The Norbury branch was quite small, and not much could be done with it – or so I was told. But it was an ideal place for me to embark on my managerial career, and I decided I was going to do something with it. I spent around eight months at the Norbury branch, working to help improve the competencies and skill mix of the staff – three elderly ladies – in order for them to work more effectively as a small team. I helped improve their sales and dispensary business before being promoted in June 1997 to manage a bigger Boots store in Bermondsey, South London. This was an average-sized store which did enough dispensing and sales business to warrant regular visits by the new area manager to make sure everything was running smoothly. It was very different to the smaller Norbury branch. It gave me an opportunity to try out new things on a larger scale, like the new prescription collection services, health promotion days, and "speak with your pharmacist" days to help bolster business and patient confidence. The events I held were a resounding success; both shop sales and the number of prescriptions went up in the first year I was there.

My second year in Bermondsey involved a somewhat new experience for me; one that distracted my attention from my normal job and had me wandering around in a very paranoid state. One day in the summer of 1998, I was opening the usual late store mail and found a letter addressed to the manager. I opened it and was flabbergasted when I was met with a one-page letter full of racist content; it told me that I was a stinking black monkey who should go back to the jungle in Africa. It also said that I should be careful when parking my car at the back of the store because one day I would get it. I was livid. I reported the matter to our area manager, who promised to investigate the matter. Nothing ever came of it.

A couple of weeks later, a shoplifter came into the shop and tried to steal some of our expensive Oil of Olay products. I confronted him and told him to put them back on the shelf, to which he said, "who the hell do you think you are, nigger?". He then pulled out a syringe which had something that looked like blood in it and said that if I didn't get out of his way, he would inject me with the needle, which he said contained a virus.

I was fuming at having yet another racist attack directed against me – and this time the person was right in front of me. I went around him, locked the store door, and told him he wasn't going anywhere until he put the products down. I also pulled out a pen that had been given to me by a pharmaceutical representative. It was shaped like a syringe and had red ink in it. I told him that my syringe also contained a deadly virus, and that it had been taken from one of my methadone patients. He continued to call me all sorts of names as we circled each other. I had decided that he was not leaving the shop with those products. He eventually threw them all on the floor and told me to open the door. I let him out whilst the rest of the customers and staff starred on in horror. I reported this second incident to my area manager, who once again promised me he would look into it.

Whilst I continued to work at the Bermondsey branch, I encountered numerous racists' incidents. Shockingly, some of them were committed by some of my own staff. Following a period of about three months of racist abuse, with no action taken by my area manager – including being a suspect when some cash went missing at my own store – I decided that enough was enough. I called the area manager and told him that he needed to move me from the store and put me back on relief pharmacist duties, otherwise I would quit the company.

In early September 1998, he pulled me from the Bermondsey store, and I was put back on relief duties. I was both pleased and grateful to leave that horrible place; it gave me nothing but awful memories and bad feelings. Being back on relief duties meant that I travelled around the different Boots stores in South London, covering managers' days off and holidays. This suited me just fine. I had few responsibilities and nobody to manage. My main responsibility when providing relief cover was to manage the pharmacy and dispensing business. I worked in nearly every branch in South London, and for a month or so I enjoyed it. It also gave me space and time to plan my next career move.

I felt that the company had not managed any of the previous Bermondsey incidents well at all. I raised this with the area manager one day when he visited the Brixton store where I was working. He tried to dismiss the matter as being in the past, which was the wrong thing for him to do – I had spent time thinking about the entire situation carefully before bringing it up. He took me into the manager's office and asked why I would not just let the matter lie. I explained to him that during the time these incidents were taking place, my life had been made a living hell by some unknown racists and some of my staff. I had been made a suspect in a theft case, and I'd had to leave a career path that I had started off on in such grand style. I believed the entire matter warranted an investigation at the least. He told me that there would not be another investigation, as it was time-consuming and demoralising for the staff involved. "You mean there has already been an investigation, and I was not told about it?" I asked. His nonchalant reply was that they had not bothered to inform me because nothing I had told them could be substantiated. By this time, I was incensed. I told him that I was leaving the company with immediate effect. He told me that was impossible, as I had to give one month's notice. He advised me not to take steps towards leaving, but I was adamant that I'd had enough of a company that didn't look after or value its staff.

The entire situation came as a surprise to both him and me, as I had not actually planned to resign. However, what he had told me had too many implications for me as a person. I was not going to compromise my outlook in life for anyone, let alone Boots. After much persuasion, he eventually convinced me to go on a nil-hours contract, which meant I would remain employed by Boots but would only work when there was a relief job that I wanted to do. The date was Thursday 16th October 1998. That day, I left Boots in Brixton, went home, and decided I needed to take time out and evaluate what I had achieved so far and where I needed to go next. I ended up spending two months at home. I had no zeal to work as a pharmacist, let alone work for Boots.

After two months at home, and doing a few locum jobs, I found it difficult to decide what to do next. I had a couple of financial responsibilities that were coming up that I would need money for, so after Christmas I decided go back to full-time work.

Back in the February of 1997, my sister Ugo had told me that one of her friends was interested in me. Her name was Valerie Mowah. I'm not quite sure what Ugo was thinking. She probably felt that a young man like me should have a girlfriend. She had introduced me to my ex-girlfriend Nnenna, so I presume she wanted to help me out. She had given me Valerie's number just before Valentine's Day. I decided not to call her around that time, as it might give the wrong impression. I waited till after Valentine's Day before calling her. After speaking with her on the phone a couple of times, we decided to meet up on the 21st February. I had seen her a few times when she came to our house to meet up with Ugo. We went out for a meal and a drink, and we talked about a lot of things.

Following our initial meeting, we continued chatting on the phone and met up when we could. Before long, we were in a relationship. Valerie lived with her mum and her twin sister, Vivian, in Balham, South London. I eventually met both of them, along with one of her aunties, who they had invited to be at the house on the day it was agreed I would visit. It was a Sunday, and a bright sunny July afternoon. They were welcoming, and although I was nervous, the meeting and conversations all went fairly well. They wanted to know where I was from, what I did for a living, whether I could speak Igbo, whether I had been to Nigeria, and so on. By the end of the meeting, we were all talking as if we'd known each other for years. My relationship with Valerie was healthy most of the time; the only issue that made me do a double-take sometimes was her temper. She had a very short fuse and she found it difficult to hold back what she had to say. It didn't bother me too much, as I was quite a calm and relaxed person – I thought we would get on fine. I was very wrong.

In 1998, Valerie and I went away to San Francisco together. Having only ever been to America once, with my sister two years previously, I was excited. San Francisco was a popular tourist destination and known for its cool summers, fog, steep rolling hills, and glorious landmarks.

I decided it would be a perfect time and place for me to propose to Valerie. I had thought deeply about getting engaged to her. I did have my reasons for being apprehensive, mainly caused by her unpredictability and quick temper. However, I kept coming back to the fact that I would have to get married one day. I spent weeks looking for the engagement ring, wanting to get the perfect one for a lady I was going to spend the rest of my life with. When I told Ugo that I was planning on getting engaged, she was surprised. She was surprised at the speed with which I was acting, arguing that I should spend a lot more time getting to know her better. She said she had introduced us so we could be friends, not get married. I told her that marriage had also been something I had been planning for since 1996.

Equally surprised was my friend Uche, who actually told me not to marry her, citing her sometimes odd behaviour and fiery temper. I agreed with both of them, but being blindly in love at the time, I couldn't see what could possibly go wrong – and I had the belief that if anything did go wrong, love would see us through.

We stayed in a very lovely hotel in the historic centre of the city, very near to Union Square and within walking distance of Downtown. We also hired a car and visited surrounding towns. We drove to San Jose to visit a friend of mine, Dr Ochaa Idika, who worked in the Silicon Valley district. I had not seen Dr Ochaa for a very long time, so it was great to spend some with him and his family. We also drove to Oakland, and to Los Angeles, taking the scenic coastal route, 101. In Los Angeles, we visited another friend of mine, Enitan, who had relocated from London a couple of years before. Even though I took the engagement ring with me wherever we went, I struggled to find the perfect moment to propose to her. Then, one evening, when we were having dinner in a lovely restaurant I had picked on Fisherman's Wharf, a popular tourist attraction area, I finally plucked the courage. I got down on one knee and asked her to marry me. She said yes. It was a surreal moment for both of us as the thoughts of what lay ahead floated in our minds; thoughts of buying our own house and starting out on our own. The rest of our time in San Francisco was bliss. We talked excitedly about how and when we were going to tell my parents, when we would tell her mum, when we would tell friends and other family members. We decided to tell everybody as soon as we got back; she couldn't exactly hide her engagement ring. We decided to set the wedding date for 11th September 1999. That meant we had just under a year to plan.

After Valerie and I got back from San Francisco, some of the boys and I decided to go away to Tenerife for a short break. It would probably be my last break before I got married. Eventually, we decided to join the music entertainment group RJS, who organised big groups that go abroad to party and have fun.

Our group consisted of Paul Oladipo, Joe Maduaka,

Nicky Dreads and me. As we were starting to plan for the trip, I got a call one day whilst I was at work. It was Nicky. He explained that he had been arrested by the police and needed me to come to Bromley police station, where he was being held, immediately. I told him I'd be there as soon as I finished work. When I got to the police station later that evening, I was informed by the police that Nicky had been arrested on suspicion of rape, but that he would be released on bail pending further investigations. Nicky appeared to be in good spirits; he said he was happy he would be able to come with us to Tenerife. He told me it was a case of mistaken identity and would all be cleared up very soon.

The trip to Tenerife was amazing. RJS had chartered two planes, which were carrying about 390 people between them. Most of the people on our flight had bottles of brandy and other types of alcohol with them. At first, the cabin crew tried to prevent people from drinking alcohol unless it had been purchased on the plane, but eventually they gave in and succumbed to bringing us plastic cups and ice.

By the time we arrived in Tenerife, most of us were a bit tipsy. Before the four of us had left home, we had all agreed that we were going to be good boys. Apart from Nicky, we were all in serious relationships, so we couldn't afford to mess around. We had, however, agreed that flirting was okay. I shared a double room with Nicky, while Joe and Paul shared a double room next door. The men were outnumbered by girls at least two to one, so there was a lot of competition between the girls to find a man to befriend for the week-long trip. Nicky was the first to go out and look for a girlfriend while the rest of us sat by the hotel pool, taking in the beautiful exotic scenery. Before long, Nicky joined us with a lady in tow. We tried to dissuade him from getting involved with anyone, especially that early in the trip, but our advice fell on deaf ears. That night, I had to sleep out on the balcony, while Nicky and his newfound lady friend romanticised indoors. I didn't mind because it was quite warm, and we had been out partying most of the night, so it was not long before daybreak. We partied every night, we consumed a large amount of alcohol, and we engaged in some casual flirting with the girls. During the day we slept, played a variety of sports, or just relaxed and drank by the pool.

Unfortunately, we did have some trouble with one of the DJs of the After Dark UK crew, who had been hired by RJS. On one of the afternoons, we decided to have a small room party. We had come prepared – I had brought a small but powerful music set and had put together a great compilation of songs. We cooked lots of food, bought some drinks, put the music on at full blast, and left the door open. Women came streaming in. Unknown to us, one of the After Dark UK members was celebrating his birthday in one of the rooms on a different floor and was expecting to pull a huge crowd. Unfortunately, a lot of the women who might have gone to the After Dark

UK party came to ours instead. The crew came to our room and commanded us to stop the party. Obviously, we ignored the instructions. From then on, we became enemies, but that did not bother us – we were in Tenerife to have fun. At the end of the trip, I was happy to have gone along and had a good time, as it was my last trip abroad as a single man, and my last opportunity to have so much fun with the boys.

In January 1999, I contacted my Boots area manager and asked him to put me back on the relief manager rota, full-time. He gladly obliged. I went back to work the following week. When I went back to work full-time for Boots, my intention was to save as much money as possible, mainly for the wedding. This meant I had to cut down on my record-buying and partying. By this time, I had thousands of records, which occupied my entire living space. I was a well-known DJ and music expert. The fact that Valerie and I had fairly well-paid jobs and both lived at home meant we were able to save very easily.

In February, my dad (who had travelled to Nigeria) came back to the UK. As was the usual routine, he brought us all up to speed with what was going on in Nigeria. He also told us that our cousin, Nnenna Oko Nnachi, was very unwell, and that the doctors couldn't find out what was wrong with her. Less than a week after he returned, on 3rd March 1999, we received news that Nnenna had passed away. She was 27 years old. The news was a huge shock to me; we were quite close, as I had lived with the

O.O. family for some of the time I was in Nigeria.

Early in 1999, Valerie and I started house-hunting in preparation for our future family life. However we had little success finding anything, and property prices were rising rapidly. We were not desperate, as we would always have somewhere to live, but we did want to find a place we could buy and call our own. We also had to be realistic about house-hunting and planning a wedding at the same time. Eventually, around May, we decided to put house-hunting on the back burner and focus on the wedding planning. Whilst we were planning for the wedding Nicky was rearrested for rape and held in custody at HMP Belmarsh. His lawyer said they were going to use me as a character witness. At the time, I was not particularly bothered by the entire situation; even though I didn't know everything about Nicky, I knew he wasn't a rapist. I had seen him around countless girls, and although he was very intrepid and forthright, he also had a very good-natured side to him which endeared him to some of my female friends and to my sisters. By June, I found myself extremely bogged down by the Nicky case, as I had to meet with his solicitor very frequently to prepare for the case. He had been charged with rape. I was also very busy with the wedding plans.

In amongst all that was happening around me I was fast becoming a transformational and reliable leader. I was working for YIBOSC, where I had been elected vice president. I was also working with a group of young Igbos to help them establish their own Igbo organisation, Igbo Cultural and Support Network (ICSN), which they believed had a different outlook to YIBOSC. I was very active with my state union, Ebonyi State Union UK, where I was serving as interim secretary. I had also started playing amateur Sunday football. I still DJed at house parties and some night clubs. I was also an active member of Interfinance, a small group of ten black friends who bought and sold shares on the stock market. It was a very busy time in my life.

Things Fall Apart in 1999

On the 17th June 1999, an incident occurred that would change my life for ever. This was the same day Thabo Mbeki was sworn in as president of South Africa.

I was working an early shift at the Elephant & Castle, South London branch of Boots and looking forward to my 4pm finish when I received a phone call from our area office asking if I could cover the Brixton branch as soon as I finished work at Elephant & Castle. I reluctantly agreed. The fact that it was Brixton helped me make up my mind – I had intended going to Brixton after work that day anyway to buy some records from a shop called Red Records in preparation for a party I was going to be playing at on the 19th June. After work, I quickly went home for a short break before walking to the Boots store in Brixton. On getting to the store, I realised I had left my wallet at home, so wouldn't be able to buy the records as planned.

Around 6.30pm, the store quietened down somewhat. That's when I made a huge mistake that would change the course of my life. I told our dispenser, a lady called Lucy, that I was going to borrow £60 from the till to buy some records and I would replace the money the following morning when I opened up the shop. When I explained that I had forgotten my wallet and wouldn't get another opportunity to buy the sample records I needed, as they would likely sell out by the next day, she agreed. She was my witness. Some senior members of the pharmacy team occasionally borrowed money from the till, with a witness present, and replaced it later.

Unfortunately for me, immediately after I took the money, the store became busy again and I worked flat out till 8pm which was closing time. I had forgotten I still had the money in my pocket. I locked up the store, and just as we were about to leave, our plain-clothes store detectives showed up and asked to search all the staff. They discovered the £60. I began to explain how I had obtained the money, stating that I had a witness, Lucy the dispenser. She flat-out denied everything I told the detectives. I didn't know why she did that. At that point, I knew I was in trouble. The detectives confiscated the money and told me they would speak with me soon. On my way home, I got a call from the area manager telling me to go to the Walworth Road Boots branch rather than the Brixton branch the following day. The entire incident left me feeling very unpleasant, remorseful, betrayed and stupid.

I didn't tell my family about the incident, as I was unsure what was going to happen. The next day, whilst I was working at the Walworth Road Boots, the same store detectives turned up again. They invited me into the manager's office and asked me to sit down. When I sat down, a lady knocked on the door and walked into the room. The detectives explained that the lady was from the HR department of the company and was there as a witness. They questioned me again about what had happened the previous day. I repeated my story. When I had finished, they told me to wait for them and left me in the room with the HR lady. After about ten or so minutes they came back, but this time they had two police officers with them. I had my rights read to me. I was under arrest for theft. My entire world collapsed. I didn't know whether to cry or scream. I was handcuffed and led outside and into the waiting police car. They took me to Brixton police station.

I was taken into an interview room, where I was put through a lengthy interview. The police officers interviewing me appeared to feel sorry for me as they appeared to understand my dilemma. They asked me a lot personal questions; about my family life, financial details – whether I was in debt. I told them I had a well-paid job and I lived at home with my parents, not paying rent or any substantial money for my upkeep. After what seemed like hours of questioning, I was released on bail. I was in a very bad state but hid it from my family.

The following day, after speaking with Valerie, I wrote my resignation letter to Boots in preparedness for Monday. We had agreed that it would be better to resign than to wait for the investigation and possibly be found guilty, and then be sacked.

On the Sunday, 20th June, I went to one of the usual YIBOSC monthly meetings in Highbury, North London. As it was Father's Day, there were some drinks and other refreshments to celebrate the occasion. I joined in the celebrations and tried to drown the nightmare of the past days by drinking more alcohol than I should have done, as I was driving. After the meeting, a friend of mine asked if I could give him a lift to Victoria, from where he would make his way to work. I obliged. Just as we were approaching Victoria station, I took my eyes off the road for what must have been a second. That's when I crashed into the back of the car in front of me that had stopped at the red traffic lights. I knew immediately that I was going to be in trouble. I told my friend to get out of the car and go to work, as I didn't want him involved in any ramifications.

Very soon, the police arrived on the scene. They asked if I had been drinking, and I admitted that I'd had a couple of bottles of Guinness. I was breathalysed. I failed the breathalyser test. I wasn't surprised. I was taken to the Belgravia Police station on Buckingham Palace Road, where I was breathalysed again with a more accurate piece of equipment; again, I failed the test. I was led to a cell, where I was kept until an officer was available to interview me. I spent little time feeling sorry for myself, and explained my entire situation to the officer. I told him that the situation with my employer Boots was the main reason I had decided to make the foolish mistake of drowning my woes in alcohol, then getting into the car to drive home whilst under the influence. I was charged with drinking and driving and bailed to return to the City of Westminster Magistrates Court on Wednesday 23rd June 1999.

At this point, I was at an all-time low. As I got outside and the cool June night air hit my face, the reality of my position began to dawn on me. As I walked along Warwick Way, I burst out crying, loudly. As I continued along Vauxhall Bridge Road, the cold chill of the River Thames hit my body, and I could not help thinking what a cruel turn of events had hit me, all in one go. I broke down crying again, quietly at first – but after a while I was unable to contain myself any longer, so I wailed out loudly. Halfway across the bridge, I stopped and looked into the calm water below. I had never had any real suicidal tendencies in the past, even when things were really tough in Nigeria and I felt I had reached the end of my tether. But here I was, looking into the River Thames, contemplating whether I should put an end to all the wrong things that were happening to me, once and for all. I thought of all the things I had dreamt of achieving in life. I thought of all the hope my family had resting on me. Maybe it was just too much. I wanted it to be over.

I am thankful to the car driver who slowed down beside me and beeped the car horn. I'm not sure whether or not the driver had read my thoughts and tooted the car horn to snap me out of the state of mind I was in, but the sound of the horn brought me back to reality. A sudden chill ran down my spine as I hurriedly walked across the rest of the bridge and into Vauxhall to catch a bus to Camberwell.

On Monday, I took my prewritten resignation letter to the Boots area office on Putney High Street and handed it to the area manager. My resignation was with immediate effect, of course. He wished me luck with my future career. I told him I was disappointed in the company and how they had handled this and other matters. I made sure I pointed out to him the company's terrible track record of not supporting me, which went as far back as 1997. When I got back home, I immediately registered with a couple of locum pharmacy agencies, telling them I would be available for work from the end of June.

On Wednesday 23rd, I made my way to the City of Westminster Magistrates Court, located on Horseferry Road. This was my first ever time in a court for an offence. I had been to court when I was in Nigeria, but that was to correct my surname – hardly a terrifying affair. I was not scared about going to court; I was actually upset that I had been so foolhardy as to put myself in this position, and I still had the unknown situation of the police enquiry about the Boots incident to contend with. I was given an 18-month driving ban, with the opportunity to attend a drink-drive rehabilitation scheme and receive a reduced ban of 12 months. I decided not to go for the rehabilitation scheme, so was told I had to serve the full 18 months. As if matters couldn't get any worse, when I got home there was a letter from the police asking me to attend

Brixton police station on July 6th for another interview regarding the Boots incident.

My brief suicidal episode along Vauxhall Bridge had somehow given me some determination to get through what I now viewed as a rough patch in my life. And even though I kept asking why these things were happening to me, I was determined to get everything behind me and continue with plans for the wedding in September.

I started working as a locum on Monday 28th June in a modern pharmacy in Soho. I was quite used to working as a locum, where there is little or no managerial responsibility, as this was similar to my role as a relief pharmacist with Boots. My main tasks were to dispense and check prescriptions and give over-the-counter medicines advice. The job was quite dull; being in the heart of central London, the pharmacy mainly dealt with emergency contraception and with migraine and headache queries. But it paid well. I tried to keep myself busy during the weeks leading up to my visit to the police station for my interview.

Early July, Dr Mark Abani, Chief Felix Ibiam, myself, and the rest of the interim Ebonyi State Union UK team held an Ebonyi Day Launch at Africana Restaurant, Camberwell, with an aim to raise awareness of the newly created State in the South-Eastern region of Nigeria. This took my mind off matters for a couple of hours. When the 6th of July finally came, I attended Brixton police station, where I was questioned again about the Boots theft. They also asked me how many times I had stolen from Boots. When I told them that this was the only time I had ever taken anything from the company, they told me they had evidence which incriminated me as being responsible for the theft of thousands of pounds, which had mysteriously gone missing from most of the stores that I had worked in.

At this point, I told them to go to hell. I told them I had made a very silly mistake and I was happy to pay for it, but if they thought I was stupid enough to fall for their sly antics they were going to see the other side of me. I was aware of money going missing from some of the stores that relief pharmacists worked in. This usually happened because the store manager who the relief pharmacist normally covers for is away, and it is not a relief pharmacist's job to manage the staff. I had my suspicions in some of the stores I worked in as a relief pharmacist, but couldn't quite identify who the culprits were, and nor did I want that responsibility – not after the lacklustre manner in which they had handled my racism case. I couldn't quite believe what was happening. The police, colluding with the Boots head of security, Gavin, trying to get me to admit to stealing from other stores. The interview ended very shortly after that, and I told the interviewing officer that I was no longer interested in helping him with the investigation, and they should go ahead and press charges.

Whilst I continued to work as a locum in central London,

I also started avidly looking for a full-time pharmacy job in South London, closer to home. It wasn't very long until I found something suitable with the Day Lewis Group. It was a pharmacy on Brixton Hill, where they needed a new pharmacy manager to develop the pharmacy business. It was a great opportunity to broaden and improve my skills. Taybi Mohammedbhai, who owned some of the Day Lewis stores with Kirit Patel, was very happy for me to have a free rein and apply my transformation skills to improve the business. I had informed the manager who interviewed me about my incident with Boots, but he told me that it should not stop me progressing my career. I started working at Day Lewis early August 1999. I was delighted to get the job; it was local, and I knew a lot of the local people and GP practices, having worked in the Brixton area before. I got stuck in.

On 10th August, I attended Camberwell Green Magistrates' Court, where I was charged with employee theft. I had very little in my defence, and I did not have a lawyer to argue my case. I was convicted of employee theft of £60 and told to pay a £500 fine. The judge was baffled as to why I took £60 from my employer; he had not been filled in with all the details of events that led to me making that decision. I just wanted it all to be over so I could concentrate on my future, earn some money and plan for the wedding, which was one month away.

Whilst all this was going on, Nicky's solicitors kept hounding me to help them with his case. They wanted me to help them because I had been with Nicky at Porky's wine bar in Streatham, South London, sometime in 1998 when he met the lady he was alleged to have raped. Nicky had warned me and his solicitor that it was going to be a very big case. At the time he told me this, I had no idea how big it was going to be, nor why.

On Saturday 11th September 1999, Valerie and I got married. It was a glorious day; the sun was out, and both families were looking forward to the occasion. We had agreed we would not have a church wedding, as Valerie was a Catholic and I wasn't; I didn't want to get married the Catholic way just for the sake of it. We got married at Wandsworth Town Hall, and the ceremony was attended by over 70 people. The reception was held at Tooting Leisure Centre, just off Garrett Lane in Tooting. We had invited 120 people, but in true Nigerian style, there were over 200 people at the reception. Thankfully, we had anticipated an overspill. My sisters, brother and family friends Joe, Charity, Nnamdi, TY and Harrison, alongside the caterers, helped make sure the day was a success.

After the wedding, I went home, whilst Valerie was brought to our house later that evening by her family – an old Igbo tradition. They came singing songs and with loads of fanfare. My dad hosted them whilst we all engaged in small talk until the early hours of the morning. When everyone had finally left, we collected our already-packed suitcases and took a taxi to our pre-booked hotel near Heathrow airport in preparedness for our honeymoon in the Caribbean island of St Lucia. The following day, we decided to visit and thank Valerie's mother, and her brothers who had come from the United States for the wedding. After more talking, eating and drinking, we took a taxi back to our hotel and got some well-earned rest. The next day we flew off to St Lucia. St Lucia was such a beautiful place to choose for a honeymoon. We had booked the right place to relax; an all-inclusive hotel. It was relaxing and hot, with lots of beaches, lots to drink and lots of food. We stayed there for two weeks.

Whilst out in St Lucia, I bumped into a lovely couple, Abraham and Beverley. They had gotten married on the same day as us, somewhere in Dulwich, South London, and were also on their honeymoon. We warmed to each other very quickly and started hanging out together. It transpired that Abraham and I had both played for the same football team, Norton FC, at different times.

Valerie and I decided that when we got back to London, we'd put all our energy into looking for a house to buy now that the wedding was out of the way – and that is exactly what we did.

A New Millennium
(2000–2003)

The year 2000 – Y2K, as it was popularly called— brought with it hope and prospects of a very bright future for me. It was a new millennium, and many people were positive about what lay ahead. I was happy to see the back of 1999; it had been a most terrible year for me. Generally, the New Year however got off to a very bad start, though: Dr Harold Shipman was found guilty of murdering fifteen patients and sentenced to life imprisonment; a Kenya Airways Flight crashed into the Atlantic Ocean, killing 169 people; and Alaska Airlines crashed into the Pacific Ocean, killing eighty-eight people. All these things happened in the first month of the new millennium. For me, the year brought with it an intense feeling that my life was headed in a new direction. In January, we found out that Valerie was pregnant, and this put more pressure on us to urgently look for a house to buy.

We stepped up our house-hunting and looked at one house every single day after work. We had different tastes as to what sort of house we wanted, and eventually I left it up to her. After house-hunting for nearly six months, we finally found and bought a house in Crofton Park, South London. We moved in on the 1st June 2000.

Less than three weeks later, on the 21st June 2000, my whole world veered into another dimension. My lovely, precious daughter and princess Nkechi Kiah Olugh was born. I finally got to understand the feeling a person gets when their new baby is brought into the world. I was overwhelmed with joy and a heap of other emotions I couldn't explain. I did know that I was happy, though. I had been waiting for this moment for a very long time. I knew I was ready to be a father, and I was not just going to be a father, I was going to be a good one. I saw that as my next challenge – I was going to give her the best possible start in life. I gladly got stuck into fatherhood.

One day in September I received a letter which was to set me on a "panic path"; it was from the disciplinary committee of the Royal Pharmaceutical Society of Great Britain, which was the statutory regulatory and professional body for pharmacists. They had been informed of the employee theft incident at Boots and had invited me to a hearing on the 11th December 2000 – my birthday. The letter detailed the allegations and the fact that I had been charged and found guilty. It also stated that following the disciplinary hearing, I could be suspended or struck off the register. This would mean I could no longer practice as a pharmacist in the UK.

I was in total shock and broke down crying. I had worked so hard to get to the position I was in and now it seemed that everything was about to be pulled from underneath my feet. What have I done to deserve all this? I asked myself. I informed my employer, Taybi, about the hearing, and although he wished me luck, we both knew he couldn't do anything to help me. I spent the next three months waiting and agonising over it. It drove me insane knowing that the hearing would spell certain doom for my career. Although I was able to function tremendously when I was at work, as this was a distraction, immediately after I finished work all the worry came pouring into my mind. This led me to try and numb my feelings with alcohol. Eventually, this became a vicious circle; work hard during the day, drink after work.

Finally, the day for the hearing arrived. I had taken a day off work to attend the hearing, which was to take place at the Royal Pharmaceutical Society's base at 1 Lambeth High Street, London. On getting there, I was ushered into a small room and asked to wait. I was asked whether I had a representative; I said no. I didn't think it was necessary – I had already pleaded guilty in court, and had been fined, so what was the use in trying to defend myself at this point? I was finally led into a very large room where there were five people, all members of the committee. I took one look at their faces and knew I was in deep trouble. A Mr Geoff Hudson, of Pennington's solicitors, placed the facts of the case before the committee. When he had finished, they asked me if I had any counter-arguments or questions for him, or had anything to add, to which I replied that I didn't. I was then led back into the small room, where I waited for what seemed like eternity. Eventually, I was led back into the big room with the mean-looking, scary faces. I was told to stand up before the decision was read. Giving the committee's decision, the chairman of the committee, Lord Fraser of Carmyllie, QC, said that the case involved a serious breach of trust, and that stealing money from an employer was an activity that could not be countenanced by the Society. The committee ordered that my name be removed from the register. That was one cold-hearted birthday present. I was numb and speechless. After a few minutes, they asked if I had anything to say. I said yes; I told them that I was sorry for what I had done, and that it was a genuine mistake. I told them that I had let the profession down, but that more importantly, I had let my family down.

It felt like my whole world had come to a crashing end. Why was it that when things were just starting to go so well, I had to have my feet cut from underneath me? So many different thoughts and emotions were swimming around in my head that I found it impossible to think straight. I don't even know how I managed to get home. I told Valerie the outcome of the hearing; I cannot remember what she said. Eventually, I went out and bought a bottle of rum, which I started drinking before I got back home. I sat downstairs drinking and thinking about my life until very late in the night. All the suffering I had endured over the years, all the hard work I had put in through university to eventually qualify as a pharmacist – and I had been a pharmacist for just five years. Just as the going was beginning to get good, I had been struck off the register. My career path to a successful life had been cut short; hardly the good example of a leader or role model.

As I sat there, I decided that there was nothing left in this world for me. I might as well be dead; that way nobody would have to worry about the continuous shame and trouble that kept following me around. With all these venomous thoughts swirling through my mind, I went to the kitchen and got a sharp cooking knife. I tested it on my skin to make sure it was sharp enough. It was. I went and sat back down. This time I sat on the floor next to the music system. I switched it on and turned the volume down low so that it wouldn't disturb Valerie and Nkechi, who were sleeping upstairs. I prayed, asking for God's forgiveness for what I was about to do. I begged for my daughter's forgiveness too; I was about to leave her without a father. I had seen people slash their wrists before on television, and I knew it was painless, so it would not be difficult for me. I felt I had no choice anyway. I had a final swig from the bottle. I held the knife to my left wrist, making sure I had the right spot. As I was about to apply pressure and cut through my skin, an apparition of my daughter appeared in front of me. Her eyes were looking straight at me – sad, questioning eyes. I held her gaze for a couple of seconds before she disappeared.

That very brief experience saved my life once again. I felt an inner energy overcome my entire body. I kept repeating to myself "be strong, I am strong, be strong, I am strong". I got up and put the knife back in the drawer in the kitchen. I sat back down on the floor and started crying, thinking to myself, what have I just nearly done? Nkechi doesn't deserve to be without a father; it isn't her fault that I have fucked up my life.

I had to find a way out of this mess. I had to get myself into shape to be able to look after my family. The image of my daughter appearing before me at such a low moment in my life had to have some significance. Maybe it was a way of telling me I was needed here on earth to look after her, and to accomplish many things. At that moment, I made a decision to take everything that came my way on the chin. Life is like a deck of cards where we don't get the opportunity to choose the cards we are dealt. You either quit when the going gets tough, or you continue to play the cards you have, and play them smartly. The thought of taking my life and leaving behind my loved ones with so much heartache and so many questions now didn't seem like a great way to go after all. It had appeared an easy choice at the time. That experience of despair, for the second time in two years, was to change my approach to life forever. I decided that I would intentionally go out and prove to the world and myself that I was a good person, capable of achieving anything I wanted to. I was going to be the leader I had set out to be, and a role model for my daughter.

The next day, I summoned the courage to go to work. When I got there, I called Taybi and told him of the outcome of the hearing. He asked whether I was going to appeal the decision. I told him that I did not intend to prolong the agony of my catastrophic journey. He told me I would be missed, and he would have to find another pharmacy manager. Later that day, he called me and told me that I could continue to work for him, if I wanted to, as a dispenser at his South Norwood pharmacy. He also told me that I would have to take a pay cut; from earning just over £32,000, I would be earning a more modest salary of £16,000. This was an unpleasant revelation for me, and it was not going to please Valerie either. I begged him to increase it to at least £20,000, but he refused, giving me all sorts of reasons why he could not. They were, however, genuine reasons. He told me I was actually lucky to still be in a job and he didn't need a dispenser so was doing me a favour. I thanked him for the offer and took it. When I got home after work, I told Valerie the bad news about my job. We discussed how we would be able to manage our now squeezed income. We had our mortgage, bills and other outgoings to pay for; it would be a struggle, but we agreed it was manageable. I sensed a morose time ahead.

The next day, I reported to work at the Day Lewis Chemist branch in South Norwood. The manager there was a guy I knew called Tunde Williams. He was from Sierra Leone, although his family were originally from the south-west of Nigeria. Working with him would make things a little easier to digest. When he asked me what happened, I explained in much detail the affairs that had led up to the hearing, and its outcome. He was sympathetic. He also told me to give it some time, then book myself onto a "Return to Practice" course, which would be the beginning of my journey to get myself back on the pharmacist register.

With Christmas less than two weeks away, I decided to take some time off, get my head in the right place, and return in the New Year with a redefined sense of purpose and hope.   I was thankful for the birth of my daughter because her arrival had brought me lots of joy, comfort, determination and resolve. I returned to work in January 2001 with newfound energy and enthusiasm. The days were generally exciting, and I enjoyed working with the pharmacy team there. I was seen as the assistant manager and was in charge of most projects. In February, Valerie went back to work after six months' maternity leave, and Nkechi started staying with a child-minder, Debbie, who lived on the same road as us.

In June 2001, I planned and executed the first YIBOSC Festival of Arts and Culture (FESTAC) event. It was held at St. Mary's Banqueting Hall, Camberwell New Road, South London. It was supposed to be compered by the footballer John Fashanu, who I had met whilst working with the Arsenal legend Kanu Nwankwo for his heart foundation. As the event was about to start, I couldn't see him and began to get worried. I gave him a call. When he answered his phone, he sounded pissed off. He told me that he was in Scotland and had forgotten about our arrangement. I gave him a rude piece of my mind then hung up. I had to beg news presenter Henry Bonsu to step in and compere the event at short notice. Gladly he understood my position and took over. The event was a great success.

In August 2001, an incident happened between Valerie and me which was the first warning sign of what was to become a very difficult and acrimonious relationship. When I got home that evening, I asked her what was for dinner. We normally took turns to cook: I would cook one week, then she would cook the following week. She told me that she hadn't made anything for me. When I asked why, she said that it was because I had not cooked on Sunday night, when I had been at a meeting. Therefore she was not going to cook. She had eaten dinner with some work colleagues before coming home. I told her it was unfair and not the way married couples treat each other. My appeals fell on deaf ears.

About a month later, on the 11th September 2001, the world witnessed a massacre that was to go down in history as the deadliest terrorist attack of its time. Tunde and I were watching television that morning in the dispensary, with the volume off, as we normally did, unaware that the images being shown on TV were actual live pictures of the events. We thought it was a movie at first. Then we began to pay more attention and turned up the volume, realising what was transpiring before our eyes. It was a horrific event which changed the world forever. The entire world was in shock as to how such a catastrophe could happen; how suicide bombers could cause destruction of human lives on such a scale. Some members of the pharmacy staff were in tears as the pictures were replayed constantly on the television, as were some patients who came in to either hand in or collect their prescriptions. Everyone was visibly shocked. Of course, Valerie and I cancelled our planned second wedding anniversary celebrations for that evening. We had booked a table in a restaurant in central London; the restaurateurs were very understanding.

The rest of the year went by without much incident as I worked feverishly with a variety of Nigerian community organisations to develop and achieve their objectives. I was instrumental in transforming both Ebonyi State Union UK and YIBOSC to greater heights. This included working with the YIBOSC president to apply for £20,000 of Big Lottery funding. Our application was successful. I also singlehandedly successfully applied for £5,000 for Ebonyi State Union UK. I took over management of an adult football team, renaming the club London Nigerian Football Club, and used it to attract young adults from the Camberwell and Brixton areas of South London who were susceptible to falling into criminal activities. I also remained heavily involved in Interfinance, as this provided a much-needed extra income stream for me.

I had been furiously looking for a job that would pay me a bit more money. In March 2002, I received the good news I had been praying for. I was offered a job as manager of a smoking cessation project at NHS Lambeth Primary Care Trust (PCT). I jumped at the opportunity. Taybi was very supportive and gave me a good reference. I was very happy to be joining the NHS. My final day at Day Lewis was on the 5th April. There were no leaving parties although Tunde was a bit sad to see me go as we had built up a good working relationship over the past 15 months or so.

I took to my new job almost immediately. The salary was just under £26,000, which was a lot more than I had been receiving in my previous job. My role was very challenging right from the start, as I had to set up the new smoking cessation service in the borough. I had no previous experience of working in the NHS, and the entire culture, ethos and mentality was new to me. It took me up to eight months to figure out what I was supposed to be doing. This was not helped by the fact that my line manager, Anne Ford, left very shortly after I joined. I also moved offices from St Thomas Street in London Bridge to new offices on Waterloo Road. I had no manager to assist me, nor did anybody in my office know what I was supposed to be doing.

It was a painful time for me, as I spent a lot time sitting at my desk doing nothing and wondering whether I had made the wrong decision to join the NHS. Then, in April or May 2003, the Chief Executive of Lambeth PCT, Kevin Barton, paid a visit to our offices. I was introduced to him as the person in charge of smoking cessation in the borough, and he asked me whether Lambeth had met its stop-smoking target the previous year. I was gobsmacked and embarrassed, as I had no idea what the hell he was talking about. I thought very quickly before telling him we had not met our target but that I was working very hard to make sure we did by the end of the financial year. This was something I would go on to work hard at, finally achieving it six years later. His question prompted me into action. I'd had no idea Lambeth had a stop-smoking target, and no idea how I was going to meet it either. Nevertheless, although I had no idea where to start, I knew I was going to succeed.

I had joined the PCT at a time of immense change. Lambeth, Southwark and Lewisham PCTs were being disaggregated into individual PCTs. This was why my boss, Anne Ford, left. When I moved over to the now-single Lambeth PCT in Waterloo Road, everyone was still in a state of disorientation and not quite clear of their roles and responsibilities. I decided to do some research to see what was happening in other boroughs. There wasn't much, as everyone was in a similar position. I did, however, get some ideas as to how I could start developing the service and building capacity. With my knowledge of GP practices in the borough, gained while working as a pharmacist in all the Boots Chemists' in Lambeth, and with some guidance from the Department of Health and some other organisations, I managed to get the service set up. It was commissioned through GP practices so they could deliver the service to their patients. I went on to build an entire stop-smoking team, consisting of ten people to support and deliver the service across the borough. The service went on to win numerous awards and accolades for its innovation and design quality.

Later that year, in September 2003, I was given an award at the British Pharmaceutical Conference by the National Pharmaceutical Association and the Guild of Healthcare Pharmacists. I was also given funds to set up an innovative stop-smoking service at St Thomas' Hospital. The project, `Smoking cessation pharmacy services: development of continuous care between secondary and primary care', had a specific aim to develop a robust system for referring patients undergoing smoking cessation from hospital to the community sector. It would involve hospital pharmacists, community pharmacists and GPs across the boroughs of Lambeth, Southwark and Lewisham. It was the first project of its kind in the UK. It was ironic that I had won an award for my work in an area I could no longer work in as a professional.

I was finally beginning to blaze a trail of success, and my work ethic was getting attention. My life seemed like it was coming together once again.

Breakdown of My Marriage
(2003–2008)

By the end of 2003, I realised that my marriage was not working. I had actually sensed something was not quite right before 2003 but had ignored it, believing it was my paranoid side playing tricks on my mind. We argued a lot, sometimes over petty things. Valerie was not as sociable as me. I liked having my friends round to the house to talk to about a lot of different and inspiring things. She was always tense and unwelcoming when my friends came round. She also tried to prevent me from going out to visit my friends. She did not have many interactions with Nigerian community groups and did not see any benefit in getting involved. I was the exact opposite and spent considerable time working for the community. On many occasions, I would take Nkechi to Ebonyi State Union UK meetings and Valerie would refuse to go. Her excuse was that the meetings were a waste of time and had nothing good to offer. We would also regularly visit her mum and spend time chatting. This was normally on Sundays. Sometimes I would visit her mum on my own and we would spend time together as in-laws. However, Valerie was very reluctant to come with me when I asked her to visit my parents with me.

One day, when I came home from work late, Valerie was upstairs in bed. I got changed, we talked for a while, and then I went downstairs to eat. I couldn't find any food anywhere, so I went back upstairs and asked Valerie if there was any food for me. She said that if I wanted my Nigerian food, I should start cooking for myself. This came as an utter shock to me. It sounded aggressive, and it was out of the blue, although it was not the first time this had happened. We argued about it but got nowhere.

That night I made an entry in my diary, lamenting what I believed was the beginning of the end of our relationship. I spent the next couple of weeks thinking about what I could do to salvage the deteriorating situation.

Diary entry 1 – Triste disclosures

The day is Friday 28th November 2003, 2320hrs, and as usual I am up thinking hard about my life and where I'm heading, what I'm trying to do, who I'm trying please, who I'm trying to help and what all that does for me in a world where being dissatisfied is more of a guarantee than anything else.

Thoughts of my marriage have kept me awake for many nights; the more nights I spend thinking, the more I wonder where my marriage is going, how long will it last and who is going to be the loser. These thoughts only keep me awake because I feel that I am at fault, I must be the one to blame, and I am the loser. I've given other people marriage support and guidance so many times, so if I cannot get it right then something is wrong; the fault is mine.

I feel frustrated, trapped, empty, sad, suffocated, demoralised and spiritually weak. I was not told that this was part of the marriage package. Maybe this is part of life's lessons, maybe it's my destiny, maybe I was told but I did not understand because I must have been in love, or maybe I just did not want to listen.

The first thing that comes to mind is that I cannot disappoint my parents. I can imagine what people would say; the first son, the one who was sent to Nigeria and who against all odds returned to the UK and proved everyone wrong and did everyone proud, made his parents feel happy and content – but he was just waiting for the right moment to drop them right down in shit and disgrace them. My parents would die. Then again, they would not. If I file for divorce it would shock everybody who knows us. We are the perfect model couple that every parent would like to boast about to their friends and family.

We are not the perfect couple that people think we are, and I am not the perfect husband I thought I would always be, I am on the very edge of mental and spiritual exertion, trembling and irate that this is not marriage the way I planned. However, I do know that I am the perfect father. My joy is my daughter, Nkechi, without whom I probably would not even be alive to complain about a marriage that has failed. I always knew I would be a great dad. Nkechi needs siblings to give her more love; I need love to give her more love.

How do I explain to my parents, my sisters? Gosh, they'd kill me themselves. I remember how much they put into our wedding, my brother who looks up to me for support, advice and guidance, my friends, my relatives in Nigeria and elsewhere abroad.

Damn. How could this be?

But unfortunately, I know better than anyone and I will always do what I want to do. At times like these, I sometimes wish that I had died in a road accident or had been shot in the head by mistake. Now I have to do the hard work and stay alive and look after my dear daughter.

Damn! This life is a con. If I had my chance I would not have been born.

How can love be so blunt? And this time there's nobody to blame — I'm all grown up now.

I miss my grand mum!

I believed it would be a shame if we didn't try to work something out, especially considering the total cost of our wedding four years ago and the fact that our families and friends had been heavily involved. There was also the stigma of being divorced. Valerie and I started talking about ways we could improve our relationship and keep our marriage on an even keel.

It appeared to work, and in June 2005 we were blessed with a baby boy, Obinna Reuben Olugh. His Igbo name, Obinna, which meant "Daddy's heart", was given to him by me; just like I had given my daughter her Igbo name Nkechi, which means "belongs to God". He was also named after the biblical Reuben, the first and eldest son of Jacob. I was over the moon when my son was born and doted over him at any opportunity. He was also doted over by Nkechi which was heart-warming to see. I was going to teach him everything I knew, just as my dad had taught me. The birth of my son helped improve my relationship with Valerie – or at least it was a distraction, for a little while. We argued less, spent more time together and I believed our future was looking bright.

For no obvious reason, in November 2005 I decided to stop eating meat for a couple of months. During Christmas, I avoided meat with ease and felt very proud of myself. In February 2006, a friend of mine had invited me out for a vegetarian meal to an East London restaurant. As I was getting ready, Valerie called from downstairs to tell me someone was urinating on our bin outside and was ignoring her calls to stop. I found that strange, as our bin was on our drive and very close to the house; in fact, it was very close to our living room window. I stopped getting dressed and went downstairs. I didn't have a top on, as I wasn't expecting to go outside. I opened the front door and saw the man as he had just finished. I went to the first step and asked him why he was urinating on our bin. He apologised, saying, "sorry mate, wrong bin". Slightly intrigued by his answer, I asked him which bin he had intended to urinate on. His second response was totally different to his initial one. "Fuck off, you black cunt," he said.

I was surprisingly calm. I went to the bottom of the steps and told him there was no need for that sort of language, but he repeated his comment and came rushing towards me. As I moved backwards, he came crashing into me. I fell backwards, banging my head on the concrete steps behind me. He was a huge guy, probably six feet tall and weighing nearly 100 kilos. Then he was on top of me, punching me in the face as I tried to defend myself. I eventually managed to roll him over. I stood up and made use of my Timberland boots, kicking him several times in his midriff but being careful not to kick his face.

As this was going on, out of the corner of my eye I saw a lady and a young man appear from near the hedges. I recognised the young man as the son of one of our neighbours a couple of doors down; he started hitting me from behind. I stopped kicking the guy on the floor and turned to the young man to ask him why he was getting involved in a fight that didn't concern him. Within that split second, the guy on the floor got up, grabbed a concrete slab the size of a brick that was part of our partitioning wall, and slammed it into the left side of my face. I heard Valerie shout "don't do it! don't do it!" before the slab landed. I was knocked unconscious. I came to probably some seconds later; the two guys were now kicking me whilst I was on the floor. I remember thinking to myself, shit, is this how I'm going to die? With that thought came the strength to pick myself up and start to fight back.

One of our neighbours had called the police. As they arrived, sirens blazing and lights flashing, the two guys ran off, jumped into a van with the lady at the wheel and drove off into the evening. I was concussed, and the side of my face hurt like mad; it was sore, but there was no blood, so I felt somewhat relieved. The police began to question me about what had happened. As I started explaining, one of the female officers asked if we could go inside my house to continue the discussion. I obliged, and we continued our conversation inside. I got the impression that she didn't believe me when I told her there was no provocation before the man attacked me. After they had taken as many notes as they could, they left and said someone would be in contact with me to inform me of developments.

I soon realised that I wasn't going to be able to meet up with my friend, so I sent a message to explain the situation. As I sat at home, I analysed what had happened. I had many questions. What had really provoked the man to attack me? Why hadn't Valerie or her sister, who was at the house at the time, called the police? Soon, my jaw began to throb. It got steadily worse, and by 8pm that night I couldn't bear the pain any longer. I asked Valerie if she could drive me to the hospital, but she refused, so I walked to Lewisham's hospital.

Following a quick examination and an X-ray, I was told that my upper left jaw had been fractured. The staff at the hospital couldn't do anything about it as they did not have the appropriate equipment. They told me to go to King's College Hospital on Monday. I was given a referral form and sent home. I was in excruciating pain throughout the weekend and popped painkillers as if they were going out of fashion. On Monday, I went straight to King's College Hospital, where they confirmed I had a fractured upper left jaw which needed fixing. I was booked in on the Wednesday for major surgery to mend the fracture. My mum was by my side when I went under my first ever anaesthetic, and she was there when I came round. Valerie did not have the time to visit me in hospital. The consultant working on me said that had the blow been an inch higher, I would have lost my left eye.

The entire incident left me feeling vulnerable, upset and traumatised. I was signed off work for three weeks with painkillers and antibiotics. I had to have my food through a straw, as I wasn't able to chew anything. I couldn't play football or any other contact sport for over two months. I vowed that the culprits would be brought to justice, although I was unsure how.

A couple of months later, the detective dealing with the case came to the house to give me an update. They had caught the young man. Almost a year later, the son of our neighbour stood trial and was found guilty of causing grievous bodily harm. He was sent to prison for 18 months. The case of the main culprit was complicated because the police had already had him under surveillance for drug smuggling before his attack on me. The police hadn't wanted the drugs investigation to be hampered, so I had to wait a long time before he was finally charged in my case. After a very lengthy trial, he was found not guilty. The judge deemed his actions to be self-defence. This was a huge blow for me and my confidence in the British judicial system. I felt let down, but there was nothing I could do.

During the time I was recuperating at home following the incident, it had occurred to me that if I had died that evening, Valerie would never have known where I was from in Nigeria. I decided it would be a good idea for us to go on holiday to Nigeria as a family. Valerie, however, didn't think it was a good idea, and suggested that I should go alone. When I told her that going alone defeated the purpose and explained the reason why I wanted all of us to go, she said that it was my country and she had little interest in going there. I then suggested that I could go with the kids; I knew Nkechi would enjoy Nigeria, as she'd been going on about wanting to visit for a few years now. Still Valerie disagreed. After days of wrangling and arguing, she agreed to go and take Nkechi, but she refused to take Obinna, stating that he was too young to travel. She also said that she wasn't going to incur any expenses, as it was not her idea; she was only going along with it because she felt I had forced her to.

I told her I was happy to foot the travel bill if she felt she didn't want to contribute. I was furious, however, that she wouldn't let Obinna come with us to Nigeria; he was nearly ten months old. I was so furious and devastated that I called Valerie's mother to explain the situation and asked her to help me convince her daughter to let Obinna come with us to Nigeria. He was my only son, and in true Nigerian cultural style I wanted him to visit his country of origin. Valerie's mum said she needed time to think it all through. A couple of days later, she called me back and said that her daughter was right to not let Obinna travel with us. She said that Obinna was going to be staying with her whilst we were in Nigeria. I had not even been part of the decision about where my son would stay for three weeks when we were in Nigeria.

I was devastated by all this, but at the same time I felt there wasn't much else I could do. At this juncture, I felt that our trip to Nigeria would either solidify our marriage or break it. We decided to visit Nigeria over the Easter holidays so that Nkechi didn't miss too many days of school. I made all the necessary arrangement; vaccinations, visas and everything else.

We left for Nigeria on the evening of the 21st April 2006, arriving in Abuja, the Nigerian capital, early in the morning of the following day. We passed through the arrivals section fairly easily and without any problems, and after a 30-minute wait, my friend Ibom appeared in the waiting lounge to pick us up. After long hugs and introductions, we made our way to his car, and he took us to a hotel not far from his flat. After checking in and having a brief rest, Ibom and his wife, Chinyere, turned up. We repeated the introductions before we left for some sightseeing. Nkechi loved the fact that it was very hot and there was lots of space. She also loved that there were lots of people, all of whom were either her uncle or aunties and who were very nice and fond of her.

After a couple of days of sightseeing in Abuja, we flew to Owerri, the capital of Imo state, where we were chauffeured to Aba, my old stomping ground. An old friend of mine and former member of the House of Representatives, Honourable Irem Ibom, had lent me his jeep and driver to use over the entire holiday. Honourable Irem was the man who tried to kick me out of the survival party hosted by Ndukwe nwa ma Grace back in the 1980s. I knew Irem's driver, Ideghe, quite well. He was slightly younger than me, but we had moved in some of the same circles when I lived in Nigeria, so this made his company quite useful.

My two sisters also arrived in Aba on the same day as us; they had travelled through Lagos and spent a couple of days there with my cousin and friend Nobel's. My parents were already at Aba. It was a great family reunion, even though my younger brother Olugh was not there. It was also the first time in a long while that we had visited Nigeria together. The difference this time was that we no longer had to stay at 15 Onyembi Street with Okoro Ikpo and Rosaline, the wicked aunty and uncle. It would have proved impossible for me to stay there, especially with my family in tow. Our new, big family house at Ndusoro Road provided the much-needed comfort, space and privacy that we all needed.

Valerie initially refused to let Nkechi eat any food cooked in our family house unless she had seen the food being prepared herself. She also refused to let Nkechi out of her sight. Everyone thought it was very odd and infuriating behaviour, especially considering the fact that we were in our well-protected family home This continued for a couple of days until Nkechi's complaints and pleas to let her out finally got to Valerie – she eventually let her mingle with the rest of the family and with her cousins and the other children her age, who were begging for her to go downstairs and play with them. Nkechi enjoyed this and would often have her morning shower, have her breakfast, and then disappear downstairs to play; she would stay downstairs playing and eating until dusk before coming back up to have her shower and go straight to bed, exhausted.

The holiday provided a much-needed break from the usual hustle and bustle of London for us – and of Los Angeles in the case of my sister Onyemachi, who had moved there some time ago. We visited the village and went to see all our relatives and some of my good friends. We mostly travelled around together and enjoyed being together as a family

Valerie's lack of cooperation throughout the holiday made me sad as I thought back to the main reason I had wanted us to embark on this holiday in the first place.. I had a sudden realisation that our marriage was coming to an end.

When we got back to the UK, I knew it would be a difficult time for us. We tried to pretend that the holiday had been wonderful. We were lying to friends about our wonderful experiences, but deep down we were both wondering: what now? how do we talk about this? what will the outcome be? The arguing escalated to heights that were intolerable for me and we started spending less time together in the house. After work, I would either go to my parents' house or to my friend Esther's house. I also increased my participation in my community and other extracurricular activities.

At home, we cooked separately, and we took turns to look after the kids individually. We could go days without speaking to each other. This carried on sometime in May 2007. It was nearly a year after our trip to Nigeria, and we were arguing about a utility bill which we both believed the utility company had overcharged us for. Valerie said she had called the company to find out why the bill was so high. I told her to give me the bill so I could follow it up when I got to work. As the argument escalated Valerie told me she was going to get me thrown out of the house and called the police. When they arrived, and after a couple of questions I was asked to get changed and come with them to the police station.

I got changed, but as I was about to go downstairs where the other officers were waiting, one of them said he needed to put handcuffs on me. When I asked him why, he told me it was procedure. I begged him not to, explaining that I was willingly coming to the station, but he did not relent. He slapped the cuffs on, and we made our way down the stairs. As I was coming down, I saw my daughter, who was in the sitting room with Valerie. The look on her face ripped my heart to shreds. It was a look of distress and pity. That was the moment I knew I had to divorce Valerie, otherwise I would probably see Nkechi looking like that more often, which I couldn't bear.

I asked the officer whether he could get my wallet and my keys from the sitting room, to which he responded, "you can have your wallet, but your wife has to decide whether you can take your house keys, considering her grave allegations". The officer asked Valerie if she was happy for me to take the house keys, to which she said she was. I was put in the back of a police van for the fourth time in my life. Although I was very calm during the journey, I was furious inside and was already planning how I was going to go through with the divorce.

I was taken to Lewisham police station. Before they locked me into a cell, I asked to make a phone call. I called my mum, and then my manager at work. When I got through to my mum, she insisted on coming to the station, but I managed to dissuade her, telling her I would come to the house immediately I was released. I told my boss I had an emergency to attend to and I would hopefully be in the following day. I was locked in a cell for about an hour before they took me to an interview room where I was questioned for over two hours. I was finally released without charge. The police stated that there were inconsistencies in the witness statement Valerie had given them earlier that day. I went home and was a bit surprised to see Valerie there – but it presented me with the perfect opportunity to tell her what was going to happen. "You know it's over, don't you?" I said. She said that she did.

On my way to my parents' house, I called a good lawyer friend of mine, Sharon Sawyer, to get some advice on what to do and to find out if she could recommend any suitable lawyers who would help me with my divorce proceedings. She told me that we should try mediation first. She did, however, give me the name of a top-class law firm in Bexleyheath, London – Chancellors Lea Brewer.

When I got to my parents' house, I explained everything to them. They said they supported me in filing for divorce, as I was constantly unhappy – and the fact that Valerie had called the police once meant this was a tactic she would probably continue to use until I became frustrated and did something stupid.

When I contacted Chancellors Lea Brewer, I was put in contact with Adella Thomas. I met with Adella a few days later and immediately warmed to her, as she exuded confidence and knowledge of the law. She would go on to work with me on my divorce and other matters over a stressful fifteen-month period. During that first meeting, we went through the details of my unfortunate and regrettable marriage and what had led to the breakdown.

After my explanation, Adella suggested we try meditation before doing anything else. I agreed, reluctantly, as I was certain that it would not work. I had asked Valerie some months back to attend mediation with me, but she had said it would be a waste of time.

I was right; Valerie refused mediation again. That actually suited me perfectly because I had no intention of mending the relationship. For me, it was over. She still had a surprise for me, though. When I asked her how we were going to go about the divorce process, she said that I wasn't going to get anything from the marriage. She said she was going to take the children away from me, keep the house, and take anything else she could get her hands on. I foolishly thought she was bluffing. I suggested that we should agree how much she could afford to give me to enable me to move out of the matrimonial home, pay a deposit towards a new place, and start my life afresh. She wasn't bluffing. She wasn't having any of it.

That was the moment I knew I had to fight for myself and what I knew was right. It was going to be the battle of my life, and I knew it. We had both saved up to put a deposit down for the house seven years ago. I had contributed a lot more than Valerie, as I thought I was earning more than her. We had both saved and contributed to make numerous structural amendments to the house, and I was not going to just get up, pack my bags and disappear into the abyss with nothing. What hurt me the most was when she said I was a bad father to the kids and that she was going to make sure I never saw them again. I was willing to fight in any way necessary for my kids, and I did.

A couple of weeks later, I went back to Chancellors Lea Brewer to explain the situation and kick-start the divorce proceedings.

Diary entry 2 – May 2007

The rot in our marriage is now there for all to smell – constant arguing, avoiding each other, no more caring words. I guess we are not surprised; the writing has been on the wall for a very long time. I can honestly say the rapid descent started in February of last year, just after I was racially attacked outside my house and left with a smashed jaw.

I will not rummage through the entire details of the divorce, because it would be very unfair on my lovely kids to read about what happened between me and their mother. I will, however, highlight some important facts and timelines.

The divorce papers were eventually served at the end of May 2007. My solicitor had advised me to leave the country if I could, as she feared Valerie's reaction when she received the papers – she had experience of such situations. I took her advice and decided to go to Nigeria. I like to think that I decided to go to Nigeria to find the inner strength, composure and tolerance I would need throughout the divorce battle. I spent three weeks in Nigeria, and I did prepare myself mentally whilst out there; I vowed never to give up. When I came back and went back to the matrimonial home, I was greeted with abuse and accusations. I had known I was in for a very tough time, so I was ready. Adella had advised me not to abandon the family home, otherwise a lot of decisions would go against me; moving out might even help substantiate some of her claims that I never stayed in the house to look after the children. Valerie's twin sister had been through a divorce a couple of years earlier after being married for about three years. The discreet and meticulous planning her family had gone through in order to get as much as possible from the poor guy gave me some insight into what was to come. But I had promised myself that this was one fight I wasn't going to lose.

In July 2007, shortly after coming back from Nigeria, I lost my driver's licence for failing to produce a breath sample when I was stopped by the police. I was taken to Lewisham police station in the back of a van (my fifth time in a police van). The arresting officers wanted to charge me with dangerous driving and driving under the influence of drugs, citing the fact that I was on my mobile phone whilst driving. I was indeed on my phone, but I have never taken drugs and I had not been drinking.

After stopping me, the arresting officers had asked me what I did for a living to be able to afford the BMW that I was driving. I said it was none of their business asking such personal questions at the side of the road, unless they had any suspicions and probable cause. They were not happy, and told me to stop being a smart-arse. I refused to cooperate with them any longer – a silly, stubborn mistake that I paid for with another driving ban.

The divorce was very messy and acrimonious. It cost me over £40,000 and went on for 15 months from May 2007 till August 2008, during which time I was verbally and physically abused, arrested by the police due to Valerie's false allegations of theft, drug-dealing, murder, and many other things. I was lucky to have solid support from my parents, siblings, Greg and Dr Mark Abani. I was always on the phone to them, pouring out my heart, crying, or planning the next move. I used to sleep in my son's room with a bible and a knife under the pillow. I had made up my mind that I was going to see the divorce to the end and get on with my life, no matter how difficult things might seem.

Excerpt of an email I sent to my solicitor on Monday 16th July 2007

Around 10.40pm last night, Valerie unleashed a barrage of verbal assault aimed at me.

I had asked her how we were going to look after the kids over the six weeks of the summer holidays. She said that we should take three weeks each, to which I agreed, and said I would like to take the last three weeks of the holidays. She then said that during my part of the holidays, I should not take the kids to Esther's house (Esther has been a friend of the family for a very long time, since 1991 or so. We are also from the same town). She didn't want me taking my kids to her house because they live on an estate, and her kids are "hood rats" and would be a bad influence on the kids. Nkechi and Obinna are good friends with all four of her children and enjoy going there. I replied that what I did with the kids during the holidays was up to me, so long as I made sure they were safe at all times. She then said that she knows where Esther lives and would tell her about herself when she goes there. When I refused to respond to her, she started screaming and shouting at me. I told her to stop shouting; she then said that she would shout because she wanted everyone to hear her. She then said that she was going to get me arrested again by calling the police, and that the police were already onto me. She then said that she was going to call the police and tell them that I said if she went to Camberwell I was going to shoot her; something I did not say, and took great offence to. She then called my daughter, Nkechi, and said, "did you hear what your daddy said? He said he is going to shoot us if we go to Camberwell". Our daughter said that she did not hear anything and started crying, something that really upset me. I came downstairs to eat and also to tell my parents what had happened. She came down and told me she would not let me sleep. I went to get some clothes together in preparation in case she called the police and I got arrested.

After getting my divorce decree absolute in September 2007, I had to move onto the next battle; the fight for the custody of my two children. Valerie wanted to have a Sole Residence Order in respect of the children and wanted my contact with them to be defined. She also claimed that I had had little input in the children's upbringing and that my contact with them on separation should be reflective of this fact. She also stated that she knew I had a plan to remove the children from the country and take them to live permanently in Nigeria. CAFCASS had to get involved to ascertain who was telling the truth about how the kids were treated and looked after as our views and statement differed too much. Two CAFCASS officers interviewed Nkechi on her own at the house. After the interview, they came downstairs and spoke with both of us.

The hearing in respect of Valerie's application for custody of the children took place at Bromley County Court in October 2007. My barrister, Alison Easton, was very knowledgeable and was eager to ensure that justice was delivered. Some of my evidence that was presented at court included witness statements from all four child-minders we had used over the course of the children's upbringing. They literally all said the same thing about me. The CAFCASS report was also produced as evidence.

After a two-day trial, the judge ruled that we were to have joint custody of the children. The judge had seen through all the lies and deceit and made the right judgment. The fact that I would get to see the children regularly filled me with immense joy. I would continue to be the father and role model I aspired to be. I was extremely happy with the decision because some months earlier I had been given the opportunity to work in Nigeria as a consultant for a company called Socketworks Limited. I decided that if

I took the job and moved back to Nigeria, the country I had left in search of better pastures nearly two decades earlier, I would give up the right to my kids. I had made the decision to stay in the UK and fight for the custody of my children.

After the custody court case, my next battle was to prevent Valerie from taking all the assets, including the matrimonial home, and leaving me broke and homeless.

My barrister and I tried to convince Valerie to settle out of court and agree a rational decision as to how much she could afford to give me. She was not having any of it.

After over 90 minutes of deliberation, the female judge instructed Valerie to give me £60,000, which she reasoned would be enough for me to put a deposit down on a flat or something reasonable. I couldn't believe my ears when I heard the judgment. I don't think Valerie could either. She also gave me an absolute date by which I needed to move out of the house: 8th August 2008. That was the same day Valerie needed to pay me my £60,000. I could not wait.

Freedom
(2008–2009)

After leaving the court, I met up with Greg Abani and Mike Ndukwe to reflect. I really needed to; it had been a tortuous fifteen months, during which time I could have been killed. I was elated that it was all over. It had been a nightmare since 2001, but I was now free. I was happy that I would be able to be a father and role model to my kids. That was the most important thing in my life.

I finally vacated the house on deadline of the 8th August 2008. Once Valerie transferred the £60,000 into my account that she had been ordered to pay me so that I could start over, I left. I moved all my belongings into a storage facility and took a small suitcase to go and stay with my parents in Camberwell, South London. It was somewhat surreal, going back to live with my parents. However, as the saying goes, there's nowhere like home. I hadn't lived with my parents since moving back from university, when had I lived in my own ground floor flat in their house, so it was an odd feeling. I travelled to work from there each day; it was actually a lot easier getting to Moffat Health Centre in Kennington from Camberwell than it was from where I had lived with Valerie in Crofton Park. On the 9th August, I headed out to Berlin for a stag weekend for Jamie Okoro, a friend from YIBOSC. It was a much-needed break. However, the most important thing for me was that it was all over and I had not only survived, I had the rest of my life ahead of me.

At my parents' house, I slept on the floor in the living room on the first floor, waiting until everyone had gone to bed before retiring for the night – although my mum would always come in very late at night to talk to me about one thing or the other. I guess we used my time with my parents as a sort of catch-up period.

One Saturday night, I went to a work-related event in Brixton with a friend of mine called Charity and my younger sister – we had gone out to celebrate the success of my stop-smoking service. On the way home, we got jumped and mugged by two guys only a couple of minutes from my parents' house. They took us by surprise, jumping out from behind a brick partition while brandishing a knife. They demanded that I give them money. I had £150 on me which I had withdrawn from the cash machine in order to pay for our football club's activities the following day. I took out my wallet, retrieved £20, and threw it on the floor. I had no intention of giving them any more than that. The guy who appeared to be the leader picked it up and then demanded another £20 for his mate. I told him I was not giving them anymore. By this time, Charity, who I had told to keep walking, had managed to flag down a passing car and came to my rescue. The guys ran off into the darkness.

I was livid with rage. This had happened around the corner from where I lived. How dare they? I thought. When we got home, I walked Charity down the road to Camberwell Green so that she could get a taxi back home. On my way back, I decided to go looking for the two miscreants who had robbed me. I had an idea of where they would be. I searched the back streets that streaked off Coldharbour Lane, familiar with every nook and cranny from my years of growing up and living in the area. I eventually saw them, on Lilford Road, buying drugs. I had suspected they were druggies. I shouted out to them from the other side of the street. When they saw me they froze. I told them not to worry; I would get my money back from them some time in the future. When I got home, I did wonder why I had gone out to look for them, and the dangerous consequences I could have faced.

A couple of days later, while returning from the gym, I bumped into one of the muggers – the quieter one. He recognised me immediately, but before he could run off, I grabbed him by the waist of his trousers. He started pleading with me. Eventually I let go. I asked him why he was outside at night robbing people. He explained that his friend had convinced him to go out that night. He went on to explain that he was an 18-year-old Ghanaian student and lived with his aunty, who largely ignored him – he was left to fend for himself. He had a sad look in his eyes. When I asked him where he was off to, he said he needed to look for food to eat. I gave him £5 and told him to be careful with the company that he kept. I had thought of asking whether he played football so I could encourage him to join my football team, but I didn't – I don't know why.

While living with my parents, I still maintained my parental duties, which meant I had the kids every other weekend and for half of any school holidays. I also had to collect them on Tuesdays and Wednesdays from the child-minder. They would stay with me from around 6pm till 8pm, at which time I had to return them to Valerie. Most of the time, we would wander around Catford or Lewisham, house-hunting and reminiscing about how different life would be once we found a place to live. When I had them over at the weekends or during holidays, they would stay with me at my parents' house. They slept on the floor in sleeping bags, whilst I slept on the sofa. I felt sorry for them, as it wasn't their fault that things were rough for us. However, they seemed to enjoy it and saw it all as an adventure and a bit of fun.

One of my work colleagues, Yinka, had tried very hard to get me to meet a girl friend of hers. She must have felt sorry for me. She wanted to introduce me to a woman that she knew I would really like and get on with. When I asked her who this woman, was she gave me a name and told me to check her out on Facebook. A couple of days later, I went onto Facebook and had a look at the woman's profile and picture. After many days of procrastinating, I eventually made contact with Bonita Ikoku via Messenger. After that, we contacted each other every couple of days or so and eventually agreed a date and place to meet up in North London.

I was very nervous at the prospect of meeting Bonita for the first time. The meeting went well and we agreed we would meet again soon. Over the following weeks, we spoke with each other every day, usually at night. After a couple of months of meeting and talking, we formally entered into a relationship.

During the October 2008 half-term holiday, I had arranged to take my children to Spain for a short break. After confirming everything with Valerie, I booked and paid for the tickets. However, when the time came for us to go away, Valerie decided to spite me and refused to let me take the children. She had all their travel documents, so there wasn't much I could do. I couldn't get a refund for the booking either, so ended up losing nearly £700. I still went to Spain with Bonita and her children, and we had a great time, although I did feel sad at times as I knew Nkechi and Obinna would have enjoyed themselves too.

After several months of house-hunting, I eventually managed to find something that I liked and could afford. The children liked it too. In January 2009, I finally put a deposit down on the house and got a mortgage. The house was situated on a quiet street off the Bromley Road in South London. I fell in love with the house and the street immediately. The following day, I took my dad to see the house so I could get his opinion. He agreed that it was a lovely place too. Although it needed some minor work, it was good enough for me.

I was able to close the purchase quite quickly, and at a time of deepening recession and turbulence in the financial markets, it was a favourable time for me to get back on the property ladder. Just after I completed the purchase, house prices started to rise again. I was over the moon to be able to have a place to call my own. I was also happy for my kids, as I knew they would enjoy living in the area. I gradually began to move my belongings into my new house.

Unfortunately, my long-awaited joy was cut short a couple of days later as a series of events played out and threw my life into a chaotic spiral of anxiety and pain.

On Monday 2nd February 2009, it had been snowing for most of the night. Nkechi and Obinna had been with me over the weekend, and I was about to take them to school when I got a text message from Valerie explaining that the school was going to be closed that day due to the severe weather conditions and the difficulty people would have getting to school. The kids were happy that they didn't have to go to school, and I was happy that I didn't have to negotiate the slippery roads to try and get them there.

I played in the snow for a while with the kids until my

dad's long-time friend, Kalu Udu Orioha, paid my dad a visit. I have always enjoyed listening to his stories and discussions with my dad. They mainly talked about English and Nigerian politics, traditions and finances. They also always reminisced about the times when they were younger and lived in Nigeria. We all went into the house to warm up. I took Mr Orioha upstairs to the living room, where my dad was resting. After a couple of hours' discussion and debate, Mr Orioha decided to leave. I decided to see him off to Camberwell Green. On getting back, I went to the kitchen to prepare lunch for the kids. When I opened the oven door, an oven tray dropped out and fell on my left foot. I sustained a very small cut – so small I could hardly see it. A couple of hours later, I began to feel cold, and soon after that I was shivering uncontrollably as if I had contracted the flu. I presumed I was coming down with a cold or a bout of the flu, having exposed myself to the cold weather in the morning whilst playing in the snow. I decided to go to bed early and see if that would make me feel better.

I was woken up later by what felt like someone sitting on my leg. When I looked, my leg had swollen to almost twice its normal size; it was the throbbing that had woken me up.

The following day, after struggling to take the kids to school, I went home and stayed indoors on my sister's bed, wracked with pain. By Wednesday, I had to get Ugo to take me to the Accident and Emergency Department of King's College Hospital, which was only a short distance from my parents' house. After waiting for around three and a half hours, I was finally seen. I had my blood taken and was eventually given two different types of antibiotics, Amoxicillin and Penicillin, and sent home. I was told to go and see my GP in three days' time. I was unable to attend our siblings' dinner event that evening, which we had planned for Onyemachi, who was visiting from Los Angeles. Diligently, I stuck to my instructions, but my condition was deteriorating quickly – my foot got bigger and more painful than ever.

Friday the 6th February was quite comical. I was lying on the sofa in the sitting room enduring my pain, and Ugo was lying on the floor, also in terrible pain. We all thought she had food poisoning from the dinner two days before. Ugo was in so much pain that her screams were scaring me. Eventually, my mum had to call an ambulance. She and my mum were taken to King's College Hospital. My dad and I waited up most of the night, expecting them to come back home or to get news of her situation. No news came, and my mum had not taken her mobile phone with her so there was no way of finding out what was happening. My mum finally came back just after midnight. The news she had was shocking and left everyone speechless. Ugo had a cyst which had ruptured into her stomach, and this was the reason she had been in so much pain. She had just had an emergency operation. However, things had become even more serious after the operation; her organs had begun to shut down, and she was taken to the Intensive Care Unit. All of a sudden, my foot problem seemed minuscule. I began to think of all the things Ugo and I had done together. I thought of our last argument; the last time I had said no to her. I prayed to God that He would pull my sister through this very rough time. After getting some rest, my parents went back to the hospital to see how Ugo was doing. They came back late on Saturday night. Ugo was still in the ICU.

By Sunday, my own condition had become intolerable. I was in so much pain that tears were running down my face, although I was not actually crying. My brother decided it would be best if I went back to the hospital, so he called an ambulance, and once again I was taken back to King's College Hospital. They looked for my blood test results, but they were not yet back. When the consultant finally came to see me, he told me that he felt it was a case of skin blistering; a very serious case of skin blistering. He said he hadn't seen anything like it in his 21-year career. He took me into a room and proceeded to cut open the blister that was on my foot. He took a sample of the fluid and bandaged me up. I then had to wait in a wheelchair in the corridor of the hospital for three hours before finally being wheeled to the Lister ward. I had a feeling this was going to be a very long stay in hospital.

I couldn't sleep much that night, nor on subsequent nights, because the hospital lights were always on and there was just too much noise. I was put on three different intravenous antibiotics – benzyl penicillin, flucloxacillin and metronidazole – to try and cure the suspected infection. I was also put on chlorpheniramine, an antihistamine, to help with the itchiness in my leg. The antihistamine meant I spent a lot of time feeling drowsy. For the earlier part of my stay at the hospital, the days seemed to roll by without me realising. However, by 11th February, the fifth day of my stay, I began to feel a lot better. On that day, I woke up at 5.38am. Around 7.30am, a nurse came round and gave me my antibiotics, although they had been due around 6am. Around 9.15am, one of the junior doctors popped his head round the curtain, had a quick look at me, then said he'd be back with his boss soon. That meant in a few hours, if I was lucky.

Breakfast wasn't bad; two slices of cold toast with jam, washed down with water. I then had some moi moi my mum had brought me the previous evening. I needed to pass the time, so I did some reading. Then I had my lunch of fish, chips and beans, which I hadn't ordered. I was just about to have a nap when the suits (the name I gave the consultants, who usually came in the mornings) arrived. They obviously knew it all – that's why they spent a maximum of a minute looking you over and then decided what to do with you until they resurfaced again the following day. The junior doctor unwrapped my leg and the senior consultant had a good look and decided the antibiotics were working well. It was decided that I should be kept on them. The consultant explained that the bacteria

I had contracted could have come from anywhere and that the swelling provided a unique breeding place.

On the afternoon of the sixth day, my dad, my sister Onyemachi, and my niece Minelli came to see me. They all looked tired, and I understood why; there was so much going on. Having my sister in intensive care and me in the hospital too was taking its toll on everybody. I truly felt sorry for Onyemachi, who was in the UK on holiday and was having to spend her time running around looking after her sick siblings.

Later that day, a young boy who couldn't have been more than 15 or 16 was moved to my ward. He was a gunshot victim and had been in the ICU for a couple of days. When he was admitted to my ward, he came with armed police to guard him – I presume either to prevent a further attack or to prevent him from escaping.

On the seventh day, my mum paid her usual visit. She too looked very tired, and I felt sorry for her. I spoke to Olugh and told him to buy me some beef and beans, and some snacks; that's what I felt like eating that evening. When he finally arrived, the disappointment nearly knocked me off my bed. He did bring what I had asked for but instead of having the beans and beef in one container, they were in different containers, which meant I had to ask for a plate from the nurses. I hated asking them for anything. I did manage to eat my lunch from the two containers, after which I spoke with Bonita who lifted my mood a somewhat.

By the eighth day, I was missing home and the freedom of the great outdoors. After an early morning check-up, I was told I'd be going home soon, as long as progress with my recovery continued. Ugo was moved into a ward on the first floor, and I was able to visit her a few times that day, which cheered us both up. I think we were both just happy to still be alive, although we didn't talk about it.

Around 9pm, after reminiscing with Ugo for a while, I went upstairs to get hooked up with my drugs. This time, it was Sister Siobhan on the late-night shift. She was a reverend sister, and was quite lovely – cheerful, helpful and very professional, all in one. She was always checking on patients, asking whether they needed anything or just checking they were fine. Sister Siobhan told me to buzz her when my infusion ran out, which would be around 1.30am, so that she could give me a top up. When the time came, I buzzed her to get my refill – but to my horror, the nurse I had nicknamed "the bull" appeared, aggressive as usual. "What is it? Why are you buzzing so late in the night?" she demanded. I tried to explain as meekly as possible that I needed an additional dose of my medication. With a huff, the bull reluctantly hooked me up with my final dose for the night and waddled off into the ward. I had nicknamed her because of her attitude two nights before, when she had huffed and barked at all the patients whilst she was on the night shift. She had also nearly managed to rip my arm out of its socket when she tripped over my infusion.

By the tenth day, the hospital was beginning to feel like boarding school. Everything was so routine and dictated by the clock. Boarding school would have been a lot more fun, though. The fact that I couldn't walk around at all made it a very difficult stay for me. Around 10am, I heard the rowdiness of the suits approaching. Very soon, they appeared at the foot of my bed. The consultant picked up my folder, had a brief glance, then had a thorough look at my leg. After what seemed like eternity, he told me I wouldn't need an operation after all, but I did need another ultrasound to find out if there was still any pus in my leg.

Later that day, my dad came by as usual. He came in quietly and sat down on a chair facing my bed. He went through the normal routine of asking how I was, whether I had slept well, and whether I'd had my food. He looked like he had an awful lot on his mind, which was understandable, considering the circumstances. After a while, he got up quietly, said goodbye, and left.

On the eleventh day, Bonita came by. Her visits always brightened up my day and lifted my mood. She brought some delicious yam, beans and stew; I told her I would eat it in two parts just to make it last longer. She also brought me two books to read; Half of a Yellow Sun and Purple Hibiscus, both by the same author, Chimamanda Ngozi Adichie. We spent some time talking about all the things I had missed, programmes on TV, and other news. My mum came by briefly before everyone was ordered to leave, as it was way past visiting hours. Minelli also came by but was not allowed to stay.

On the afternoon of Friday 19th February, the thirteenth day, I was finally discharged. My happiness was difficult to conceal, although the day did have its drama. Very early in the morning, about 4am, the bull came over to hook me up to my infusion. She struggled to find any veins on my arm; unsurprisingly, they had all collapsed. I had been on intravenous antibiotics for nearly two weeks. Unhappy that she couldn't find any veins, she insisted on hooking me up, by hook or by crook. She stuck the needle into a swollen part of my arm, took a brief look at me, then waddled off. After the early morning handover of nursing staff, one of the nurses came over to make sure I was okay. He took one look at my arm and shouted, "who the hell put this needle in your arm?" Without waiting for an answer, he quickly took the needle out. He said that whoever had put the needle into my arm had risked giving me a very serious infection. I was just happy to be going home.

I thought being discharged from the hospital would be the end of my worries. I was wrong. When I got home, my problems began in earnest. I was discharged with a course of antibiotics, which I took for a couple of days. Just as I thought I would be getting ready to go back to work after such a long time off, my leg started to throb. When I took the bandage off my foot, there was a foul smell coming from it which engulfed the entire room. It was coming from one of the open sores on the instep of my left foot. I assumed it was just a minor infection which would soon disappear, especially as I was on antibiotics. I was very wrong. A couple of days later, the sore had doubled in size and the smell had become unbearable; everyone was worried. Eventually, when my antibiotics finished and I realised they were not helping with the smelly sore on my foot, I returned to hospital to raise my concerns. After hours of tests, they decided that the wound needed to be debrided. Debridement is the removal of unhealthy tissue from a wound to promote healing.

After debriding the sore, they covered it with some special ALLEVYN dressings, I was also given some extra packs to take home and shown how to change them. When I went back to the hospital four days later for a check-up, I was hardly able to walk. The consultants had worried looks on their faces. The lab results from the tests they had done on some of my debrided skin had returned. They gave me the bad news. I had contracted something very similar to necrotising fasciitis, a flesh-eating bacteria, and they were racing to save my left leg. All the intravenous antibiotics I'd had whilst in hospital had not killed off the bacteria. I was given a seven-day dose of 500mg Metronidazole and Clindamycin; I was also given a pump, which was connected to my waist and had a long tube that was fitted to cover my wound and suck up the pus into a reservoir, which I emptied every day. The machine made a farting-type noise and smelt foul. I had to take it everywhere with me. I also had a pair of crutches because I was unable to walk unaided. I felt totally handicapped.

I had to keep visiting the hospital to see the consultants, who would make some decisions on my progress, followed by a nurse, who would dress my wound. This went on for many weeks, with little or no improvement; the infection lingered. In between these demoralising hospital visits, I had to go back to work and also look after my children on my allocated days. It was a very tough and low time for me, but I willed myself to keep going, no matter what. I hated the fact that my children had to see me so incapacitated, weak, and unable to do much with them. However, I had made up my mind that I would get better so that we could continue to have fun together and I could continue to be a good role model for them.

I still had to visit the new house, and Bonita was very helpful in chauffeuring me back and forth and unpacking my things. I do not think I would have managed during that difficult time without her assistance. As the weeks ticked by, the infection gradually disappeared, leaving a huge scar on my foot. The consultant considered doing a skin graft to replace the skin there. The infection had damaged some of the nerves in my foot, which meant I had lost quite a bit of movement in it. It would take time for the nerves to grow back, if they ever did. I was glad my ordeal appeared to be finally over – it had cost me nearly three months of my life. I was finally able to make arrangements to move into my new home, settle down with my kids, and focus on rebuilding our lives.

In May 2009, my brother and Bonita helped with the final move into my new house, four months after I had originally bought the place. The kids were excited, which was to be expected; we had spent months house-hunting, and they'd had their ideas of what type of house they wanted me to buy. I had done my best to accommodate their requests.

I had saved some money to buy some furniture, but a friend had asked me to lend him £3,000, which was essentially the amount I had saved. I had known him since we were kids, and he had always worked and invested money in a lot of different investment schemes. I therefore had no doubts that he would give me the money back. Seven months after lending him the money, I hadn't managed to get it back. In fact, whilst I was in hospital, I called his wife and found out that I was just one of a long list of family and friends who had been swindled out of money to feed his gambling addiction. I'd had no idea he gambled.

I was furious, because he had initially asked me to lend him £10,000. I wouldn't have gotten that back either, and it would have prevented me from buying my house. I had actually considered making the loan, but had told my mum, who advised me against lending such a huge amount of money to anyone without any collateral. When I next saw him and started giving him an excuse as why I couldn't lend him the money, he quickly changed his approach, telling me he had managed to get most of the money he needed from his savings and only needed £3,000. I didn't hesitate. I never did get my money back, so I had to start from scratch to save for all my household items. In the meantime, my kids and I had to sleep on the floor of the house because I could not afford to buy a bed for them.

This lack of money was further magnified by the fact that I had put my name down as a guarantor for another so-called friend, Sunny Ikwor Ejah Nnachi, who needed to take out a loan to get married in Nigeria. He was working; he actually had two jobs, so he had no problem paying off the loan in the allocated time. Things went sour for him and he simply disappeared off the face of the earth. By the time the loan company contacted me to pay off the loan, it had accumulated a lot of interest, and the total amount owed was over £5,000. Sunny eventually did contact me and apologised for his absence. He had been incarcerated. He promised to pay me back very soon. He eventually relocated to America and refused to pay me back the money he owed. Needless to say, I learnt my lesson about lending money to people; I vowed I would never lend money to anyone again. After a while, I managed to save some money, and eventually we did buy all the things the house needed. The kids and I settled in, and we began to look forward to our life ahead.

Moving Up
(2009–2019)

The complex interlacing of CANUK, work and personal life

During my time at Lambeth PCT as a project manager, I had established and managed the borough's stop-smoking service, which went on to gain national acclaim for its innovation and good outcomes. It was the best stop-smoking service in London in 2009, and the service met its government-set target for the first time. This was something that, back in 2003, I had pledged that I would do.

In order to take a more innovative approach to the way the service operated and create some ground-breaking methods, I started working with private sector organisations like Dr Foster Intelligence, with whom we used mosaic segmentation to carry out social marketing campaigns – the first of their kind in the UK. I also joined forces with an organisation called One Deep Breath; we worked with the famous Choice FM DJ, Daddy Ernie, to target people from Black and Asian Minority Ethnic groups and support them to give up smoking. We also worked with Her Majesty's Prison Brixton to support prisoners give up smoking.

Having spent seven years at Lambeth PCT and achieved everything I possible could, I decided it was time to move on. I did try to stay within the organisation, but this proved impossible, especially after I was not offered a job I was expected to get. I had spent three months working temporarily in the role of locality manager, and the person who had left the role briefed me on any gaps in experience I had, but I was not even invited for an interview for the job. When I asked for feedback, it was refused. My manager at the time advised me it was time to look for a job outside of Lambeth PCT. He pointed to the fact that a king is not always recognised in his own country.

Baby mama drama

In June 2009, I was offered a new job with Greenwich PCT. It was a good time for me to move on. I decided to take a holiday to Nigeria to regain my energy, prepare for my new job, and help my parents with some family business. I thought it would also be a good idea to take the kids with me, knowing they'd enjoy the trip – especially Obinna, who still hadn't been to Nigeria. I couldn't have predicted the sequence of events that unfolded during the process. It came as a total shock to me when, with just four weeks to go before our trip, I received a court order explaining that I could not take my children outside of the jurisdiction of the UK. It also stated that Valerie feared I was going to abduct my children and never come back to the UK.

I was summoned to court, again. I had to see if I could take the children on a holiday that we had already agreed they could take. This time, I had barrister Nicholas Baker prepare my case, which was to be heard at the Royal Courts of Justice at the Strand on the 8th and 25th of June 2009. My appeal to take my children on holiday to their country of origin was eventually refused on the basis that Nigeria is a non-Hague Convention country. The judge said he didn't believe I was not planning to return with my children to the UK, but he was still mindful of the fact that if for whatever reason I decided not to return, Valerie would struggle to get them back.

Once again, I had already booked and paid for our flights. I was fortunate to get most of the money back from the booking agent. I did, however, have to fork out more than £5,000 for the court case, which left me penniless yet again. After the court case, Mr Baker advised me to keep my distance from Valerie. My former barrister, Alison Easton, had given me the same advice. They both said I should always communicate with her by email in order to have an audit trail.

Whilst in Nigeria, I was able to reflect on my life and plan for the future. I believed that I was very fortunate to still be around, and that there was a reason for that. Whatever the reason was, I was going to snatch the opportunity and forge ahead with my life. I was going to prove to myself that giving up wasn't an option, and I would continue to push myself to be a better person. My children gave me so much hope, inspiration and joy – I knew I had to be a good dad for them. They deserved it. I promised myself

I'd be there for them at all times until I grew old – then they could look after me. I took the entire episode as a stepping stone that would take me higher, and to better things.

Obligation to do the right thing

When I came back from Nigeria in October 2009, I started my new job at Greenwich PCT. It was a new role, so I had the opportunity to mould it to my own vision. Full of energy and enthusiasm, I got stuck in and made a good impression very early on.

Earlier in the year, Bonita had asked me why I had never bothered to try to get back on the pharmacy register. I told her I'd lost interest in the profession, and in any case, I had been put off by my experience with Boots and was actually doing very well in my alternative career in the NHS. She, however, persevered and encouraged me to try and get my name back on the register. Using the impetus of my newfound energy and enthusiasm, I contacted the Fitness to Practise committee of the General Pharmaceutical Council to find out what the procedure was to have my name restored to the register. It turned out to be a very onerous process, but I decided I would follow it through to the very end. At least I could feel content in the fact that I had tried my best. I obtained written references from two notable pharmacists who testified to my fitness to practise. I also obtained as much evidence as I could to support my application. I submitted my application and waited for a response.

Whilst I was waiting for the General Pharmaceutical Council to get back to me, I decided to get more involved in the affairs of the Nigerian community. I made a concerted effort to take my voluntary community and leadership work to another level. Dr Mark Abani, who was the chairman of the Central Association of Nigerians in the United Kingdom (CANUK) at the time, had been encouraging me to get much more involved with the organisation. I felt the time was right.

CANUK had been set up in 2005 by the then Nigerian high commissioner to the UK, His Excellency, Dr Christopher Kolade. It was established in the wake of the July 2005 London bombing, when the Nigerian High Commission realised there was no coordinated way of contacting Nigerian organisations to establish whether any Nigerians had been affected by the atrocities. CANUK, as an umbrella organisation, would serve that purpose. I had served on the social committee of CANUK between 2006 and 2008, in my capacity as the manager of the London Nigerian Football Club. I had helped organise the Nigerian family fun days with people like Mrs June Douglas and Fola Odetoyinbo of the London Nigerian Rugby Club.

As the tenure of the founding members was coming to an end, it seemed like the perfect time to join the new incoming executive team. It would provide me with an opportunity to work more closely with the Nigerian community. As the nomination period approached, Ebonyi State Union UK opted to put the previous president of the Union, Ochiora Mike Ndukwe, forward for a position on the CANUK executive council. However, at one of the Union's monthly meetings, where a final decision was to be made, Mike Ndukwe was unable to attend. That was my opportunity. The members decided to nominate me, especially because I had worked closely with Dr Abani both at the Union and at CANUK. I decided to run for the position of first vice chairman of CANUK. I wasn't sure who I was up against, or how many people, at the time, nor did I have any indication as to whether I would win or not.

It was whilst I was waiting for the CANUK executive nomination list to be published that the Fitness to Practise committee contacted me. They had set the date of the restoration hearing as the 24th May 2010. I travelled to their headquarters for the hearing, where they considered a range of factors. After about three hours of deliberation and cross-examination, the committee granted my application to have my name restored to the register – nine and a half years after it had been removed. My name was restored to the register on the condition that I completed 100 hours working in a pharmacy and gained experience of advanced pharmacy services. At this point, I really knew that I was going to surge forward and climb some of my highest mountains, just as I had dreamed. A huge cloud had been lifted. I had decided, though, that I wasn't going back to work in community pharmacy. I preferred to stay in the NHS because it provided me with a great work/life balance, which I knew community pharmacy couldn't offer.

Eventually, when the CANUK nomination list was published, around August 2010, I found out that there was one other candidate for the position of first vice chairman; Mr Toyin Ibrahim-Igbo. He was the incumbent second vice chairman of CANUK, and a friend. I had my work cut out; being an incumbent member of the executive council, he had an advantage. With the elections due to take place in November 2010, I set up a strong campaign team and hit the campaign trail, vowing to give it my all. The election results were released on 10th December, but before they were made public I received a telephone call from a member of the electoral committee congratulating me on my success. I had won, and it was a landslide victory. I would be the new first vice chairman of CANUK. I was over the moon. At the 2011 CANUK Annual General Meeting, before the founding CANUK executive council handed over power and the new executive team were sworn in, I was awarded a certificate of merit by the outgoing CANUK executive. This was for the ambassadorial role I had played for CANUK over the years and behind the scenes, raising the profile of Nigerians in the UK.

I served the Nigerian community for four years, with other good and well-meaning patriotic Nigerians like Chief Bimbo Folayan, Dr Biodun Fakokunde, Remi Ayela, Yusuf Tokan and June Douglas, to name but a few. Under the leadership of the newly elected chairman, Chief Bimbo Folayan, CANUK expanded its remit and engaged with Nigerians across the country. Immediately after I was sworn in, I resigned my position as player manager of the London Nigerian Football Club. I felt I was unable to give the team the undivided attention that I had dedicated to it over the past eleven years.

During my two terms of office in CANUK, I was so dedicated to enhancing the organisation and developing the Nigerian community that I was given the additional roles of head of projects, registration secretary, and deputy secretary. I tried to use these roles to sew the different Nigerian organisations together and to encourage them to participate in Nigerian events and projects. Eventually, most organisations started to engage, including those that were sceptical of the Nigerian High Commission.

However, my life just never seemed to settle long enough for me to enjoy it before something troubling came along. Whilst I was enjoying my role in CANUK, my work life started to get challenging. My manager who I'd originally had a good relationship with, began to challenge some areas of my work, and sometimes my overall approach to certain projects. The growing tension in our relationship came to a head in May 2011. This was immediately after I had formed a private healthcare company, Consult

Health Ltd. I was due to due a presentation at Olympia, London on how to improve outcomes of prevention, using diabetes as an example – a successful project I had worked on with GP practices. My name had been published on the conference organiser's website and I was listed as director of Consult Health. My manager called me into an emergency meeting to get more detail about the company and what it did. When I told her that the company was dormant and not conducting any business, she did not believe me, so she ordered an investigation. Following the investigation, she decided there was enough evidence for me to face a disciplinary panel for misconduct.

She alleged that I had formed the company without getting her formal approval to do so and that I had tried to use the NHS as a platform to promote my company. I didn't take the allegations lightly. In preparation for my disciplinary hearing I countered her allegations, with evidence. Consult Health was listed as a dormant company as I had not completed the business plan for the company and had merely registered the name with Companies House to avoid losing the name. This meant it was not doing any business at the time. To further support my case, I explained that although she was my manager, I hardly got to spend any time with her, as she worked from home three days a week and was only in London on Tuesdays and Wednesdays. With hindsight, I could have informed her about the business by email, but I had wanted to tell her during my one-to-one session with her. In the event, she found out before the session. I explained that I had not kept the information about Consult Health a secret – far from it; I had informed all my work colleagues because I was quite excited to have my own private venture.

Most of my colleagues thought it was quite harsh of my manager to pursue a disciplinary, as quite a few of them had their own private businesses and even charged the NHS for work carried out outside working hours or for separate work undertaken by their companies.

In the lead-up to the hearing, my manager and I tried to be as professional as possible; it helped that she was hardly in the office. I knew the disciplinary procedure would be a difficult time, so I asked my good friend, Greg Abani, to accompany me for moral support. I was glad he was able to attend and help me through the very challenging process. The panel consisted of our director, Dr Hilary, who was a good personal friend of my manager, and someone from the human resources department. I had asked if I could also bring a representative from the union as an observer, but this request was turned down. Greg and I decided we were going to record the proceedings on our phones, without the panel's knowledge.

On arrival at the venue, I began to feel scared. Our director was such a busy person that it was very difficult to get a five-minute meeting with her, but here she was, dedicating an entire day to this disciplinary hearing. We set our phones recording before we went in and put them on the table. As we were about to begin, Hilary asked us to give the panel five minutes, so we left the room, leaving our phones where they were. After about ten minutes, we were all called back in and the proceedings got under way. They lasted the entire day.

The outcome was that I was given a final written warning, which would stay on my file for 18 months. My manager was advised to schedule regular supervisory meetings with me to ensure she was kept up to date with all the projects I was working on. She was also expected to attend training to support supervision of staff. She was not happy.

I wasn't happy with the outcome either, but I was relieved to still have my job. I felt some remorse, and I understood how the whole affair could look to an outsider – especially when our director, in her summing up, explained how bad the whole situation could have turned out if she had been approached by any of her peers and asked about my company. She would have been unable to answer, which would have made her look very silly and unprofessional.

After we left the building, Greg and I went for a beer to calm our nerves and mull over the day.

As I was now able to get on with my life unperturbed, I thought it was time to have a second chance at marriage. I always knew I would remarry. My marriage to Valerie had been a sham, and I knew marriage had a lot more to offer than I had experienced so far. On 29th December 2011, Bonita's birthday, I took her to dinner at a lovely Mediterranean restaurant in North London. Just as I was about to propose, a man who was having dinner with his partner had an epileptic fit. I had to go across and help to make sure he was okay. When the episode was over, I waited for the right moment and proposed to Bonita. It was an entirely surreal moment. She was speechless and emotional, and so was I. When I told my parents, they were happy for me.

During one of the weekends that my kids were staying with me, I sat them both down and explained that I was going to get married to Aunty Bonita, as they called her. They were enthused by the news, which was great for me. They had become quite fond of Bonita. On most of the weekends when they were with me, we would travel up to Islington, where she lived and spend time there, usually going back to South London on Sunday evening in readiness for school the following day.

An achievement

With the London 2012 Olympics on the horizon, the capital was buzzing with activity, new developments and the promise of great things to come – from the competing athletes, from organisations and companies in London, and from individuals. As head of projects for CANUK, I believed the Olympics presented a great chance for the organisation to showcase its ability to unite Nigerians in the UK. After spending a couple of hours brainstorming ideas with Dr Mark Abani at my house on a cold day in December 2011, we came up with a plan of ideas to launch CANUK into the limelight. I put together a 2012 Olympic proposal for the executive committee to consider; it included a series of events and workshops involving Nigerians, both in London and across the rest of the country. The proposal was eventually signed off by the executive. I successfully apply for the London 2012 Inspire mark. The Inspire programme was a national programme established to recognise outstanding non-commercial projects genuinely inspired by the London 2012 Games. The Inspire mark acted as a promotional tool and enabled the CANUK projects to connect with the Games and reach out to new audiences.

From January 2012, I spent my time planning the CANUK Olympic projects; I hardly had any time for my family as I went from one meeting to the other after work, meeting anyone who was half-interested in taking part. Things took a very positive turn when I received a call from Engineer Sani Ndanusa, the president of the Nigeria Olympic Committee. Dr Abani had given him my details during a chance encounter on a flight to Nigeria. He wanted Team Nigeria to work with CANUK to deliver some of its Nigeria Olympic Committee projects.

When the Olympics finally arrived, CANUK managed to successfully deliver a couple of the planned projects. The most high-profile of all the projects was the renowned Team Nigeria community reception dinner, which took place on Sunday 8th July at a venue in North London. It was a reception hosted to gather the Nigerian community in the UK together to wish Team Nigeria good luck in their endeavours and encourage the athletes to do well at the Games.

The main newspaper caption (in Nigerian Watch and Nigerian Voice) read: Nollywood superstars Olu Jacobs and Justus Esiri are leading other colleagues to welcome Nigeria's team to London 2012 Olympics as Nigeria gets set to stun the world with promises of more medals than has ever happened in Olympic history. Also at the centre-stage of the night of sports and entertainment skill empowerment is the Nigeria Bank of Industry with a strong team of business and economic planning executives racing higher in its continued effort to put Nigeria on the spotlight of investment attraction to the other world.

It was attended by Nigerian government officials, sports personalities and celebrities. The Nigerian high commissioner to the UK, Dr Sarki Dalhatu Tafida OFR, CFR, led a strong team from the embassy as special guest of honour. The Nigerian federal minister of sports, Mallam Bolaji Abdullahi, and the chief host, the president of the Nigeria Olympic Committee, Engineer Sani Ndanusa, were all at the centre of the empowerment speeches that took place that evening. It was a great success for CA-NUK, for the Nigerian community in the UK, and for me as the main organiser and coordinator.

Unfortunately, Team Nigeria was unable to win any medals at the Games, which was a huge disappointment for Nigerians living in the UK who had gone the extra mile to support the team. The Nigerian Paralympic team, on the other hand, amassed a haul of medals and were handsomely rewarded for redeeming the honour of Nigeria.

I was very relieved to see the back of the Olympic planning. Unknown to my CANUK colleagues and a lot of other people, at the same time, my fiancée and I were also planning our wedding, which was scheduled to take place on Saturday 14th July, six days after the Olympic reception dinner – so I was under a huge amount of pressure.

When the big day finally came, I wasn't nervous about getting married, although I was quite anxious about the smooth running of the day itself. The anxiety was, however, overshadowed by extreme excitement. We had agreed we were not going to have a very large wedding and would try to keep it reasonably modest, only inviting family and close friends. About 120 people attended the reception, which took place in Beckenham, South London. The weather was on our side – it was a gorgeous day. My best man was my good friend, Greg, and he put in a lot of effort to make sure everything was on time and went according to plan. It was great to be surrounded by good friends and family on such a great day. I was glad I had decided to give marriage another try. I was quite emotional, although I tried not to show it. I was happy for Nkechi and Obinna, as they were pleased to see me so happy. Our wedding website captured how we felt about each other. It said: Whatever are souls are made of, yours and mine are the same.

About Us

About me

Popularly known as Mr C, a free spirit, with a constant smile, I like to make sure everyone around me is content and happy. My 2 kids, soon to be 5 are my cod liver oil that keep me young and energetic. I have 3 younger loving siblings, who are also my good and candid friends. I am a dedicated and focused individual, motivated by love, passion, values and beliefs. My lovely lady, Uzoma, has been a joy since day 1; Uzoma has brought me content, joy and love too. Thanks darling! Gotta thank Yinka, Facebook and Yahoo messenger for your covert assistance.

About Chima

The first day I spoke to Mr C ..,I knew ..This guy is mine! We spoke for hours ! He's gentle , loving, attentive , hardworking , caring and intelligent. He is my friend and since we have been together, life has been wonderful in good times and bad.... I hope it's stays that way for eternity...He truly is a wonderful person! Love you C xxx Oh and thanks Yinx!

About me

I am the oldest in my family. A typical Capricorn! I have two beautiful kids soon to become 5! I love to have fun, to be happy, free spirited, loyal and love being around my family and kids. I do have my serious side although a bit too serious sometimes ;). I am a late starter but I always get the best of what I wanted in the end..... Mr C ..I promise you , life will never be boring..we will enjoy what we have with our family with God on our side always..

About Uzoma

Uzoma is a wonderful , sensitive and caring woman who always puts other people before herself.She has a great sense of family and family values and tends to share that with people who are also close to her.Apart from being all the above. Bonita is also a friend and soul mate who makes my heart flutter all the time.

How we met.....(Bonita's story)

We met through a good friend of mine Yinka...who insisted that he would be perfect for me , Thanks to face book! Once Mr C saw me , he just could not resist! Could you C? lol.. The rest is history and so much has happened...good things mind you...

The proposal

On my birthday! 29th December 2011 at a lovely Meditarrenean restaurant on Exmouth Street...I was speechless and so emotional

Being married seemed to bring some stability and focus into my life. At the same time, it was quite humbling; I had been single for quite a long time and had become used to doing most things the way I wanted, so this was a huge change for me. I had thought deeply about the type of relationship I would have with my stepchildren. I really hoped they would not see me as an invasion, as they were used to having the undivided attention of their mum. I also made sure that being married did not slow down my community work, and Bonita encouraged me to work hard and try and give back to the community.

Less than two weeks after the wedding, my work life took a turn for the worse again. My manager accused me of making an error of judgement during a pharmacy procurement exercise we had both been involved in a couple of months earlier. She said that I have given out commercially sensitive information to one of the unsuccessful bidders of the service and reported me to the deputy director, who immediately ordered an investigation into the matter. I felt a sense of déjà vu. In August 2012, I was invited for a formal investigation meeting with the deputy director and someone from HR. I was questioned for over an hour on the events leading up to, during, and after the procurement exercise. I explained that after the exercise, one of the unsuccessful bidders had called me and asked what the value of the contract was. I had told them that the contract value was something in the range of £60,000. Having carried out numerous procurements, I knew I was allowed to give them a value range.

During the meeting, I explained that I wanted it to be noted that I felt the allegations made by my manager were malicious. I explained that ever since I had left Lambeth PCT in 2009 with a hugely successful and impressive track record and had joined NHS Greenwich, my career had been subject to malicious assassination attempts. I also told them that the very first error in the procurement exercise was committed by my manager; as the lead for the process, she had failed to identify a very serious con-flict of interest for one of the interview panel members. This gross oversight had landed our team in trouble with the local pharmaceutical committee, who were unhappy that the conflict had not been detected earlier and de-clared. I went on to say that I was happy for the investi-gation to take place, as long as they also took these events into account. This would have far-reaching consequences for my line manager.

Later on that month, as I was driving to Walthamstow, East London, for the burial of a good friend, Andrew Nwachukwu, the deputy director called me. He had called to explain that following his investigation, he had decided against a referral to a formal disciplinary hear-ing. The news came as a relief. If it had gone to a dis-ciplinary hearing, I would most likely had lost my job, as I was already on a final warning notice. It would not have been a great start to married life, and the situation was a stark and scary reminder of a similar set of events immediately after my first marriage in 1999. I put it all behind me, drew courage and belief from my inner soul, and soldiered on. The obstacles that kept getting in my way would only make me more resilient and determined to win my battles and build myself into the person I want-ed to be.

On the 6th October 2012, our daughter Obiageli Dan-iella Agbogho was born. Her arrival brought huge joy to both us. It was her siblings who chose Daniella as one of her names.

Other achievements

In 2013, as I continued to work very hard with the Nigerian community through CANUK, I was rewarded for my efforts in community work – the Nigerian UK-Based Achiever's Award (NUBAA) organisers recognised me with an award for my commitment and contributions to the Nigerian community in the UK. I was pleased to get the award of appreciation, although I told the organisers and the audience that my work was a way of me trying to make a change in society. A little later that year, the diabetes prevention project I had worked on and given many presentations for was shortlisted for a Health Service Journal award. Although the project didn't win, it was uplifting that it had been shortlisted and recognised for its good work.

Late in 2013, I started planning for the 2014 CANUK family fun day, which has always been the pinnacle event of the organisation. As it was going to be the last one during my term, I decided to give it my all. It was scheduled to take place on the 24th August 2014 in Catford, South London. I established and led a formidable 30-man project team, made up mainly of well-known community leaders, young up-and-coming leaders, and people who had a track record of delivery. The project team met up every three weeks between November 2013 and the 23rd August 2014. Most of those involved were dedicated to the project and gave it their all to ensure it succeeded. Having previously successfully delivered the 2012 Olympics reception dinner, I was under some pressure to ensure the event went well.

The event was a huge success and was very well-attended. Once again, the high commissioner, Dr Dalhatu Tafida, led a big delegation from the Nigerian High Commission to the event. A lot of non-Nigerians also attended, which I had been keen to ensure happened. This would help CANUK showcase itself to the outside world. It was also proof that I could attract an audience – and not just a Nigerian audience. I also handled the project budget very diligently, despite the competition for funds from other projects.

The coordination and project management of the Nigeria family fun day took its toll on me, so after completing the evaluation of the project I decided to take time out from serving my community. I took a two-week break and avoided all emails and most telephone calls.

One day, whilst I was at home resting, I received a telephone call. I did not want to answer it, but something told me I should. The call was from the Royal Pharmaceutical Society (RPS). I had been shortlisted for the Public Health Pharmacist of the Year Award, and they had not received a response to an earlier email they had sent some weeks ago. The awards programme celebrates and

acknowledges the achievements of teams and individuals within the pharmacy profession. The awards also recognise and reward excellence and innovation in pharmacy and those setting the highest standards.

I apologised and explained that I would check my emails and respond. When I checked my emails, there was an invitation to the awards ceremony, which was scheduled to take place on the 7th September 2014 as part of the RPS annual conference dinner at the National Exhibition Centre (NEC) in Birmingham.

After a lot of thought, I decided not to attend. The awards were on a Sunday evening, in Birmingham; although I was happy to have been shortlisted, I thought it was unlikely that I would win, and I would have to stay over, which meant getting an early train back to London to get to work. It was all too much for me. However, my wife convinced me to acknowledge the invitation and attend, so I booked my train ticket. I left on Sunday afternoon and was met at the station by one of my brothers-in-law, Charles. We went to his house to relax a little before he dropped me off at the NEC.

Receiving my Public Health Pharmacist of the Year 2014 Award

To my utter surprise, that Sunday evening I won the RPS Public Health Pharmacist of the Year 2014 Award. It was presented to me by David Allen, chief executive of the Faculty of Public Health. I won the award for my work in the area of cardiovascular disease and the extension of the provision of NHS Health Checks in local pharmacies. I was gobsmacked, elated, over the moon and filled with emotion. From being removed from the pharmacy register by the pharmacy regulators, to nearly losing my job at Greenwich over the procurement process of a project, to winning an honourable award from the RPS was simply a moment in my life that made me proud of myself. I wished my grandma had been alive to witness this huge achievement. I was proving I could be successful, and I was starting to enjoy the acknowledgement for my hard work.

The following day, on the way into work from Birmingham, I sent a message to my manager and explained my good news. She informed our director that I had won a prestigious award. When I got to work, a couple of people in the office came over to congratulate me. One of the runners-up had called a colleague to find out more about me, and that was how the news had gradually spread. Our department had staff briefings every two weeks, and this was where any news was announced or brought to the attention of the directorate. My award win never did feature in any of the briefings.

It took me a couple of weeks for the euphoria to settle.

It also took me just about the same amount of time to realise that it was time for me to look for a new job. I felt unappreciated by many members of my senior team, and the awards situation simply heightened my awareness of how I felt. I knew I had to end my flustered affair with Greenwich.

The CANUK saga

Whilst I was on top of the world, still brimming with my newfound success and eminent status, a major issue had started to develop in CANUK. Unknown to many people at the time, the growing issue was going to cause huge and acrimonious divisions within the Nigerian community. It also led to many friends falling out. It was also an enormous test of certain people's tempers. I definitely had to lean heavily on my morals, integrity and desire to always do the right thing.

In early October 2014, the CANUK executives began to prepare for the 2015 Annual General Meeting and main elections. Some people had assumed that, as first vice chairman and a man with a lot of experience working within CANUK, I would challenge for the position of chairman. They knew that I commanded a lot of respect from Nigerian community leaders and had the integrity and leadership qualities required to take the organisation to the next level. Some members of the Nigerian community had asked for the constitution to be reviewed to enable executive members to serve more than the mandatory two consecutive terms allowed. Although it was a sensible request, the CANUK executive felt that an extensive review of the constitution was needed and that this was not something the current executive could commit to, especially in light of the forthcoming elections. Additionally, the change would have benefited many serving executives, including myself, which we all felt was morally wrong. At one of our executive meetings, we decided it wouldn't be in the best interest of the Nigerian community to amend the constitution at this late stage of our tenure, so we all voted against it.

There were obvious early signs that the journey to the 2015 CANUK elections was going to be difficult and convoluted. Mr Babatunde Loye, who had been co-opted into the executive to serve as assistant social secretary, harboured ambitions of taking over from Chief Bimbo Folayan as the chairman. When it became obvious that I was not going to contest the position of chairman, he began to approach numerous influential people within the Nigerian community, including some members of the executive, asking for their support and backing.

When he approached me, I explained that I didn't believe he had enough experience or had quite perfected the qualities needed to lead an organisation like CANUK. Therefore I was not in a position to give my support. Some other members of the executive felt the same way and did not offer their backing. What then followed, up to the day of the elections and beyond, was a game of wits, coercion and political strategy.

A well-orchestrated process that undermined most of the serving executive and flouted CANUK's electoral processes and regulations commenced. One of the first things the assistant social secretary did was to set up a shadow CANUK executive with himself as the chairman. The plan was that members of the shadow executive would support each other during the election period and would get their own supporters to support their fellow members. They held regular meetings in central London as they planned their campaign process. Unknown to the main organisers, the details of most of these meetings were fed back to me and the chairman.

Around November 2014, the plans started to become more unethical and aggressive and were in no small way connected to the ramped-up tactics used by the co-opted treasurer, Peters Osawaru Omoragbon. Some members of the executive felt betrayed, as we had supported the process to co-opt these two individuals. I had specifically carried out a mini interview-type process to shortlist and eventually appoint Peters to the position of treasurer.

After setting up their shadow executive, Babatunde and Peters proceeded to send in new applications of mainly non-operational organisations that were interested in registering with CANUK. The aim was to inflate the size of the electorate so that the people registered would be eligible to vote for them when the 2015 elections commenced. As I was the registration secretary of CANUK, these application requests mainly came to me from Peters or Babatunde. During my time as registration secretary, I had spent a great amount of time developing and implementing a robust and systematic method of registration for interested organisations. The correct method of applying for registration was to complete an application form and send it to me. I would verify the authenticity of the organisation through a variety of checks, including making some telephone calls, speaking to people, checking the internet etc. before making a recommendation for registration. After this, if my recommendation was passed by the executive, I would notify the organisation and ask them to pay their registration and delegate fees. On several occasions this system was circumvented or flouted. On several occasions, registration monies had been collected from organisations without following the due process set out for registration. In December 2014, I had so many organisations asking to register with CANUK that I had no option other than to highlight my concerns to the executive team.

At our January 2015 executive meeting, following the registration concerns I had raised, the executive instructed me to carry out a thorough due diligence process with all organisations that had expressed an interest to register with CANUK in the three months prior to December 2014. It was also agreed that organisations that had registered after the 31st December 2014 would not be eligible to take part in the 2015 elections. Furthermore, I had a very frank discussion with both Peters and Babatunde, where I explained that I knew what they were trying to do and would make sure their plans did not succeed. I told them that their strategy of setting up a shadow executive was flawed and would bring discontent within CANUK member organisations, as it would be viewed as campaigning at a time when the commencement of the electoral process had not formally taken place (it had be signalled by the electoral committee, which had not yet been established by the CANUK executive). I also explained that the setting-up of a shadow committee would incur problems for the new CANUK executive, as not all members of the shadow team were going to win their respective elections; this would result in the creation of two teams within a team.

The CANUK executive team gave me 28 days to carry out the due diligence exercise, which I managed to complete. When I fed back my findings to the executive, I explained that I had a gut feeling that some of the organisations were either non-existent or were simply one-man enterprises. However, this was very difficult to prove, as when I contacted the so-called organisations, they had already been primed and knew what answers to give. I was hassled throughout the 28-day process – steps were taken to confuse me, throw me off my guard and even intimidate and threaten me. I received a constant barrage of rude and belligerent emails about my approach. These would be followed up with phone calls in which those involved pretended to pacify me. I didn't fall for any tricks. I was very concerned for the Nigerian community, as I sensed they were on the verge of inheriting some charlatans for leaders.

The politics and games continued in the run-up to the elections. Some members of the shadow executive were disqualified for various reasons. On my part, in order to try and disrupt their plans to seize power at all costs, and out of frustration at their antagonistic and fraudulent methods, I actively campaigned against some members of the shadow executive. Heated and abusive emails were exchanged on a daily basis, full of accusations, counter-claims and threats. I was, however, determined not to waver; in fact, I just became more diligent and resolute in my work to ensure due process was followed.

The elections of all executive positions except that of the chair were conducted electronically a few weeks before the May 2015 AGM and the election of the chair. The overall results of the electronic elections were bittersweet. In the fight for the position of general secretary, Peters lost to Dr Coker. That was a great relief for me and other members of the Nigerian community. Some disgruntled members disputed the outcome for the position of general secretary and appealed the decision. The denunciations were looked at, investigated, and duly dismissed for lack of evidence and substance. Some of us had tried very hard to preserve the image of CANUK, and at a great cost.

It is needless to state that many individuals were revealed as wolves in sheep's' clothing; covers were totally blown, and gloves had come off. After the election results, I received numerous tirades of foul-mouthed, ignorant and shameless emails. There were also emails threatening blackmail and insults. I found it extraordinary that individuals who wanted to lead the Nigerian community in the UK could display such behaviour. However, this was just a glimpse into the chaos that was about to be unleashed on the unsuspecting Nigerian community in the UK.

Saturday 11th April 2015 was the day of the election of the CANUK chairman and the AGM. Babatunde was able to use some of the organisations that he had registered to solicit a very marginal victory, defeating Mrs Ronke Udofia and Dr Boma Douglas, both exemplary community leaders who had campaigned elegantly, even as friends. In the second run-off, Babatunde beat Dr Douglas by two votes in an election that went to the wire.

My personal opinion is that either Dr Douglas or Mrs Udofia would have made fine CANUK leaders. However, that happy ending was not to be. The election and swearing-in of the new executive in 2015 heralded the deterioration of CANUK as an organisation.

The inherent lack of leadership skills, community experience and knowledge of the Nigerian community terrain was clearly evident for all to see. It was obvious during the campaign period and through the approach to the elections, and became even more obvious during the very controversial and embattled reign of the chairman. This was not helped by the fact that there was no attempt to unify and align the member organisations that had not voted for the chairman. That gesture would have expanded his endearment to the community, and I had advised him to do so one day after the elections. My advice was ignored. Also, as I had predicted the previous year, the newly elected executive was split in two. The chairman was desperate to become the chairman for personal ulterior motives, and the signs of this began to surface almost immediately. Despite all his flaws, he did have a support base – but I believed that support was misplaced and would lead to definite failure of the leadership.

The CANUK chairman's reign was characterised by the predicated split executive team and by a constant disregard for the rules, regulations and goodwill that had guided the organisation in the past. There was neglect of most of the Nigerian community that the organisation had been set up to serve. The leadership's belligerent attitude was displayed clearly at the 2016 AGM. CANUK AGMs are usually held at the Nigeria High Commission in London. On this occasion, the approved delegates' attendance list had been tampered with to illicitly prevent certain member organisations from gaining access to the

AGM. Private security guards were also hired to control entry into the High Commission. This was a scene that the Nigerian community had never witnessed before, and people were obviously shocked, upset and angry. The blatant disregard and disrespect that many CANUK delegates witnessed brewed the perfect storm. Most people who were banned from entering, together with many who had already gained entry to the building came together and rebelled against the illegal processes being used. The security guards soon realised that things had taken a turn for the worse. They left the High Commission in a hurry. The meeting that followed the incident was rowdy, disorganised and full of illegality. In one instance, the leadership tried to coerce members to adopt a financial report which was riddled with inaccuracies. More importantly, the financial report had not been approved by the executive, which was the normal procedure, prior to it being presented to delegates at the AGM for adoption. Needless to say that the finance report was not adopted.

During the short term in office, there were also attempts to alter the constitution to enable executive members to serve longer than the mandated maximum four-year term – an alteration that would favour his desire for a third term in office. However, the alteration to the constitution was met with fierce resistance from unrelenting community leaders and member organisations, who had decided to put an end to the tenure.

CANUK went from being a reputable welfare organisation to one that seemed to be stuck in limbo. It was very painful to watch an organisation I been involved with since 2006 disintegrate into a shabby representation of its old self. During the turbulent reign, I lost respect for many community leaders who had put personal ambition, greed and dishonesty before selfless service of people. I had no time for individuals who were dishonest and immoral.

The beleaguered two-year reign eventually came to an unceremonious end, in May 2017, amidst confusion and arguing between the two different factions within the executive. There was immense resistance to any alteration of the constitution, and this included resistance from within the executive team by dignified and courageous people like Dr Coker, Chief Achebe, Dr Sawacha, Mrs Anyiwo and Charles Sylvester. The joint effort of those courageous executive team members and some experienced Nigerian community leaders thwarted the third term plot and sacked the leadership in what was an audacious and polished strategic lesson in due process, community politics and community resilience. This bittersweet lesson was dished out at the May 2017 AGM. Dr Douglas was sworn in as the new chairman after an election in which he was the only candidate. The community had regained their organisation and the rebuilding had started.

My constantly unpredictable journey

When my community work with CANUK ended in

2015, I decided it was a good time to turn more of my energy and attention to managing the Ex-Blues Junior under-elevens football team. I had already started managing them at the start of the football season in September 2014, but the affairs of CANUK had meant I was not able to focus as much as I wanted to on their development and mentoring at the time. I was happy to be in a position to mentor the younger generation and also be able to watch them develop and progress in football, at school, and in life.

I also decided it was a good time to re-evaluate my career options and look for some opportunities in the job market. Moving to Greenwich had seemed like an ideal move, but my time there had been quite turbulent. The final straw was when a job opening came within our team. The rest of the team believed it was a good idea for me to apply, even though it would mean I would be managing them. Sheila Taylor, a good friend, was adamant that the role was perfect for me. I approached my manager, as the role would report into her, to tell her about my intention to apply for the job. She said that there were still gaps in my knowledge and that she thought the post was for someone more senior. Her comments put me off applying for the job. I was also absolutely put off working for Greenwich.

The senior management team eventually recruited to the post. During one of our team meetings, the new manager told us that she had been contacted and asked to apply. This was obviously the reason I had been discouraged from applying. With that knowledge, I found it very difficult to continue to dedicate myself to working for Greenwich. After many months of job-hunting, and with support from a good friend, Dr Nike Arowobusoye, I eventually found what I felt was the perfect job for me at NHS Tower Hamlets Clinical Commissioning Group (CCG).

The usual thing to do in a workplace when a member of staff is leaving is to circulate a card and buy a leaving present for them. I told my manager that I didn't want a leaving card or a present, as I felt it would be an insincere gesture – I felt my colleagues did not really appreciate me or my work. I also believed that I had to leave Greenwich with a clear message that I had tolerated them long enough and was not cheap or dumb enough to want a card, present or audience. My wife made the perfect leaving cake – it was in the shape of my favourite work bag, with my footsteps walking off (onto better things). Everyone at work enjoyed the cake. The irony, however, was lost on most of them. In September 2015, after six years at Greenwich, I left – and it was exactly the right time. I had spent 12 months feeling like an unwanted tenant, bored and doing the bare basics of the job I had once taken to extraordinary heights.

Tower Hamlets was an innovative CCG, and that was the main reason I was keen to join the team there. I started work there at the end of September 2015 for what I believed would be best my best job yet. Although the team I joined was new, quite a few of members had worked there for many years. I felt that this was great, as they would be able to keep everyone else up to date with any historic information. I got on with my manager and the rest of the team and eventually began to settle in.

Early in 2016, I decided to focus my attention on my planned 50th birthday party, which had been booked for the 10th December 2016. I had been looking forward to turning fifty since I was about forty-six, although I'm unsure as to why. As soon as we entered 2016, I had started planning. As December drew closer, I got more rigorous with my planning and had plenty of support from my wife. On the day of the party, everything went according to plan; that is, almost everything. There were one or two minor hiccups, with space being tight for the number of guests and some difficulties with the projector screen, but that was to be expected when planning such a large project.

Guests attended from all parts of the country. My former Leicester School of Pharmacy housemates attended, as did the former president of the Royal Pharmaceutical Society, Ashok Soni, and Honourable Rita Orji, member of the Federal House of Representatives, who was in the country at the time. Hon. Orji said she had been directed by numerous Nigerian community leaders to attend the party of the supposed Mr Diaspora, so she obliged. The party was packed full of people I referred to as my friends, some reputable members of the Nigerian community, relatives, and a wide range of professionals and business friends. When I looked across the hall, I beamed with delight at the sea of kind and happy faces smiling back at me. However, two of the most important people in my life were not there – my dad and mum. My dad hadn't been feeling well over the past couple of months, so we'd agreed he would stay at home with my mum and rest. I was sad that they couldn't attend, but the promise of having a small family gathering sometime later in December made me feel better. Despite their absence, I had a great time with my family and friends, and I received many gifts.

Sadly, life has its way of not working out as planned all the time. My family were about to be on the receiving end of one of life's sad tales. On Thursday the 29th December 2016, I was still savouring the events of Christmas and getting ready to celebrate my wife's birthday. At around 11.20am, I got a call from my mum. She sounded frantic, which is very unlike her. She told me that something was wrong with my dad and I needed to come to the family house immediately. When I asked her what she thought the problem was, she told me that paramedics were already at the house. I asked to speak with one of the paramedics so as to get an idea of what was wrong. The paramedic I spoke to told me to come as soon as possible. Moments later, my brother called and asked whether I had spoken with my mum. I explained the situation and told him I was on the way over to the family house.

When I arrived at our family house, there were three ambulances outside – two small ones and one large one. Most of the ambulance crew were in the ambulance, talking, which signalled bad news to me – otherwise they would have been inside the house attending to my dad. A member of the ambulance crew saw me walking into the house and approached me to ask who I was. Then he gave me the worst news I have ever had to receive. My dad had passed away. I rushed upstairs to the sitting room to find my mum sitting in a chair looking solemnly at my dad, who was lying on the floor as if he was sleeping. I knelt beside my dad and felt for a pulse, just in case the ambulance crew had got it wrong; there was no pulse. My mentor and teacher was truly gone, forever. I kissed his forehead, said a prayer and bid him farewell.

My dad passing away so suddenly was something that I had never fully planned for. My siblings and I had talked about it at times, more during discussions of family succession planning rather than in stark preparation for his actual departure. I was stunned for a while and unsure what to do. The entire family had been together at the house a couple of days earlier for our usual meet-up just after Christmas, and also to send off my sisters, who were travelling to Nigeria. We had all used the opportunity to spend time with our parents as we always did during Christmas. The thought that I had seen him a couple of days earlier gave me some comfort.

With my sisters on holiday in Nigeria, we were not all together to discuss what to do. When my brother arrived, I explained the situation, and he went upstairs to see for himself. Later on, we sat outside together on the front porch and sipped on glasses of whisky while we began to plan what needed to be done. It made me sad to see how the world just simply continued on as if nothing had happened. A neighbour walked by and, seeing all the ambulances on the street, casually said to me, "it looks like something has happened". I shrugged my shoulders and smiled at her. She had no clue. My brother called my sisters in Nigeria and broke the sad news. They were devastated. Later that evening, after the paramedics, police and coroner had left, my mum, my brother and I finally had some quiet to begin to think about the next steps. I asked my mum to let me and my siblings handle the funeral arrangements.

During the funeral preparations, I realised how similar all the siblings were in many respects – especially resilience. My dad had always been in love with Nigeria, and I think that as he got older, he fell more deeply in love with the country. There was therefore very little discussion as to where he would finally be laid to rest. In preparation for his funeral, we held regular family meetings. At the very first meeting, I asked to take charge of most of the Nigeria affairs; having lived there, I understood the mind-set, especially that of close relatives. I wanted to make sure we had all angles of the funeral covered. I had to make sure that the villagers were on our side and that we did not owe them any money. I made sure we did not owe our age grade organisations any money. These assurances were very important because if any of these groups are unhappy or felt they were owed money or anything else, they could scupper the funeral by not attending or not letting the body into the village.

I had to find an appropriate mortuary and arrange the catering for the expected 600 guests.   I also had to factor into the planning an amount of leverage and unknown elements. I was very pleased I did, as Nigeria is a country where not everything is as straightforward as it should be – there are always last-minute surprises that one needs to be ready for.

After we had made all the necessary arrangements, my dad's body was flown to Nigeria on the 7th February 2017. As a family, we had agreed the 25th February 2017 as the funeral date. It would take place in his village, Ogbu Edda, in Ebonyi State. Between the four siblings we could comfortably manage the financial aspects of the funeral.

All of our uncles, aunties and cousins from my mum's family were very supportive – especially my mum's two younger brothers, Oko and Onyike, and my cousins, Ignatius and Okoro, who were always on hand to help the family. This was obvious right from the day my dad died. My uncles and cousins did most of the running around and organising of meetings in Nigeria on our behalf.

Members of Ebonyi State Union UK and Edda Welfare Association UK were very supportive and paid condolence visits to my house, as the eldest son. My friends in the UK and Nigeria were also very supportive.

Many of my friends in Nigeria travelled from Abuja, Lagos and other parts of the country to be in Ogbu and support the family. However, most of our uncles, aunties and cousins from my dad's side of the family were not very helpful – although I had anticipated that. I saw early warning signs when it took one of the senior members of my dad's family over two weeks after receiving the news about my dad's death to contact my mum and condole with her. I sensed immediately how things with them were going to turn out. When they showed no initial interest in helping the family, I made sure that they were not involved or informed of what we were doing so as to avoid any potential plot of sabotage. The plan worked.

Unfortunately, a couple of days before the funeral, I became terribly ill and was mainly incapacitated for most of the Thursday and Friday. My uncles suggested I go to the hospital and get a check-up to make sure I had not been poisoned. I refused, as I was scared that I might not make it out in time for the funeral. Instead, I self-medicated for the next couple of days and eventually got better, just in time.

Saturday the 25th February came and went very quickly; the funeral went well and without any snags. My dad was laid to rest at our family home – a home that had only recently been completed, in September 2016, and one that my dad never got to spend a single night in. The sun was very intense that day, nearly unbearable, but the choice of taking cover from the scorching heat was not an option, and we endured it as we celebrated my dad's life and his achievements. My dad would have been very proud of his final send-off. We all were, and we thank God for all his wisdom and guidance during such a difficult period. As a family, we had an amazing time, all together in the village for over a week, planning, laughing and reminiscing.

Tribute to My Daddy

Papa, you were called to the Lord on Thursday the 29th December 2016, two days after your four children had gathered to smother you with companionship and love; unbeknown to us you were about to leave us.

You were the most intelligent, astute and visionary person I have ever come across. You taught me most of the things I know, the things that have guided me through my life. Your decision to send me to Nigeria when I was nine years old was a master stroke of a decision; my experience of Nigeria has made me the man I am now – thank you for that, papa. Papa, you understood me as well as I understood myself; this can only be down to your intensive attention to things that matter.

You were a man of integrity, firm when you needed to

be, but also lenient too. You were a man of few words, but you also had so much to say when it mattered; from your stories about your life in London, to tales from your numerous visits to Nigeria. When you went to Nigeria, I used to look forward to your return so I could sit down and listen to all your stories and experiences. Oh, how I will miss all that! However, I have so many wonderful memories of you, I'll keep smiling for the longest time.

You were such a humble man; you never boasted about all the great things you had achieved, and most times I found out about your philanthropic acts through other people, mainly beneficiaries. Your philanthropic acts and gestures of kindness always made me understand it is a great gift to give, a gesture I have emulated and will continue to demonstrate throughout my life. Your acts of silent kindness earned you the nickname the Humble Lion.

You were a man who had a complete life; you had the perfect wife and companion, you had raised the perfect family and instilled the right morals in all of us. You had achieved everything you aspired to, and more. For a little boy from Ogbu who was not supposed to live, to a colossus of a man who cannot be rivalled, you exceeded in all your endeavours. It would be unfair to ask a runner who has run a marathon and crossed the finish line to continue running.

Papa, you have run your marathon, you crossed the finish line in first place – you can rest now.

You will be so sorely missed, and my heart will always long for you, but I am comforted because you did everything you needed to in life. Your legacy lives on in me and my younger ones, so you can look down upon us with pride.

Rest well, papa – my mentor, teacher, super hero, and friend.

Your son – Chima Olugh.

My siblings left Nigeria first, and I stayed behind for an additional week to tie up some loose ends and support my mum with some family things. Following my return to the UK in March, I fell into a depressive state, mainly due to the death of my dad. I hadn't had time to grieve properly due to the relentless planning for the funeral, which had kept me very occupied. With that all over, and with the disturbing flow of sad news about some very close friends who had died suddenly, I felt overwhelmed and boxed in.

Faced with this, I would usually have sought solace in my good friend Greg Abani. Unfortunately, though, he was not well himself. He had recently been diagnosed with a terminal illness. This meant I was mainly alone. I was grieving the loss of my dad and upset at the news of my friend. My wife understood how I felt but couldn't do much for me.

However, I was determined to overcome my depression. I was determined to refocus on my plans and get back to my happy state. I felt I was not much use to anyone when I was depressed, so I tried very hard to break out of it — but the cold hands of depression held me firm. To make matter worse, my line manager was mostly unsympathetic towards me and piled up my inbox with endless tasks.

Eventually, in June, I could no longer handle the depression and the excessive workload and broke down at work. I was having a one-to-one with a close colleague, explaining how I felt and how difficult I was finding things, when the tears just came gushing out. I cried for a while, and she comforted me and advised me to call my doctor and get some time off work. She said this would hopefully give me time to recuperate and get myself together. I took her advice, and the GP signed me off work for two weeks, followed by a further nine days. During this time, I stayed indoors, either in bed or on the couch. I also sought professional advice; this played some part in helping me get my mind, body and soul back together again.

When I went back to work, it felt like I was being punished for taking time off. The work was still relentless, and now my manager had started to challenge some of my project decisions. Work suddenly got very tough and challenging. My manager would sometimes give me projects to manage with specific instructions to take the lead and see them to the end, and then would ask why I had not sought her approval at certain stages. When I reversed my way of working to suit her instructions, by seeking her approval at specific intervals, she would criticise me for not using my initiative. This caused me much anxiety and frustration and made me fell unwell. I started to feel anxious at night when I thought about going to work the following day. I often broke down in private, at home and at work. I asked God why all this was happening to me. Was I ever going to get a break from the challenges of life? As a strong-minded individual capable of getting up after being knocked down many times, my fighting spirit was very weak.

As 2017 drew to a close, I tried to focus on getting my healthy mind and wellbeing back and keeping my manager happy. I wanted to end the year on a high and leap into 2018 like a warrior, confident of surprising and defeating the enemy. However, that was not to be the case. The cruel hands of death dealt a killer blow on the 26th December 2017.

Greg Abani had been unwell for the eight or nine months leading up to December 2017. The prognosis for his condition had not been good, but one is never really prepared for losing someone close. The last time I saw Greg was on my birthday, 11th December 2017. I had taken the day off work and decided to spend my day with him. Fifteen days later, I received the heart-breaking news I had dreaded. Boxing Day will never be the same again for me or my family.

Greg was my good friend, my greatest critic and my best supporter, and he was always there when needed. He was the godfather to my youngest daughter, Obiageli. He was also very close to my family, and we shared many good times and difficult times together. His death left me feeling very empty; our relationship was very deep, and we understood each other very well and had a lot in common. He will be sadly missed, but life really does have to go on, no matter how difficult that is.

The fight to win

In the period between these two most painful tragedies in my life, there was something worth pulling inspiration from. In September 2017, following wide-ranging consultation and negotiation, I was elected president of Ebonyi State Union UK at our AGM. Taking on the leadership of the union was a very difficult decision for me for a number of reasons. As a founding member of the union, I had been actively involved since its inception in 1996, and I had held a range of different positions. This had enabled me to develop and implement many projects that were beneficial for the union, so I had no ambition to lead. Furthermore, I was still not back to my bouncy, happy self after my dad's death and felt I needed some time to relax with my family. However, Greg had spoken with me on a couple of occasions, and so had a couple other people. This convinced me to take on the arduous but loving task.

Once I decided to go for the position and was elected, I threw myself back into the community I have served for so long. Community leadership is something worth cracking a smile for; it is hard work, but it is good hard work and I was ready once again. With community work, it is difficult to avoid all the politics, grand-standing and egos. Therefore, in order for me to remain focused on the work I needed to do, it was important that I had a clear agenda of what needed to be done and how it could be achieved. It might sound too simplistic, but setting out a strategy with some timelines has always worked for me. That is exactly what I did immediately after I was elected president of Ebonyi State Union UK. With my clear strategy, the executive team and members were able to establish objectives and understand how they could provide the support that would take the union to the next level.

At the turn of the year, I had great plans; plans to work for the community, enhance my career and spend more time with my family. These are all normal things an individual should be able to wish for and plan, but considering my oscillating past, I could not take anything for granted – and I was right not to. In February, I was flabbergasted when my manager explained that she was unsatisfied with my work; she thought it did not meet the standard expected of someone in my position. She began a formal performance process against me. I sensed that the end of my time at Tower Hamlets was very near. We had not been on the best of terms since I returned from my sick leave. She was insensitive to the way I felt and rewarded my vulnerability with tasks full of mixed messages and the constant threat of undermining my decisions.

Despite the difficult and negative relationship with my manager, I continued to work very hard, re-examining all my projects and tasks to ensure I had covered everything. The papers that I frequently had to write and submit to boards or committees took me three times as long to complete as usual due to my extraordinary interrogation of my own work. In the past, and during the performance review period, I had received good feedback from peers and other senior managers about the quality and thoroughness of my work. My manager, however, felt that references to the commendations I had received were disproportionate, and she pursued me with a vengeance through the performance reviews. I always suspected she was unhappy that I earned nearly as much as her – she had mentioned it in passing in some of my previous one-to-ones.

The reviews culminated in a performance hearing where my fate would be decided. The thought of the performance hearing filled me with anger and despair. I knew what the outcome would be. My feelings were validated when I received my manager's case against me. The case was filled with inaccurate information, lies and half-stories. It reminded me of my previous disciplinary hearing at Greenwich. It was happening all over again.

I wanted to give up hope and leave my job, but my wife encouraged me to stand up to my manager and fight for my job, so I did. I compiled a comprehensive response to her case, with bundles of evidence. I knew how the system worked, and that it was going to be an uphill battle to defend myself against my superior. I was right. The panel sided with her story and homed in on one fact – a draft project plan that I had compiled to help me with a project I was working on. The panel chair asked me why the project plan did not have the organisation's logo on it. When I tried to explain that it was for my own use and not for use externally, she said that all working documents are expected to have the organisation's logo on them. I was bewildered. When I tried to get the panel to consider the feedback from my peers and other senior managers, they refused. I left with a written warning and three months to pull my socks up. When I came out, I had a confidential discussion with one of the panel members, who advised me to tread carefully with my manager.

Following the hearing, my relationship with my manager broke down irretrievably. This was doubly difficult because we worked in the same office, sitting about two metres apart. Whenever I said "good morning" to her, she ignored me, so after a while I stopped. I still held out some faith that my hard work and resilience would see me through. I went into work early and left late; not because I wanted to impress her, but because she had given me a very complex project. The remit was for me to pull all the homeless services in the borough under one overarching service. Although it was challenging task, I embraced it like a long-lost brother; this was my opportunity to prove what I could do. I led the project from the start. Due to the nature of homelessness, which cannot be treated in isolation, I had to pull together a big project team that included colleagues from different boroughs and different organisations. Once again, I received very good feedback from my peers on the project. The procurement of the new service that I had developed coincided with the end of my three-month review period.

A week before the formal review, I asked my manager whether we could have a discussion. Surprisingly, she agreed. When I asked her how she thought I had performed over the past couple of months, she said she could see that I was working hard, but that it was not good enough for her. This meant that she would be recommending my dismissal. I was not actually surprised; I had never really felt it would work out. However, the fact that I would now be dismissed from my job made me cry. After crying for a while, I knew I had to find a way to fight back. I knew everything was stacked against me, but when hadn't it been? Even though my back was against the wall, I still had to fight. That's what warriors do. I took some legal advice to find out what options were available. A couple of days later, with a clear plan, I asked my manager whether we could have another discussion. She agreed.

A month or so later, on the 24th August 2018, I left Tower Hamlets, one month shy of my third anniversary there.

Coincidentally, when I had joined Tower Hamlets in 2015, I had planned to give myself three years before I looked at how to make my way through the proverbial glass ceiling.

I was officially unemployed for the first time in my life. This was a whole new experience for me, but I was psychologically geared up to overcome this hiatus. I started job-hunting immediately and was instantly rewarded with an interview a week after leaving Tower Hamlets. Before I got home from the interview, I received a telephone call and was offered the job, subject to references. Unfortunately, we were not able to agree on certain terms and conditions, so the conditional offer was withdrawn.

The entire episode seemed like only a minor setback to me. I believed that with my comprehensive CV and all the value added by my community activities, finding a job would not take long. I was very wrong. I had not carefully considered the time of the year, and discovered that recruiters were not keen to take on new staff towards the year-end. I also had not carefully considered the planning needed for the Christmas holiday to Nigeria that I had booked with my mum, siblings, nephew and youngest daughter. In between job-hunting, I'd had to apply for Nigerian passports for my daughter and myself. My interaction with the Nigeria High Commission was very pleasant, and I was able to get my passport after two visits totalling just under three hours. However, there were so many other things that needed to be bought and done to ensure my daughter had everything she might need in a foreign country away from her mum and siblings. Eventually, having attended a couple of interviews, I gave up job-hunting and concentrated on our dream trip to Nigeria. I had not been to Nigeria over the Christmas period for over twenty years, and my daughter had never been to Nigeria at all.

The trip to Nigeria was pleasant but expensive. My daughter had a wonderful time meeting her cousins, great cousins, aunties and uncles. I knew she would enjoy it there even before we left home. We all had a good time together, travelling from one village or town to another. On the 29th December we held a special remembrance for my dad in the house – just the family.

We arrived back to a cold and overcast London early in January 2019. The weather, however, was the least of my worries. I was not only still unemployed; I was also broke. That was not a good feeling to have at any time, but especially not just after Christmas.

Later in January, I had started making plans to go back to community pharmacy when I got the call I had been waiting for. I was offered a job as a primary care commissioning manager, which was a lovely dream come true. It reminded me that good things do truly come to those who work hard. I started my new job in February 2019.

As I was getting ready to start my new job, I received

a call from Dr Douglas, the CANUK chairman. He explained that CANUK was about to start its 2019 electoral process and that the executive had nominated me to take charge of the 2019 CANUK electoral committee as the chairman. It is always an honour for me when I am recognised not just my work ethic but also my integrity and affection for due diligence. Once again, I was duty-bound to do what was right for an organisation that I loved so profoundly. I accepted the offer to chair and work with the committee and we guaranteed that the electoral process and the elections would be conducted thoroughly, successfully and by the book.

My fantastic start to the New Year was crowned when I received an email in late February. The email stated that representatives of Nigerian Healthcare Professionals UK had nominated me for the 2018 Nigerian Healthcare Professionals UK Excellence Award, in recognition of my outstanding professional contributions and achievements in the NHS over the years. I did not feel anxious and took the nomination news in my stride.

The awards ceremony was being held in celebration of the seventieth anniversary of the NHS. It was scheduled to take place on the 23rd March 2019 at the Grange City Hotel in London, which was local for me. My wife, my brother and I bought tickets for the ceremony. I was not particularly concerned about winning. Making the list of the seventy most outstanding Nigerian healthcare professionals in the UK out of 207 top-class healthcare professionals was not an impossible feat, but it was a demanding one. When we got to the event and saw the calibre of the other candidates, we agreed it would be a good idea to just enjoy the occasion and revel in the fact that I had been nominated alongside such outstanding people.

The occasion was grand and was attended by some of the most famous members of British and Nigerian society. The then Nigerian minister for health was there and gave out many awards to the winners. Also in attendance were Yvonne Coghill, the director of race equality for the NHS; the Nigerian high commissioner; and Lord Victor Adebowale, the chief executive of the social care enterprise Turning Point.

When the MC started announcing the winners and the seventy most outstanding Nigerian healthcare professionals in the UK, the titles before names were quite intimidating. There were professors, doctors, consultants, and some people with a combination of two or three of these titles. As each winner was called, they had to go up onto the podium to collect their award, have some photos taken, and then go to the specially prepared area for a short interview and more photos. The list seemed to go on for eternity. And then suddenly I heard my name. I had been in deep conversation with my brother and was not paying much attention, so I was unsure why my name had been called. My brother and I exchanged astonished looks; we were both wondering what was going on. Before I had time to think, my name was called again; I heard it very clearly. As I got up and made my way to the podium, some members of the audience started clapping. I saluted them all. I was a proud award winner, again. One of the seventy most outstanding Nigerian healthcare professionals in the UK. My award was handed to me by the inspirational Lord Victor Adebowale. To once again to be recognised for doing what I love when it had seemed the entire world was against me was a surreal and very proud moment for me.

With my broad experience of life and all it has to offer, I know that my journey to where I want to be is nowhere near finished. I will continue to exploit my rich experience to make sure the other parts of my life are well-informed, full of joy and happiness, and contain as little pain as possible.

Throughout all my years of joy, suffering, torment, challenges and missed opportunities, everything often seemed like a movie with a convoluted script that was being acted out in front of me; I felt like an observer watching on in awe as this mighty warrior fought and conquered every battle that came his way. I often wondered what it would take for him to give up, lose a battle or die fighting. I sometimes fantasised that I was the mighty warrior and thought of some of the things that I might have done differently.

It took me a very long time to realise that I was never an observer watching on – I was the main character, the great warrior, the surviving warrior, of this explosive blockbuster movie.

During my life I have suffered unimaginable pain. On three occasions, I could have died and not had to put up with it all. I have also enjoyed immense love and joy, and if had died earlier, I would have been very upset with myself for giving up so easily. Whenever I reflect on my life, I get dizzy very quickly.

Could someone's life really be so unpredictable?

This is just part of the continuing story of my life. I will wait to see what happens next.

Author's End Notes

The ups and downs in my life surely have given me more than enough experience to manage any challenge that I come up against. My numerous battles have made me a resilient person who wears his battle scars in his heart and in his smile.

I am not a professional writer, nor have I taken any writing courses. I am just an ordinary man who wanted his story to be told.

When I started writing my memoirs, I shared them with some friends and family. Surprisingly, when I shared them, most people didn't believe my life experiences, claiming my understanding and interpretation of things that happened to me were unrealistic. I continued to write anyway, because I am a very committed and focused individual; once I make the decision to go ahead with something, there is no going back. As I continued to write, my life kept evolving, and I knew it was the right thing to do.

I have had an interesting life so far. I have made many mistakes and I have learned a lot. I want to be able to use my personal experiences to encourage people to always aim to be the best at what they do. Everything is possible. It is simple arithmetic. When we face difficult decisions in life, we should be in total control of ourselves we when make our choices. That way we can be encouraged to make the correct decision, and if we make a mistake there is nobody else to blame.

The actual hard work of achieving our ambitions is up to each of us alone. However, the world we live in has its complexities, which will have an impact on how we arrive at our final destination.

My parents explained to me at an early stage in my life how important it was for my word to be taken seriously. It was imperative that people believed in me and what I said. They called it integrity. I always listened to my dad but did not always do what he wanted, when he wanted – but that was me and my way of working through things in at my own pace. One thing I did learn is that integrity is not a bar; it is a ladder which has to considered and climbed with care.

As I got older and things became more difficult and complex for me, I simply strengthened my resolve to succeed in this life. My passion for imparting my learning to others inspired me to make sure that this autobiography was completed. Sometimes I feel the life I am living is a dream, as if I'm not supposed to be here. It is as if I have made up an unreal and supernatural warrior, and life, in order to escape the harsh reality into which I was born.

As a child and young man growing up in my dad's house in Nigeria, I was told so many times that I was nobody and that I'd never be anybody. During the many times that I slept on the concrete floor underneath my cousin's bed, I always asked myself what I needed to do to better myself; to be able to buy my own bed and breathe fresh air while sleeping. I was starved and beaten, and I was psychologically and physically abused. If all this could happen in the house owned by my dad, then what could I expect elsewhere? All the harsh and unkind words and acts were part of the reason I worked hard to make sure I succeeded in life. I worked hard to write my own script and prove my aggressors wrong.

As I went through life, my dream started to be realised, and I became happier. But on so many occasions, when I thought I was finally on the home straight to enjoying a comfortable life, something happened that knocked me down to ground zero. Sometimes the rollercoaster ride of my life was too dizzying for me to withstand, and thrice I thought of putting myself out of my misery for good.

Although I don't measure how much of a man I am by counting the tough times I've been through and the battles I've won, I do look at the scars those battles have left and the memories and the experiences they've given me – and I use them to teach myself and educate others about the journey of life. I feel lucky, happy, and blessed to still be here to share my journey, and I hope it inspires many who read about it.

Despite all the setbacks in my life, I have refused to give up. And in some uncanny way, I thank my aggressors;

those who tried to humiliate and subdue me when they had no business doing so. They should have embraced me as one of theirs and loved me like they loved their own children. I would like to thank them because they had a huge impact in building my resolve, confidence and unrelenting desire to succeed in this life.

I especially want to thank my uncle Okoro Ikpo Uzoh and his wife Rosaline Uzoh who tormented me throughout most of the years I lived with them at Aba. My parents trusted them with their first and only son at the time. That trust was betrayed and obliterated.

I want to thank Orji Okam Agha, aka Ojens, for telling me to fuck off to Owutu because he thought I was not worthy to be at his older brother's wedding during the Christmas of 1983. His older brother, Oko Chukwu, loved me dearly; he had engaged with me and won me over to help him with his wedding plans. I was sent away on the eve of the wedding. I was 17 years old, and that experience will stay with me forever. I could not understand why Ojens was so cruel to me.

I want to thank Pastor Orji Abia Onyike, my mum's cousin, for not believing me when I told him I didn't take his money. He had trusted me with the keys to his room; the person who took the money had climbed through the gap between the roof and the wooden part of the house meant for the ceiling. The person left a clear footprint on his bedside table. He took me outside into the village compound, stripped me naked in front of everyone and beat the living daylights out of me. That horrible experience scarred me for life.

I want to thank my aunty, Eleya Agwu Chukwu, who lied to Okoro Ikpo Uzoh that I had joined an armed gang and robbed people at gunpoint on the Aba-Port Harcourt expressway. I was only 12 years old. How could you concoct such lies against a child so young?

All these individuals were people – relatives – who my parents had entrusted with their son's welfare and childhood. Instead of being guardians and safeguarding my interests, they tried their best to subdue and frustrate anything that I did. They all tried their best to convince me that I'd never make it in this life.

I am happy that not only did they fail in their bid to undermine me, but that their immoral acts encouraged me to work hard, focus and strive to be the best whenever I could.

I have tried to live my life without many regrets. However, the sort of life I've had means there have been some encounters that I really regret and would have liked to sidestep.

I regret meeting Nicholas Webb Edwards. He was eventually found guilty of rape at the Old Bailey in London, and I had to attend his trial for one day as a witness. In nearly 20 years, Nicholas had stood trial for rape seven times but was only convicted and locked up twice. I met him before his eighth rape trail. I had no idea of how evil he was. During the trial, up to five women were allowed by the judge to tell jurors about their past ordeals with him. It was a landmark case; the first time in a rape case that the prosecution was allowed to call the 'similar fact evidence' of five previous complainants against Nicholas. He was jailed for life in 2000.

The entire episode left me hurt, angry and disappointed in myself. How could I not have seen it? I realised that I trusted people too easily without looking for faults. A couple of my friends had told me that there was something about him that didn't sit very well with them. How could a man in his thirties not have any friends? He never introduced me to any of his friends. He did not have any because he had spent most of his time in prison. The friends he did have before going to prison had abandoned him. He acted irrationally a lot of the time, and cared little for life. It was a very stern life lesson for me about friendship.

Top of my regret list, though, is getting to know, and eventually marrying, Valerie Mowah. There had been several warning signs which had alerted me that something was wrong. I had seen them on many occasions. Other close friends and some family members had also seen her odd behaviour and warned me to take a step back and observe her some more before making such a huge decision. I did not listen. What a potently poisoned chalice although if that relationship had not happened,

I wouldn't have my wonderful kids, Nkechi and Obinna.

I regret spending so much time fooling around in Nigeria when I could have been studying and taking more from life. I do believe, though, that it was how the Lord had planned it.

I regret not going to my grandma's funeral. I would have taken the blanket she told me to buy for her. I do know she is warm up there now.

There are also some things I wouldn't change in my life, including going to Nigeria in the summer of 1976. It made me the man I am now. If I had stayed in the UK, I would have been dead by now.

I wouldn't change the fight I put up against Valerie to gain custody of my kids. It is amazing what one can do when backed into a corner and there is nowhere to turn. It was the best fight of my life to date. The outcome from that battle brings a smile to my face every single day.

I didn't have a constant father figure to look up to during my time in Nigeria, but I managed to work out a lot of things for myself. I made a promise to be a great father figure for my kids. I vowed to teach them everything I could – that is the least they deserve in life. I couldn't imagine my life without my kids.

Being a very practical and sceptical man, I was very re-served about love and what people believed it meant or what it felt like. I am in love with my wife, Bonita. Before I met her, I was unsure as to how many times I'd been in love. I wondered how you really knew. I know now; I had not known real love before.

This is the prayer I have said since I was six years old:

The Lord is good to me and so I thank the Lord for giving me the things I need – the sun, the rain and the apple seeds. The Lord is good to me. Everlasting and merciful Father, forgive us our trespasses, so we can forgive those that trespass against us. Deliver us not into temptation and deliver us from evil, for thine is the kingdom, the power and the glory, forever and ever.

Amen.

Acknowledgements

My grandma, Nne Agbai, aka Ugo Uwele, Ugo Okoro – thank you for your guidance when I was young and lost. I can still hear your words of wisdom. I'll miss you always.

Thank you, Oko Ukpai, for rescuing me from the devilish hands of my uncle, Okoro Ikpo Uzoh, in Aba; had you not taken me with you to Ohafia when you did, I would not be here to tell my story today.

Thank you, Onyike Elekwa, for your doggedness and resilience in making sure I got into the Institute of Management and Technology, Enugu, and making sure I retook my exams. It was during my time with you in Enugu that I realised I had the potential to make a difference. It was whilst I was with you the penny dropped and my entire outlook on life did a 360-degree turn.

Thank you to all my wonderful and loyal friends; it is so easy to get people to walk with you in the cool of the evening, but not many people will walk with you in the heat of the day. You stood beside me during some of the most difficult periods in my life; I am grateful and indebted to you.

To Ama Orji Okoro, aka Nobel's – we are living our dream.

To Dr Mark Abani – my mentor extraordinaire.

Thank you, Greg Abani – your voice of protection follows me everywhere, my buddy for life.

To my Original Ravers crew – as young as we were, we tried our best to keep it all together.

Thank you, Imo Okoro Ikpo, my cousin – for planting the football seed. I took it to a new level.

Thank you to my wife, Bonita – for bringing back the happiness and my smile.

Thank you, my rocks, Nkechi and Obinna – for making me the resolute and dedicated dad that I am. We made the house-hunting a fun thing to do. Who would have known we were homeless?

Thank you to my parents for sending me to Nigeria during that summer of 1976. It was the single best thing you did for me; if I had stayed in the UK, I would have died very young and achieved nothing at all. I did miss you, and at times I even felt resentment – but look at me all now. I am also grateful for your dogged lessons in resilience, telling the truth, morals and integrity.

I have lost many great people during my journey through the years of my life. I guess life has that predestined ending.

My dear people I have lost along the way:

Grandma – My solid rock. Thank you for everything.

Imo Okoro Ikpo – Thanks for being my older brother and showing me how to play football.

Bolanle Marinho – We partied like there was no tomorrow.

Nnenna Oko Nnachi – I miss your proactive approach to life, as young as you were.

Ola Trouble – I still remember your wedding day.

Michael Ghana – Thanks for introducing me to swing beat, eighties. We rocked South London College. You left before we turned thirty. Damn.

Andrew Onyekwere Nwachukwu – You had so much love in your heart.

Oko Captain – We were stubborn together and terrorised Abakaliki in 1985; in a good way.

Godwin Yellow – We know they killed you.

Chief Felix Arua Ibiam – We had fun. You showed me the ropes.

Afshin Kanji – You bought me my Whitney Houston Bodyguard album in 1992. Why did you have to leave?

Eke Onyekwere (Buma Tactics) – We never did meet again.

Dr Ochaa Idika – You were such a kind and inspirational person.

Big John – Glad to have met you.

Chineke Man – My big ragged brother from Owutu,
Edda, Nigeria.

Ndukwe Basketball – Gone too soon.

Gregory Okechukwu Abani – We were awesome
together.

Francis Olaoluwa Faluyi – You left with no warning.
May you all continue to rest in peace.

About the author

Chima Olugh is a community leader, mentor, football coach, manager, multi-award-winning pharmacist, philanthropist, husband and loving father. He is the CEO of Consult Health Ltd.

The interesting details of his life journey are detailed in this autobiography.

He lives in London, United Kingdom, with his wife and children.